Table of Contents

Reading

CRAZY BIG BOOK
Second Grade

Thinking Kids®
Carson-Dellosa Publishing LLC
Greensboro, North Carolina

Thinking Kids®
Carson-Dellosa Publishing LLC
P.O. Box 35665
Greensboro, NC 27425 USA

ISBN 978-1-4838-4453-4

Name _____

Beginning Consonants: *B, C, D, F, G, H,* and *J*

Directions: Fill in the beginning consonant for each word.

Example: __c__ at

_____ ox

_____ acket

_____ oat

_____ ouse

_____ og

_____ ire

Beginning Consonants: *K, L, M, N, P, Q,* and *R*

Directions: Write the letter that makes the beginning sound for each picture.

_____ _____ _____ _____

_____ _____ _____ _____

_____ _____ _____ _____

_____ _____ _____ _____

Beginning Consonants: *K, L, M, N, P, Q,* and *R*

Directions: Fill in the beginning consonant for each word.

Example: __r__ose

____ oney

____ uilt

____ ion

____ an

____ ey

____ ose

Harvest Time

Directions: Color the path from the apple tree to the basket.

What Swims Fast?

Directions: Color the spaces with **A** blue. Color the spaces with **a** yellow.

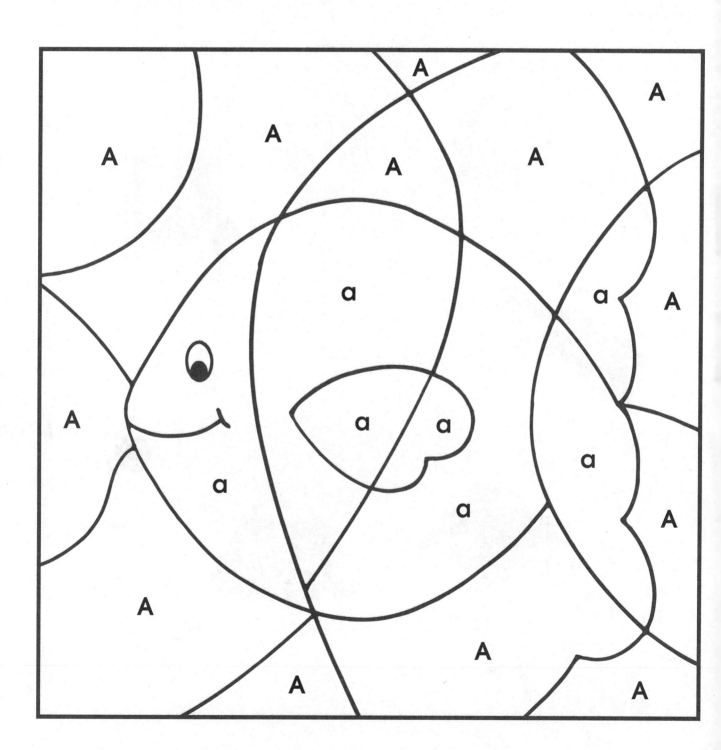

Beginning Consonants: *S, T, V, W, X, Y,* and *Z*

Directions: Write the letter that makes the beginning sound for each picture.

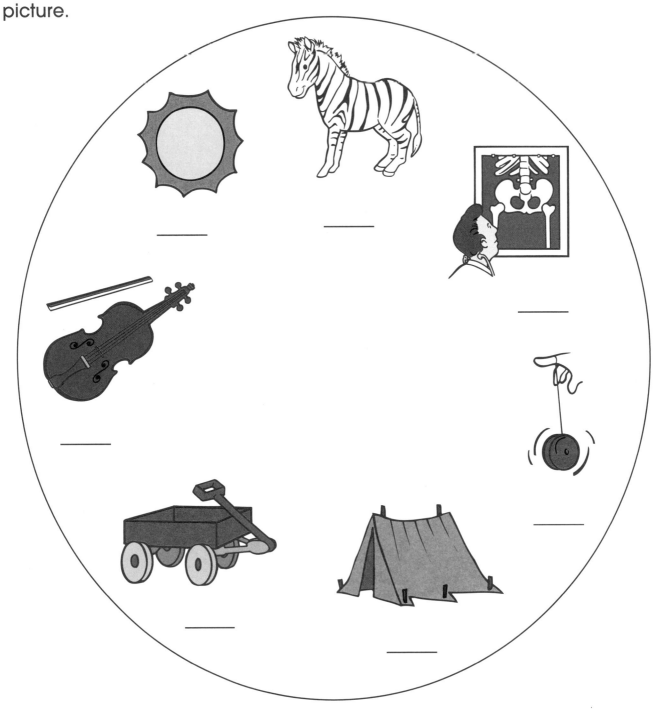

Beginning Consonants: *S, T, V, W, X, Y,* and *Z*

Directions: Fill in the beginning consonant for each word.

Example: ___s___ ock

____ ipper

____ able

____ ray

____ ase

____ olk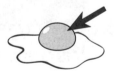

____ and

Winter

Directions: Read the clues and use the words in the word box to complete the puzzle.

| snowman |
| skis |
| ice |
| sleep |
| blizzard |
| indoors |
| shovel |
| bare |
| sled |

Across

1. This is what some animals do in winter.
2. Use this to take the snow off of sidewalks.
3. This is where to stay warm in a snowstorm.
6. It is a snowstorm.

Down

1. You can build one in the snow.
2. Wear two of them on your feet.
4. Ride this down a snowy hill.
5. This is how the trees look in winter.
7. This is water that has frozen.

What Waves in the Wind?

Directions: Color to find the hidden picture.

★ ★ ★ = purple

★ ★
★ ★ = blue.

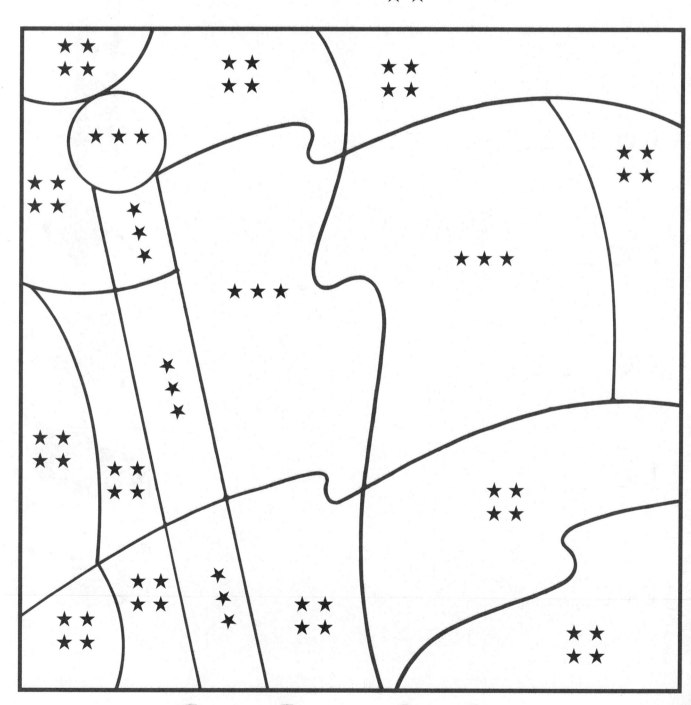

Ending Consonants: *B*, *D*, *F*, and *G*

Directions: Fill in the ending consonant for each word.

ma _____

cu _____

roo _____

do _____

be _____

bi _____

Ending Consonants: *K, L, M, N, P,* and *R*

Directions: Fill in the ending consonant for each word.

nai ____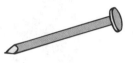

ca ____

gu ____

ca ____

truc ____

ca ____

pai ____

Home Sweet Home

Directions: Help the bee find its way home.

Plump Pig

Directions: Color each **u purple**. Then, color the rest of the picture.

Ending Consonants: *S*, *T*, and *X*

Directions: Fill in the ending consonant for each word.

ca ____

bo ____

bu ____

fo ____

boa____

ma ____

Name _____

What Lives in the Forest?

Directions: Color the spaces with **C** green. Color the spaces with **D** yellow.

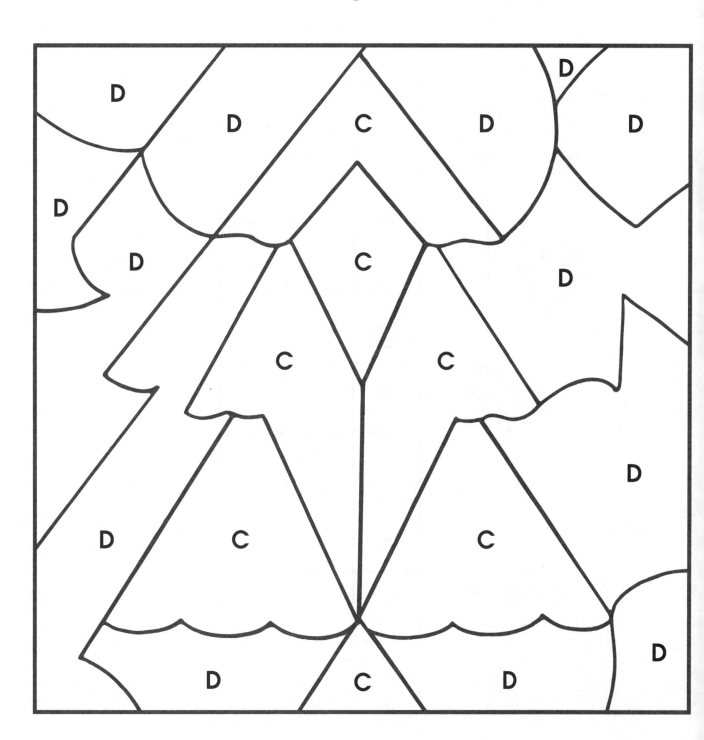

Fill Them In

Directions: Write the vowel to complete each word.

p		g

n		s	t

f		n

		t

s		

h		t

Consonant Blends

Consonant blends are two or three consonant letters in a word whose sounds combine, or blend. **Examples: br, fr, gr, pr, tr**

Directions: Look at each picture. Say its name. Write the blend you hear at the beginning of each word.

_____ _____ _____

_____ _____ _____

_____ _____ _____

_____ _____ _____

Name _____

Blends: *fl*, *br*, *pl*, *sk*, and *sn*

Directions: Look at the pictures and say their names. Write the letters for the beginning sound in each word.

Blends: *bl*, *cl*, *cr*, and *sl*

Directions: Look at the pictures and say their names. Write the letters for the beginning sound in each word.

_____ own

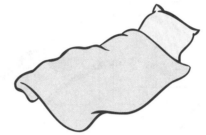

_____ anket

_____ ayon

_____ ock

_____ ide

_____ oud

_____ ed

_____ ab

_____ ocodile

Once Upon a Time

Directions: Color the path from the princess to the castle.

Up in the Sky

Directions: Write the words in the puzzle.

moon

sun

rocket

stars

Underline

Directions: Underline all the objects that do not belong in the kitchen.

Silent Letters

Some words have letters you can't hear at all, such as the **gh** in **night**, the **w** in **wrong**, the **l** in **walk**, the **k** in **knee**, the **b** in **climb**, and the **t** in **listen**.

Directions: Look at the words in the word box. Write the word under its picture. Underline the silent letters.

| knife | light | calf | wrench | lamb | eight |
| wrist | whistle | comb | thumb | knob | knee |

_____   _____   _____   _____

_____   _____   _____   _____

_____   _____   _____   _____

A Sea Giant

Directions: Color the spaces with **M blue**. Color the spaces with **m black**.

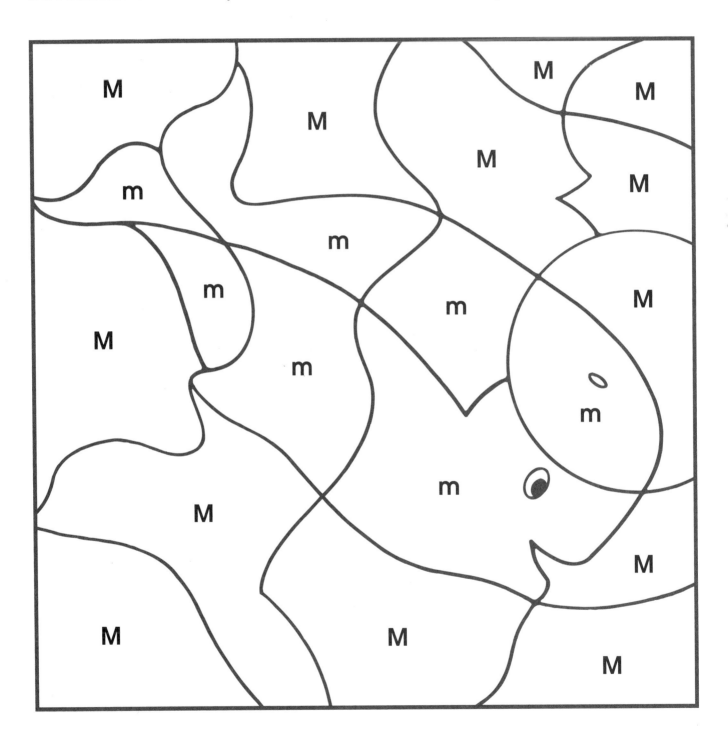

Reading

Name _____

Getting Dressed

Directions: Look at the picture clues. Then, complete the puzzle using the words from the word box.

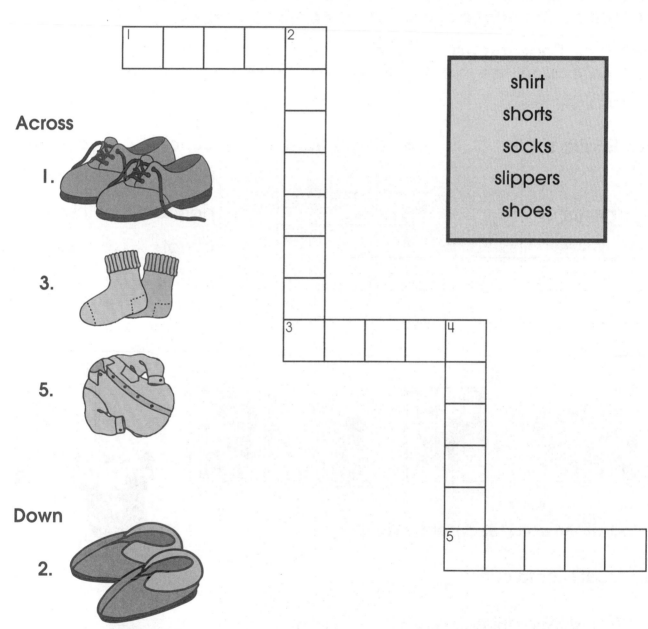

Across

1.

3.

5.

Down

2.

4.

shirt

shorts

socks

slippers

shoes

Name _____

Hard and Soft *C*

When **c** is followed by **e**, **i**, or **y**, it usually has a **soft** sound. The soft **c** sounds like **s**, as in **c**ircle and fen**c**e. When **c** is followed by **a** or **u**, it usually has a **hard** sound. The **hard c** sounds like **k**, as in **c**up or **c**art.

Directions: Read the words in the word box. Write the words in the correct lists. One word will be in both. Write a word from the box to finish each sentence.

Words with soft c

__pencil__

_____

_____

_____

_____

Words with hard c

_____

_____

_____

_____

_____

pencil	cookie
dance	cent
popcorn	circus
carrot	mice
tractor	card

1. Another word for a penny is a _____.

2. A cat likes to chase _____.

3. You will see animals and clowns at the _____.

4. Will you please sharpen my _____?

Hard and Soft G

When **g** is followed by **e**, **i**, or **y**, it usually has a **soft** sound. The soft **g** sounds like **j**, as in chan**g**e and **g**entle. When **g** is followed by **a**, **o**, or **u**, it usually has a **hard** sound, like the **g** in **g**o or **g**ate.

Directions: Read the words in the word box. Write the words in the correct lists. Write a word from the box to finish each sentence.

engine	glove	cage	magic	frog
giant	flag	large	glass	goose

Words with soft g

_____engine_____

_____

_____

_____

_____

Words with hard g

_____

_____

_____

_____

_____

1. Our bird lives in a _____.

2. Pulling a rabbit from a hat is a good _____ trick.

3. A car needs an _____ to run.

4. A _____ is a huge person.

5. An elephant is a very _____ animal.

To Bear's Cave

Directions: Color the letters **O** and **P** to find the path to the cave.

Name _____

Short Vowels

Vowels can make **short** or **long** sounds. The short **a** sounds like the **a** in **cat**. The short **e** sounds like the **e** in **leg**. The short **i** sounds like the **i** in **pig**. The short **o** sounds like the **o** in **box**. The short **u** sounds like the **u** in **cup**.

Directions: Look at each picture. Write the missing short vowel.

p __ p   n __ t   s __ ck

__ x   l __ ps   h __ t

f __ x   t __ nt   p __ n

Short Vowels

Vowels can make **short** or **long** sounds. The short **a** sounds like the **a** in **cat**. The short **e** sounds like the **e** in **leg**. The short **i** sounds like the **i** in **pig**. The short **o** sounds like the **o** in **box**. The short **u** sounds like the **u** in **cup**.

Directions: Look at the pictures. Their names all have short vowel sounds. But the vowels are missing! Fill in the missing vowels in each word.

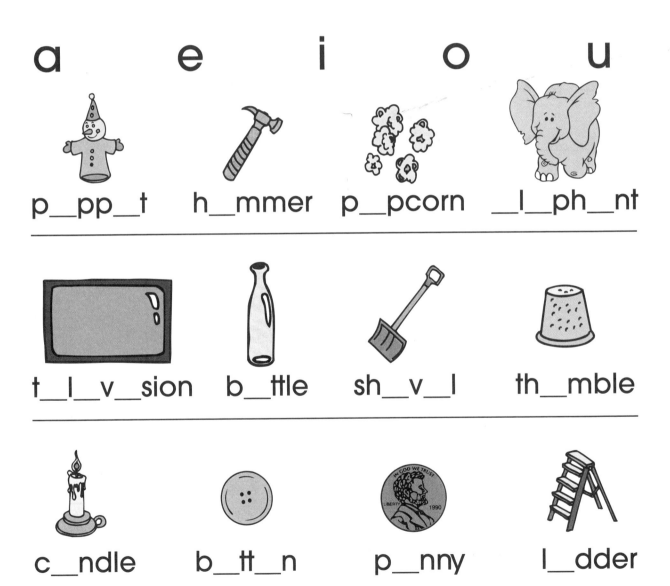

a   e   i   o   u

p__pp__t   h__mmer   p__pcorn   __l__ph__nt

t__l__v__sion   b__ttle   sh__v__l   th__mble

c__ndle   b__tt__n   p__nny   l__dder

Name _____

Autumn Leaves

Directions: Circle the leaf that is different in each row. Then, color.

Name _____

Amphibians and Reptiles

Directions: Read the sentences and use the words in the word box to complete the puzzle.

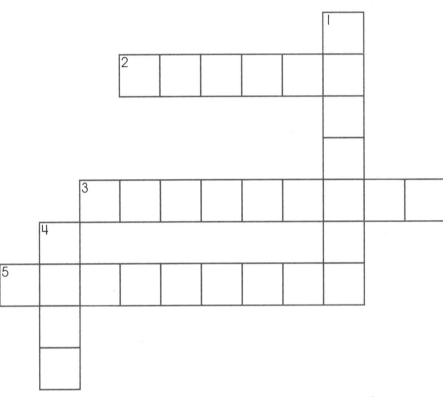

amphibian
reptile
turtle
crocodile
frog

Across

2. A _____ is a reptile that has a shell and pulls its head, legs, and tail into the shell for protection.

3. An _____ is a cold-blooded animal that has scaleless skin and lives part of its life in water.

5. A _____ is a reptile that has a long snout.

Down

1. A _____ is a cold-blooded animal that has dry, scaly skin.

4. A _____ is an amphibian that has four legs and no tail.

Super Silent *E*

Long vowel sounds have the same sound as their names. When a **Super Silent e** appears at the end of a word, you can't hear it, but it makes the other vowel have a long sound. For example: **tub** has a **short** vowel sound, and **tube** has a **long** vowel sound.

Directions: Look at the following pictures. Decide if the word has a short or long vowel sound. Circle the correct word. Watch for the **Super Silent e!**

can   cane   tub   tube   rob   robe   rat   rate

pin   pine   cap   cape   not   note   pan pane

slid   slide   dim   dime   tap   tape   cub   cube

Swoosh!

Directions: Help the skier find her hat.

Name _____

Be a Dinosaur Detective

Directions: Circle **5** mistakes that are in the picture. Then, color.

Long Vowels

Long vowels have the same sound as their names. When a **Super Silent e** comes at the end of a word, you can't hear it, but it changes the short vowel sound to a long vowel sound.

Example: rope, skate, cute, line

Directions: Say the name of the pictures. Listen for the long vowel sounds. Write the missing long vowel sound under each picture.

c __ ke

h __ ke

n __ se

__ pe

c __ be

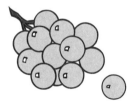

gr __ pe

r __ ke

b __ ne

k __ te

Double Vowel Words

Usually when two vowels appear together, the first one says its name and the second one is silent.

Example: b<u>ea</u>n

Directions: Unscramble the double vowel words below. Write the correct word on the line.

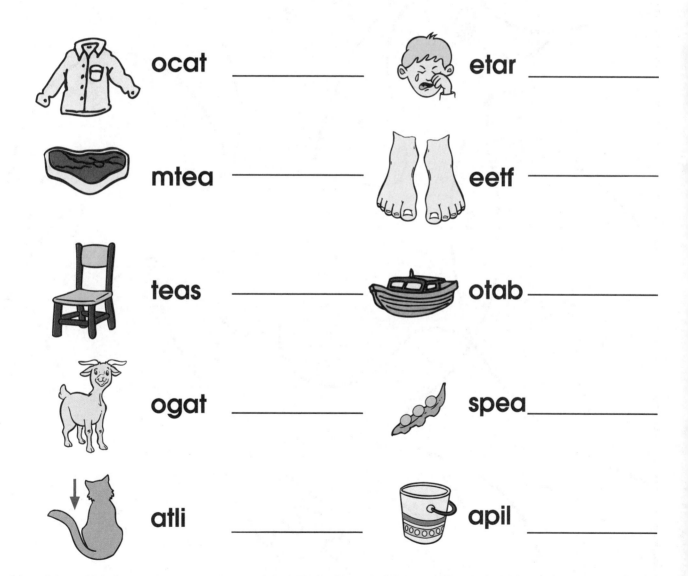

ocat _____

mtea _____

teas _____

ogat _____

atli _____

etar _____

eetf _____

otab _____

spea _____

apil _____

Who Likes to Crow?

Directions: Color the spaces with **E red**. Color the spaces with **e blue**.

Name _____

To the Mailbox

Directions: Color the letters **y** and **z** to find the path to the mailbox.

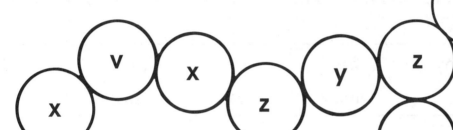

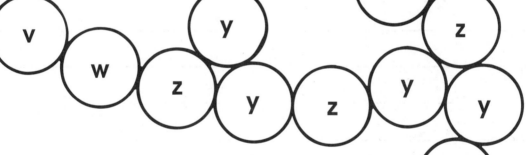

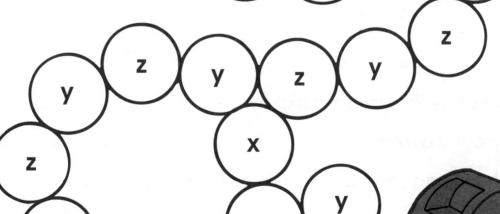

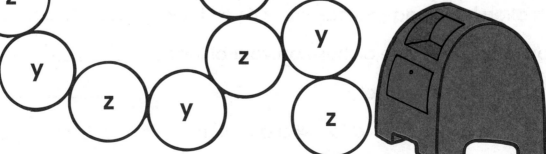

Y as a Vowel

When **y** comes at the end of a word, it is a vowel. When **y** is the only vowel at the end of a one-syllable word, it has the sound of a long **i** (as in **my**). When **y** is the only vowel at the end of a word with more than one syllable, it has the sound of long **e** (as in **baby**).

Directions: Look at the words in the word box. If the word has the sound of long **i**, write it under the word **my**. If the word has the sound of long **e**, write it under the word **baby**. Write the word from the word box that answers each riddle.

happy	penny	fry	try	sleepy	dry
bunny	why	windy	sky	party	fly

my   **baby**

_____   _____

_____   _____

_____   _____

_____   _____

_____   _____

1. It takes five of these to make a nickel.   _____

2. You might call it a rabbit.   _____

3. It is often blue, and you can see it if you look up. _____

4. You might have one of these on your birthday.   _____

5. It is the opposite of **wet**.   _____

6. You might use this word to ask a question.   _____

Y as a Vowel

Directions: Read the rhyming story. Choose words from the box to fill in the blanks.

Larry	Mary
money	funny
honey	bunny

_____ and _____ are friends.

Larry is selling _____. Mary needs _____

to buy the honey. "I want to feed it to my _____," said

Mary. Larry laughed and said, "That is _____. Everyone

knows that bunnies do not eat honey."

Y as a Vowel

Directions: Read the story. Choose words from the box to fill in the blanks.

try	my	Why	cry	shy	fly

Sam is very _____. Ann asks, "Would you like to

_____ my kite?" Sam starts to _____.

Ann asks, "_____ are you crying?"

Sam says, "I am afraid to _____."

"Oh, _____ ! You are a good kite flyer," cries Ann.

Name _____

Living Things

Directions: Read the clues and use the words in the word box to complete the puzzle.

Across

2. I can fly.
3. I am a plant. I have petals and smell pretty.
4. I have a trunk, leaves, and branches.

Down

1. I am a person.
2. I am a large gray animal with a long trunk and big, floppy ears.
3. I live in the water and can swim.

Find the Mystery Picture

Directions: Read each sentence and cross out the picture. What picture is left?

1. It is not a lube.

2. It is not glue.

3. It is not an ice cube.

4. It is not a flute.

5. It is not June.

6. It is not blue.

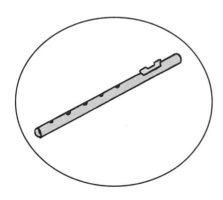
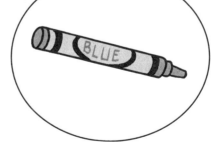

The mystery picture is a _____ .

School Words

pencil	teacher	crayons
recess	lunchbox	play
fun	math	

Directions: Fill in the blanks with a word from the word box.

1. I need to sharpen my _____.

2. I like to _____ at recess.

3. School is _____!

4. My _____ helps me learn.

5. I need to color the picture with _____.

6. I play kickball at _____.

7. My sandwich is in my _____.

8. In _____, I can add and subtract.

A Fast Frog

Directions: Color the circles to help the frog find the fly.

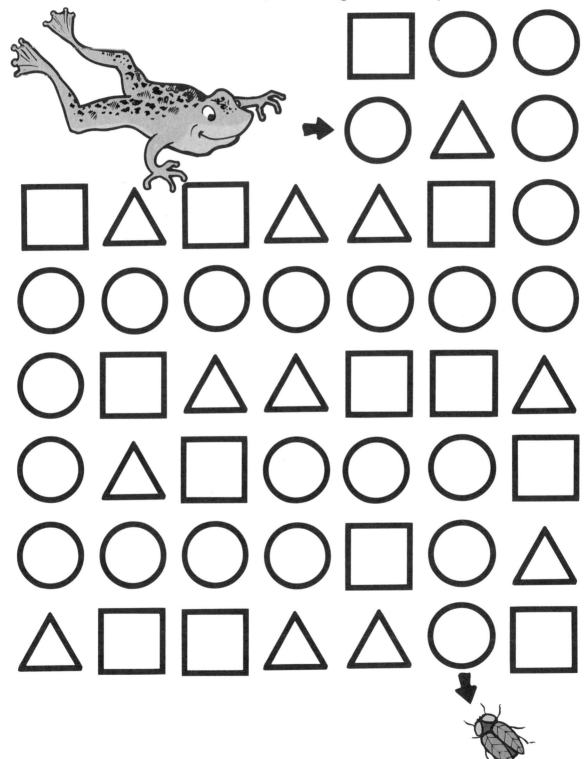

Days of the Week

Directions: Write the day of the week that answers each question.

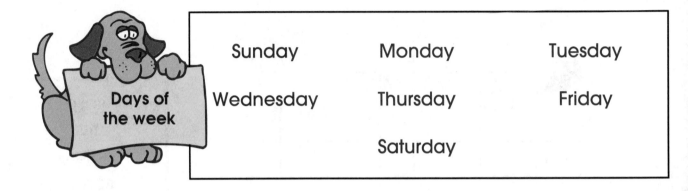

Sunday	Monday	Tuesday
Wednesday	Thursday	Friday
	Saturday	

1. What is the first day of the week?

_____

2. What is the last day of the week?

_____

3. What day comes after Tuesday?

_____

4. What day comes between Wednesday and Friday?

_____

5. What is the third day of the week?

_____

6. What day comes before Saturday?

_____

7. What day comes after Sunday?

_____

Bugs, Bugs, Bugs

Directions: Read the clues and use the words in the word box to complete the puzzle.

wasp
fly
ant
ladybug
cricket
bee
butterfly
caterpillar

Across

1. An insect that makes honey.
4. This bug may change into a butterfly.
5. This bug flies around garbage.
6. She wears a red coat with black spots.

Down

1. This bug has beautifully colored wings.
2. You might hear this bug chirp at night.
3. This stinging insect makes a paper nest.
7. This worker might like your picnic lunch.

Compound Words

Compound words are two words that are put together to make one new word.

Directions: Help the cook brew her stew. Mix words from the first column with words from the second column to make new words. Write your new words on the lines at the bottom.

grand	brows
snow	light
eye	stairs
down	string
rose	book
shoe	mother
note	ball
moon	bud

1. _____

2. _____

3. _____

4. _____

5. _____

6. _____

7. _____

8. _____

Name _____

Compound Words

Directions: Read the sentences. Fill in the blank with a compound word from the box.

raincoat	bedroom	lunchbox	hallway	sandbox

1. A box with sand is a

_____.

2. The way through a hall is a

_____.

3. A box for lunch is a

_____.

4. A coat for the rain is a

_____.

5. A room with a bed is a

_____.

Super Swimmer

Directions: Color the spaces with **D** blue. Color the spaces with **N** orange.

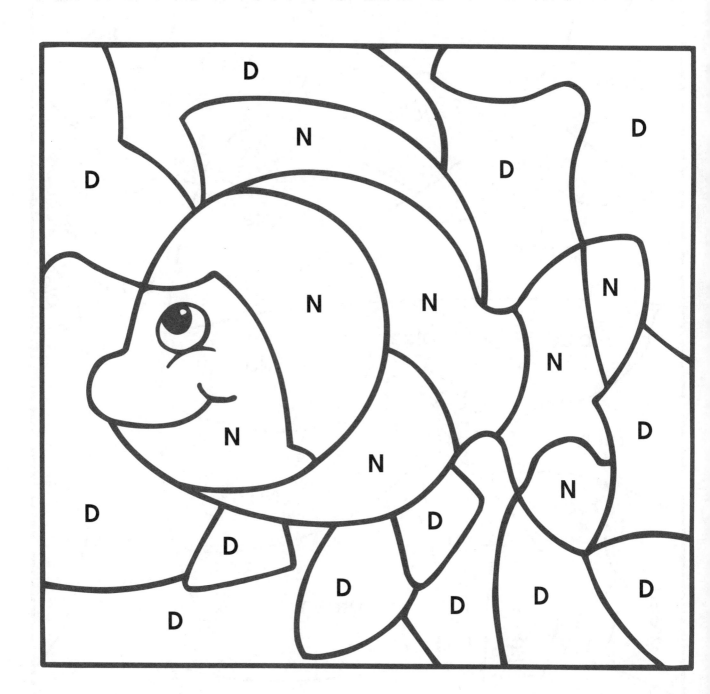

Name _____

Color Words

Directions: Read the color words. Then, color the spaces to match.

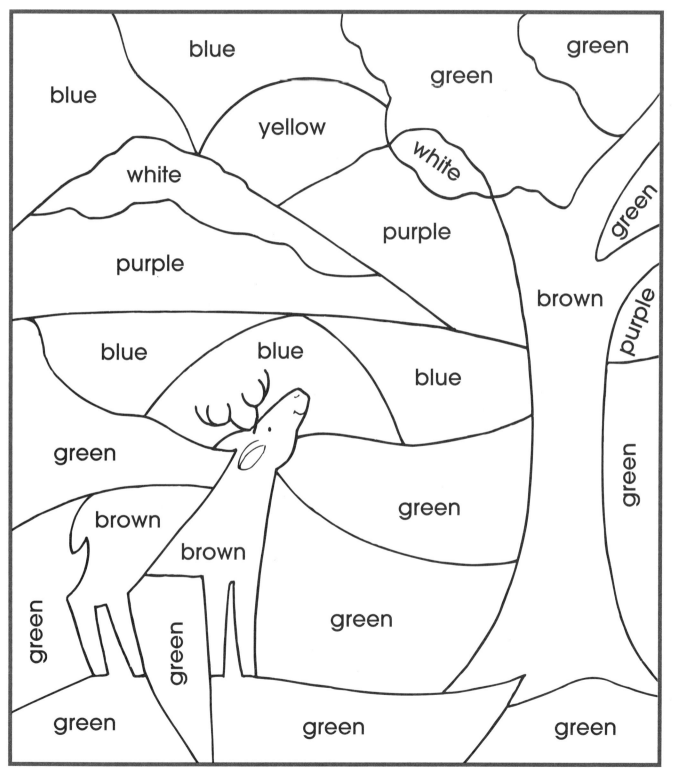

Contractions

Contractions are a short way to write two words.

Examples: it is = it's, is not = isn't, I have = I've

Directions: Draw a line from each word pair to its contraction.

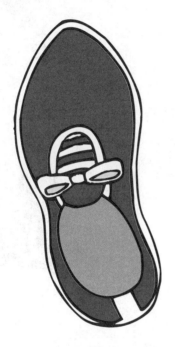 

I am	she's
it is	they're
you are	we're
we are	he's
they are	I'm
she is	it's
he is	you're

Contractions

Directions: Circle the contraction that should replace the underlined words.

Example: were not = weren't

1. The boy <u>was not</u> sad.

      wasn't   weren't

2. We <u>were not</u> working.

   wasn't   weren't

3. Jen and Caleb <u>have not</u> eaten lunch yet.

      haven't   hasn't

4. The mouse <u>has not</u> been here.

      haven't   hasn't

Contractions

Directions: Match the words with their contractions.

would not	I've
was not	he'll
he will	wouldn't
could not	wasn't
I have	couldn't

Directions: Make the words at the end of each line into contractions to complete the sentences.

1. He _____ know the answer.   **did not**

2. _____ a long way home.   **It is**

3. _____ my house.   **Here is**

4. _____ not going to school today.   **We are**

5. _____ take the bus home tomorrow.   **They will**

Name _____

Desert Life

Directions: Read the sentences and use the words in the word box to complete the puzzle.

flowers
animals
burrows
night
deserts
plants

Across

1. Desert ____ get water from the food they eat.
5. Desert ____ store water in their leaves, roots, or stems.
6. Many small animals stay in ____ underground during the day.

Down

2. At ____ , the desert animals begin to stir.
3. ____ are very hot and get little rainfall.
4. After it rains, colorful ____ bloom across the desert.

A Big Eater

Directions: Color the spaces with **B purple**. Color the spaces with **b green**.

Name _____

Forest Life

Directions: Read the sentences and use the words in the word box to complete the puzzle.

Across

3. ____ climb trees and eat acorns.
5. Many ____ crawl along the forest floor.
6. Many ____ grow in the forest.

Down

1. A little bit of ____ shines through the trees.
2. It is cool and dark in the ____ .
4. A ____ nibbles on the sweet green plants.

sunlight

forest

insects

trees

squirrels

deer

Syllables

Words are made up of parts called **syllables**. Each syllable has a vowel sound. One way to count syllables is to clap as you say the word.

Example: cat   I clap   I syllable
          table   2 claps   2 syllables
          butterfly   3 claps   3 syllables

Directions: "Clap out" the words below. Write how many syllables each word has.

movie _____   dog _____

piano _____   basket _____

tree _____   swimmer _____

bicycle _____   rainbow _____

sun _____   paper _____

cabinet _____   picture _____

football _____   run _____

television _____   enter _____

Syllables

Dividing a word into syllables can help you read a new word. You also might use syllables when you are writing if you run out of space on a line. Many words contain two consonants that are next to each other. A word can usually be divided between the consonants.

Directions: Divide each word into two syllables. The first one is done for you.

kitten   kit   ten

lumber   _____

batter   _____

winter   _____

funny   _____

harder   _____

dirty   _____

sister   _____

little   _____

dinner   _____

Syllables

One way to help you read a word you don't know is to divide it into parts called **syllables**. Every syllable has a vowel sound.

Directions: Say the words. Write the number of syllables. The first one is done for you.

straw • ber • ry

bird _____1_____   rabbit _____

apple _____   elephant _____

balloon _____   family _____

basketball _____   fence _____

breakfast _____   ladder _____

block _____   open _____

candy _____   puddle _____

popcorn _____   Saturday _____

yellow _____   wind _____

understand _____   butterfly _____

Name _____

Syllables

When a double consonant is used in the middle of a word, the word can usually be divided between the consonants.

Directions: Look at the words in the word box. Divide each word into two syllables. Leave space between each syllable. One is done for you.

butter	puppy	kitten	yellow
dinner	chatter	ladder	happy
pillow	letter	mitten	summer

___but___ ___ter___

_____ _____

_____ _____

_____ _____

_____ _____

Many words are divided between two consonants that are not alike.

Directions: Look at the words in the word box. Divide each word into two syllables. One is done for you.

window	doctor	number	carpet
mister	winter	pencil	candle
barber	sister	picture	under

___win___ ___dow___

_____ _____

_____ _____

_____ _____

Syllables

Directions: Write **1** or **2** on the line to tell how many syllables are in each word. If the word has two syllables, draw a line between the syllables.

Example: sup|per

dog	_____	timber	_____
bedroom	_____	cat	_____
slipper	_____	street	_____
tree	_____	chalk	_____
batter	_____	blanket	_____
chair	_____	marker	_____
fish	_____	brush	_____
master	_____	rabbit	_____

Name _____

Touchdown

Directions: Color the path to the airport.

Name _____

Veggie Delight

Directions: Look at the picture clues. Then, complete the puzzle using the words from the word box.

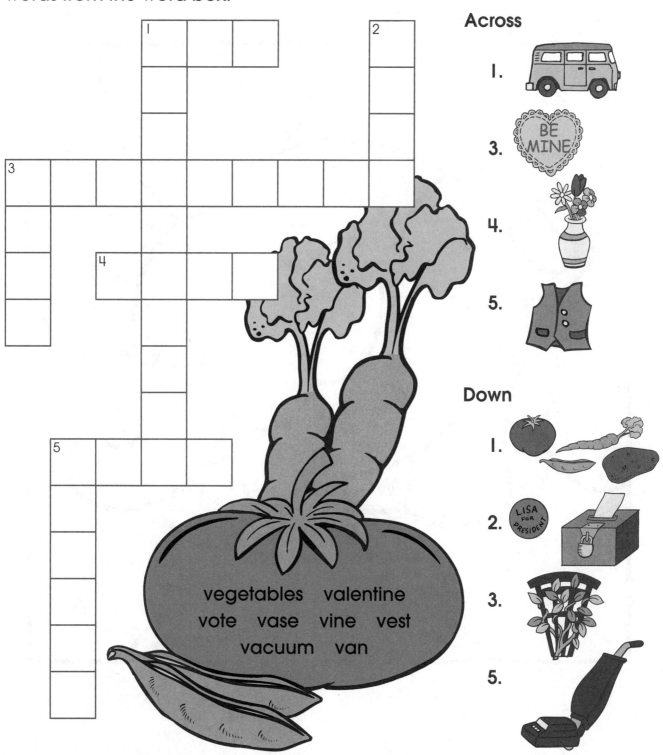

Across

1.

3.

4.

5.

Down

1.

2.

3.

5.

vegetables   valentine
vote   vase   vine   vest
vacuum   van

A Super Trunk

Directions: Color the spaces with **A red**. Color the spaces with **W gray**.

A Picture Puzzle

Directions: Can you find **9** hidden pictures that begin with **p**? Circle them. Then, color the picture.

pig

pencil

pot

pail

pin

pan

puck

pie

pear

Name _____

Tongue Twisters

Directions: Use the code to decode the tongue twisters below.

1.

2.

3.

A	
B	✓
C	✸
D	●
E	❄
F	◆
G	⚑
H	☆
I	✗
J	✪
K	❖
L	▢
M	▲
N	●
O	✎
P	▼
Q	🔔
R	✦
S	■
T	○
U	★
V	☺
W	⇨
X	🎧
Y	✿
Z	✧

Haiku

A **haiku** is a form of Japanese poetry. Most haiku are about nature.

first line: 5 syllables
second line: 7 syllables
third line: 5 syllables

Example: The squirrel is brown.
He lives in a great big tree.
He eats nuts all day.

Directions: Write your own haiku. Draw a picture to go with it.

_____

_____

_____

Shape Code

Directions: Write the missing letters **m**, **n**, **o**, **p**, or **s** for each word. Use the code to help you.

1.  ___ ct ___ ___ u ___
   ○   ○ ▱   ⬡

5.  ___ e ___ cil
   ▱   △

2.  ___ a ___ er
   ▱   ▱

6.  ___ ___ u ___ e
   □ ○   ⬡

3.  ___ ___ ther
   □ ○

7.  ___ a ___
   □   ▱

4.  ___ ule
   □

8.  ___ u ___
   ⬡   △

m	n	o	p	s
□	△	○	▱	⬡

Name _____

Suffixes

A **suffix** is a letter or group of letters that is added to the end of a word to change its meaning.

Directions: Add the suffixes to the root words to make new words. Use your new words to complete the sentences.

help + ful = _____

care + less = _____

build + er = _____

talk + ed = _____

love + ly = _____

loud + er = _____

1. My mother _____ to my teacher about my homework.

2. The radio was _____ than the television.

3. Madison is always _____ to her mother.

4. A _____ put a new garage on our house.

5. The flowers are _____ .

6. It is _____ to cross the street without looking both ways.

Suffixes

An **ing** at the end of an action word shows that the action is happening now. An **ed** at the end shows that the action happened in the past.

Directions: Look at the words in the word box. Underline the root word in each one. Write a word to complete each sentence.

snowing	wished	played	looking	crying
talking	walked	eating	going	doing

1. We like to play. We _____ yesterday.

2. Is that snow? Yes, it is _____.

3. Do you want to go with me? No, I am _____ with my friend.

4. The baby will cry if we leave. The baby is _____.

5. We will walk home from school. We _____ to school this morning.

6. Did you wish for a new bike? Yes, I _____ for one.

7. Who is doing the dishes? I am _____ them.

8. Did you talk to your friend? Yes, we are _____ now.

9. Will you look at my book? I am _____ at it now.

10. I like to eat pizza. We are _____ it for lunch.

Suffixes

Directions: Write a word from the word box next to its root word.

coming	running	sitting
lived	rained	swimming
visited	carried	racing
hurried		

run _____   come _____

live _____   carry _____

hurry _____   race _____

swim _____   rain _____

visit _____   sit _____

Directions: Write a word from the word box to finish each sentence.

1. I _____ my grandmother during vacation.

2. Ava went _____ at the lake with her cousin.

3. Tyson _____ the heavy package for his mother.

4. It _____ and stormed all weekend.

5. Cars go very fast when they are _____ .

Oops!

Directions: Use a word from the word box to finish each sentence. Then, use the words in the puzzles.

Across

1. A 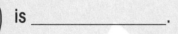 is _____.

Down

2. An 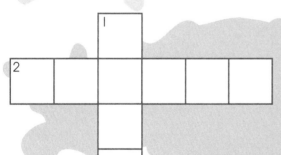 is _____.

Across

2.   are _____.

Down

1. An is _____.

Across

2. A is _____.

Down

1. A  is _____.

| brown | orange | purple | green | red | gray |

Blast Off!

Directions: Help the astronaut find the space shuttle.

Animal Parade

Directions: Circle the animal that comes next in each row.

Prefixes: The Three Rs

A **prefix** is a letter or group of letters that is added to the beginning of a word to change its meaning. The prefix **re** means "again."

Directions: Read the story. Then, follow the instructions.

Kim wants to find ways she can help our planet. She studies the "three Rs"—reduce, reuse, and recycle. **Reduce** means "to make less." Both **reuse** and **recycle** mean "to use again."

Add **re** to the beginning of each word below. Use the new words to complete the sentences.

_____ build   _____ fill

_____ read   _____ tell

_____ write   _____ run

1. The race was a tie, so Sanj and Mia had to _____ it.

2. The block wall fell down, so Simon had to _____ it.

3. The water bottle was empty, so Luna had to _____ it.

4. Javier wrote a good story, but he wanted to _____ it to make it better.

5. The teacher told a story, and students had to _____ it.

6. Toni didn't understand the directions, so she had to

_____ them.

Prefixes

Directions: Change the meaning of the sentences by adding the prefixes to the **bold** words.

The boy was **lucky** because he guessed the answer **correctly**.

The boy was (un) _____ because he guessed the

answer (in) _____ .

When Jada **behaved**, she felt **happy**.

When Jada (mis) _____ .

she felt (un) _____ .

Mike wore his jacket **buttoned** because the dance was **formal**.

Mike wore his jacket (un) _____ because the dance

was (in) _____ .

Cameron **understood** because he was **familiar** with the book.

Cameron (mis) _____ because he was

(un) _____ with the book.

Prefixes

Directions: Read the story. Change the story by removing the prefix **re** from the **bold** words. Write the new words in the new story.

Repete is a **rewriter** who has to **redo** every story. He has to **rethink** up the ideas. He has to **rewrite** the sentences. He has to **redraw** the pictures. He even has to **retype** the pages. Who will **repay** **Repete** for all the work he **redoes**?

_____ is a _____ who has to

_____ every story. He has to _____

up the ideas. He has to _____ the sentences.

He has to _____ the pictures.

He even has to _____ the pages.

Who will _____ _____ for all the

work he _____ ?

Name _____

Dinosaur Crossword

Directions: Look at the picture clues. Then, complete the puzzle using the words from the word box.

fossil

eggs

teeth

horn

claw

plate

Across

4.

5.

6.

Down

1.

2.

3.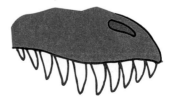

Spouting About

Directions: To find the mystery letter, color the spaces with the following letters yellow.

e   m   c   q   y   r   o   j   a

e	b	s	d
q	k	t	f
c	a	m	i
o	g	y	n
r	h	j	p

Circle the mystery letter.   d   h   m

Reading   Name _____

Crack the Code

Directions: Write the missing letters for each word. Use the code to help you.

1.  ___ ___ayon

2. ___ ou___e

3. ___oon

4. ___ta___

5. ___lou___

6. ___ a ___ ___ ot

7. bi ___ ___

8. ___ on___ey

c	
r	★
s	▲
m	⬟
d	■
k	◆

Parts of a Book

A book has many parts. The **title** is the name of the book. The **author** is the person who wrote the words. The **illustrator** is the person who drew the pictures. The **table of contents** is located at the beginning to list what is in the book. The **glossary** is a little dictionary in the back to help you with unfamiliar words. Books are often divided into smaller sections of information called **chapters**.

Directions: Look at one of your books. Write the parts you see below.

The title of my book is _____

The author is _____

The illustrator is _____

My book has a table of contents.　　　　　　Yes　　No

My book has a glossary.　　　　　　　　　　Yes　　No

My book is divided into chapters.　　　　　　Yes　　No

Name _____

Springtime

Directions: Color the butterfly's path to the flower.

ABC Order

Directions: Put the words in ABC order on the bags.

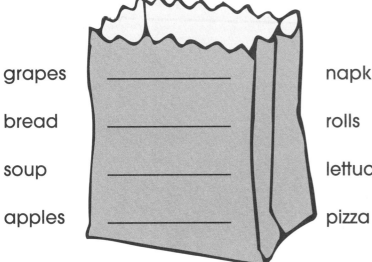

grapes

bread

soup

apples

napkins

rolls

lettuce

pizza

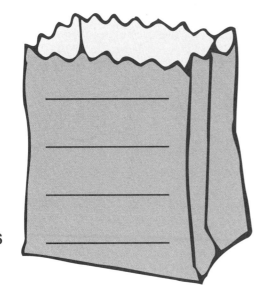

milk

carrots

beans

potatoes

meat

juice

cups

rice

ABC Order

Directions: Write each group of words in alphabetical order. If two words start with the same letter, look at the second letter in each word.

Example: **lamb**   **Lamb** comes first because **a** comes before **i**
             light   in the alphabet.

tree   _____

branch   _____

leaf   _____

dish   _____

dog   _____

bone   _____

rain   _____

umbrella   _____

cloud   _____

mail   _____

stamp   _____

slot   _____

Sequencing: ABC Order

Directions: Write **1**, **2**, **3**, or **4** on the lines in each row to put the words in ABC order.

Example:

1. __1__ bell   __4__ well   __2__ smell   __3__ tell

2. _____ bite   _____ kite   _____ write   _____ might

3. _____ tar   _____ car   _____ far   _____ bar

4. _____ sand   _____ land   _____ band   _____ fanned

5. _____ sweet   _____ meat   _____ eat   _____ treat

6. _____ hair   _____ pear   _____ tear   _____ wear

7. _____ lake   _____ bake   _____ rake   _____ take

8. _____ round   _____ sound   _____ pound   _____ found

Megan's Birthday Present

Directions: Write a word from the word box to complete each sentence.

1. Megan got a new ____ ____ ____ ____.

2. It was a birthday ____ ____ ____ ____.

3. The color is ____ ____ ____ ____ ____.

4. Megan wears a ____ ____ ____ ____ ____ ____
   when she rides her bike.

5. She wears elbow ____ ____ ____ ____.

6. She wears ____ ____ ____ ____ pads, too.

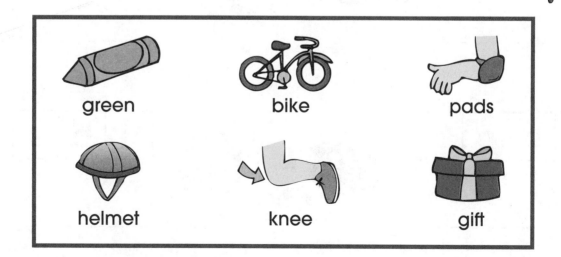

green	bike	pads
helmet	knee	gift

Fix These Words

Directions: Unscramble the letters. Use the pictures to help you. Then, write the words on the lines.

g	p	i

r	a	t	s

_____　　　　　　　　　　　　_____

u	n	s

d	e	b

_____　　　　　　　　　　　　_____

t	h	a

n	f	a

_____　　　　　　　　　　　　_____

t	e	n	s

u	b	s

_____　　　　　　　　　　　　_____

Garden Time

Directions: Find the words and color them the color shown.

pink
flowers
path
tools
weeds
pots
bench
seeds
shovel
water
sun
air
leaves

yellow
bugs
wonder
friendly
golf
travel
sailing
sofa
believe
neighbor
socks
dirt

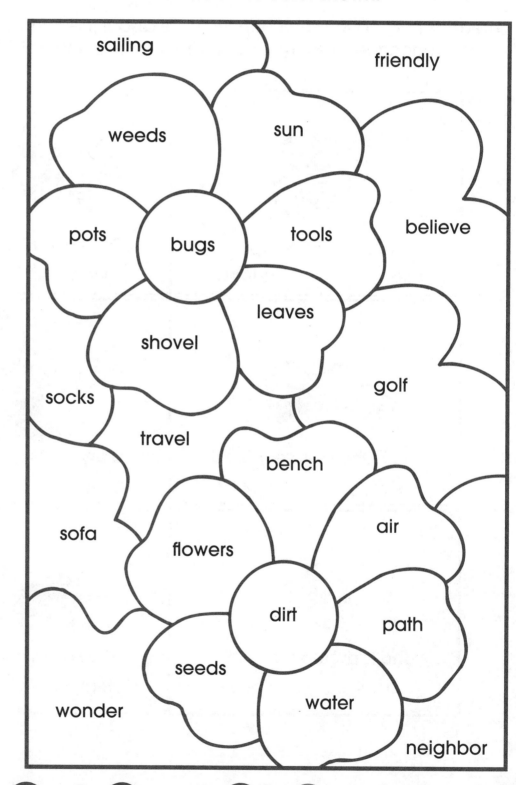

Synonyms

Words that mean the same or nearly the same are called **synonyms**.

Directions: Read the sentence that tells about the picture. Draw a circle around the word that means the same as the **bold** word.

The child is **unhappy**.

sad   hungry

The flowers are **lovely**.

pretty   green

The baby was very **tired**.

sleepy   hurt

The **funny** clown made us laugh.

silly   glad

The ladybug is so **tiny**.

small   red

We saw a **scary** tiger.

frightening   ugly

Synonyms

Directions: Read each sentence. Fill in the blanks with the synonyms.

friend	tired	story
presents	little	

I want to go to bed because
I am very <u>sleepy</u>.

_____

On my birthday, I like to open
my <u>gifts</u>.

_____

My <u>pal</u> and I like to play
together.

_____

My favorite <u>tale</u> is *Cinderella*.

_____

The mouse was so <u>tiny</u> that it
was hard to catch him.

_____

Mail Call

Directions: Unscramble the words that have to do with mail. Use the words in the word box to help you.

1. rettles ___ ___ ___ ___ ___ ___ ___

2. cpageksa ___ ___ ___ ___ ___ ___ ___ ___

3. tpamss ___ ___ ___ ___ ___ ___

4. ilam rrcaire ___ ___ ___ ___ ___ ___ ___ ___ ___ ___ ___

5. tsop oceiff ___ ___ ___ ___ ___ ___ ___ ___ ___ ___

6. axombli ___ ___ ___ ___ ___ ___ ___

7. leeydivr ___ ___ ___ ___ ___ ___ ___ ___

8. dracs ___ ___ ___ ___ ___

delivery	mail carrier	
letters	stamps	packages
mailbox	cards	post office

Off to School

Directions: Color the letters **O** and **P** to find the path that leads to the bus.

Antonyms

Antonyms are words that mean the opposite of another word.

Examples:
   hot and **cold**
   short and **tall**

Directions: Draw a line from each word on the left to its antonym on the right.

sad	white
bottom	stop
black	fat
tall	top
thin	hard
little	found
cold	short
lost	hot
go	big
soft	happy

Antonyms

Antonyms are words that are opposites.

Directions: Read the words next to the pictures. Draw a line to the antonyms.

dark   empty

hairy   dry

closed   happy

dirty   bald

sad   clean

full   light

wet   open

Antonyms

Words that mean the opposite are called **antonyms**.

Directions: Read the sentence. Write the word from the word box that means the opposite of the **bold** word.

bottom	outside	black	summer	after
light	sister	clean	last	evening

1. Lena has a new baby **brother**.   _____

2. The class went **inside** for recess.   _____

3. There is a **white** car in the driveway.   _____

4. We went to the park **before** dinner.   _____

5. Joe's puppy is **dirty**.   _____

6. My name is at the **top** of the list.   _____

7. I like to play outside in the **winter**.   _____

8. I like to take walks in the **morning**.   _____

9. The sky was **dark** after the storm.   _____

10. Our team is in **first** place.   _____

Antonyms

Directions: Look at each picture, and read the sentence. Cross out the incorrect word, and write its antonym in the blank.

When it is light, we go
to bed.   _____

When I broke the vase,
it made my mom smile.   _____

The hot chocolate is
very cold, so be careful!   _____

My pants were tight, so
I needed to wear a belt.   _____

The balloons float down
in the sky.   _____

Bouncing Letters

Directions: To find the mystery letter, color the spaces with the following letters **blue**.

d   s   x   i   z   t   o   p   c   w   f   l   y

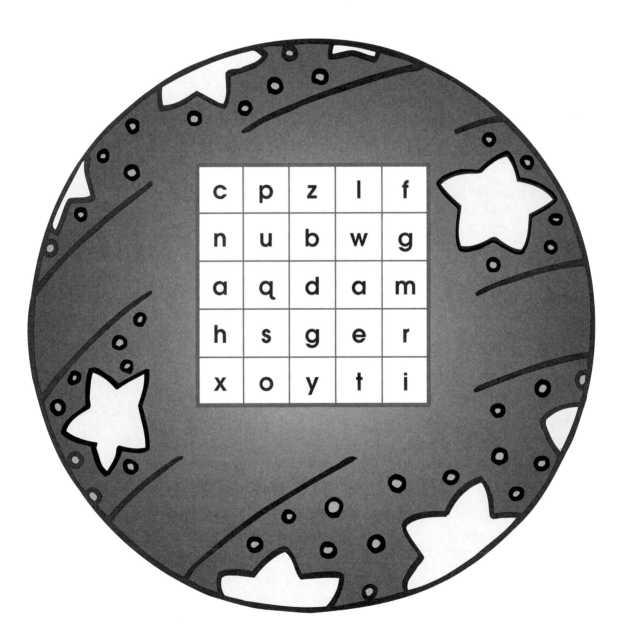

c	p	z	l	f
n	u	b	w	g
a	q	d	a	m
h	s	g	e	r
x	o	y	t	i

Circle the mystery letter.   a   t   z

Around Town

Directions: Read each riddle. Then, write the answer. Use the words in the word box to help you.

play
work
vote
shop
learn
eat
help
drive

1. Kids do this with toys and at parks. ____ ____ ____ ____

2. People go to markets to do this. ____ ____ ____ ____

3. Teachers help kids do this. ____ ____ ____ ____ ____

4. You can do this at a restaurant. ____ ____ ____

5. People earn money by doing this. ____ ____ ____ ____

6. Adults travel in cars by doing this. ____ ____ ____ ____ ____

7. Do this to be a good neighbor. ____ ____ ____ ____

8. People do this to choose leaders. ____ ____ ____ ____

What Is It?

Directions: Color the spaces with words that name vehicles yellow. Color the other spaces **blue**.

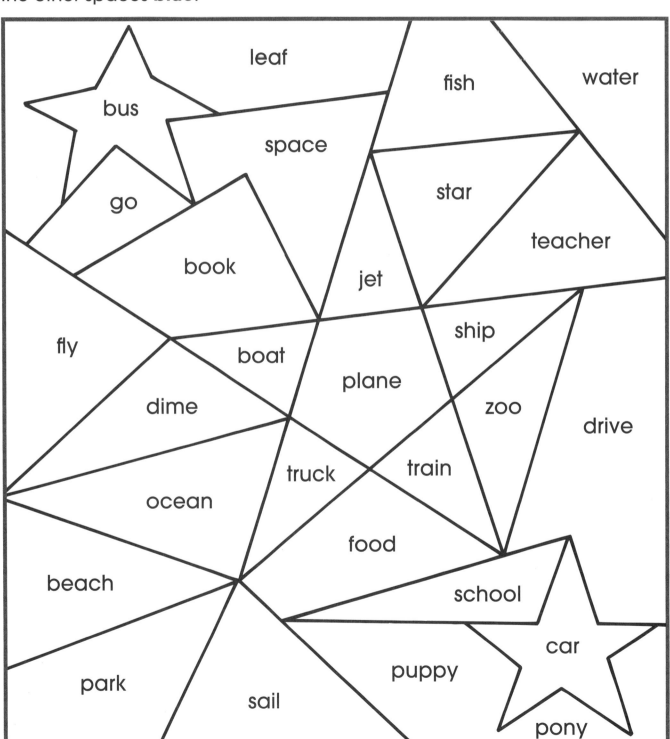

Career Time

Directions: Use the pictures and words in the word box to help you fill in the puzzle.

1.
2.
3.
4.
5.
6.
7.
8.

doctor
teacher
artist
plumber
lawyer
singer
chef
carpenter

1.
2.
3.
4.

5.
6.
7.
8.

Homophones

Homophones are words that sound alike but are spelled differently and have different meanings. Sometimes, homophones can be more than two words.

Examples:
    Pear and **pair** are homophones.
    To, **too**, and **two** are three homophones.

Directions: Draw a line from each word on the left to its homophone on the right.

blue	knight
night	too
beet	blew
write	see
hi	meet
two	son
meat	bee
sea	high
be	right
sun	beat

Homophones

Directions: Look at each picture. Circle the correct homophone.

deer   dear

blue   blew

two   to

hi   high

by   bye

new   knew

ate   eight

red   read

Homophones

Directions: Write the homophone from the box next to each picture.

so	see	blew	pear

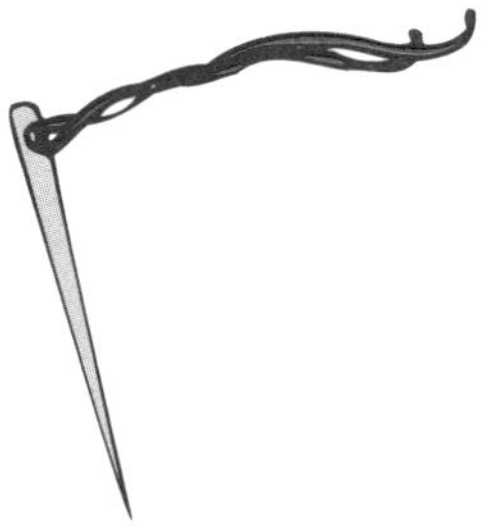

sew   _____

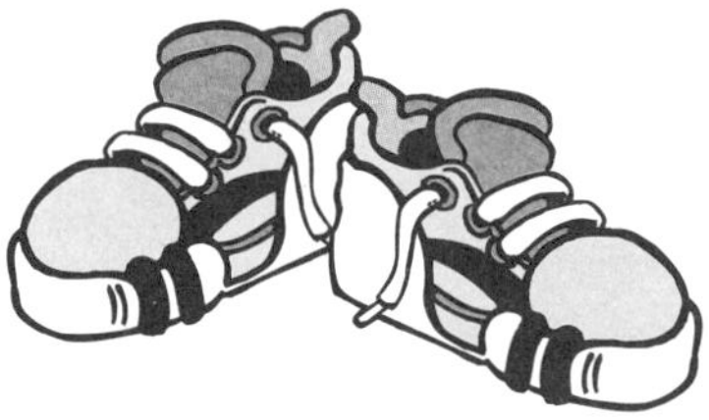

pair   _____

sea   _____

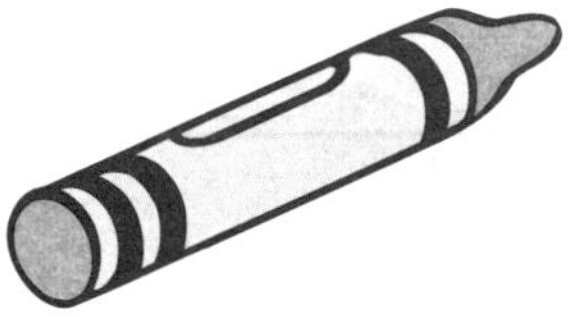

blue   _____

Homophones

Directions: Read each word. Circle the picture that goes with the word.

1. sun

4. hi

2. ate

5. four

3. buy

6. hear

Favorite Games

Directions: Travel through the maze choosing only games, sports, or things with which you can play.

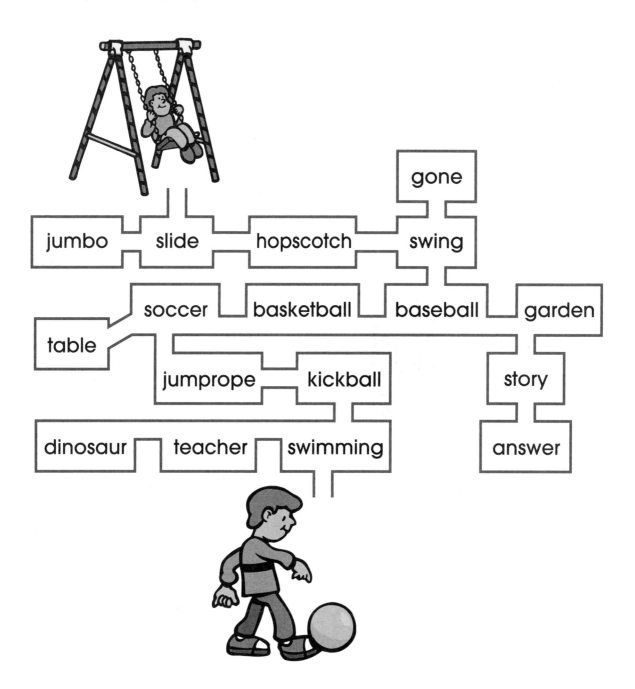

jumbo   slide   hopscotch   gone   swing

soccer   basketball   baseball   garden

table   jumprope   kickball   story

dinosaur   teacher   swimming   answer

Animal Homes

Directions: Read the clues and use the words in the word box to complete the puzzle.

word box
web
tree
nest
lodge
hive
hill
shell
pond

Across

3. This is where bees make their honey.
4. This is a home for a clam.
6. Fish and frogs live here.
7. A bird makes this home.

Down

1. Ants build one to live in.
2. This is where a spider lives.
5. A beaver builds a dam near this home.
8. A hole in this makes a good home for a squirrel.

Mystery Picture

Directions: Read each sentence and cross out the picture. What picture is left?

1. It is not a toy.

2. It is not foil.

3. It is not boil.

4. It is not coins.

5. It is not soil.

6. It is not oil.

The mystery picture is a _____ .

Wagon Wheel

Directions: Write the first letter of the words in the puzzle wheel.

Nouns

A **noun** is the name of a person, place, or thing.

Directions: Read the story, and circle all the nouns. Then, write the nouns next to the pictures below.

Our family likes to go to the park.

_____

We play on the swings.

_____

We eat sandwiches.

_____

We drink lemonade.

_____

We throw the ball to our dog.

_____

Then, we go home.

_____

Proper Nouns

Proper nouns are the names of specific people, places, and things. Proper nouns begin with a capital letter.

Directions: Write the proper nouns on the lines below. Use capital letters at the beginning of each word.

logan, utah

mike smith

_____

_____

lynn cramer

buster

_____

_____

fluffy

chicago, illinois

_____

_____

Proper Nouns

The days of the week and the months of the year are always capitalized.

Directions: Circle the words that are written correctly. Write the words that need capital letters on the lines below.

sunday	July	Wednesday	May	december
friday	tuesday	june	august	Monday
january	February	March	Thursday	April
September	saturday	October		

Days of the Week	**Months of the Year**
1. _____	1. _____
2. _____	2. _____
3. _____	3. _____
4. _____	4. _____
	5. _____

Plural Nouns

Plural nouns name more than one person, place, or thing.

Directions: Read the words in the box. Write the words in the correct column.

hats	girl	cows	kittens	melon
spoons	glass	book	horse	trees

_____   _____

_____   _____

_____   _____

_____   _____

Plurals

Plurals are words that mean more than one. To make a word plural, add **s** or **es** to it. In some words ending in **y**, the **y** changes to an **i** before adding **es**. For example, **baby** changes to **babies**.

Directions: Look at the following lists of plural words. Next to each, write the word that means one. The first one has been done for you.

foxes   __**fox**__

bushes   _____

dresses   _____

chairs   _____

shoes   _____

stories   _____

puppies   _____

matches   _____

cars   _____

glasses   _____

balls   _____

candies   _____

wishes   _____

boxes   _____

ladies   _____

bunnies   _____

desks   _____

dishes   _____

pencils   _____

trucks   _____

Facing the Sun

Directions: Read the clues and use the words in the word box to complete the puzzle.

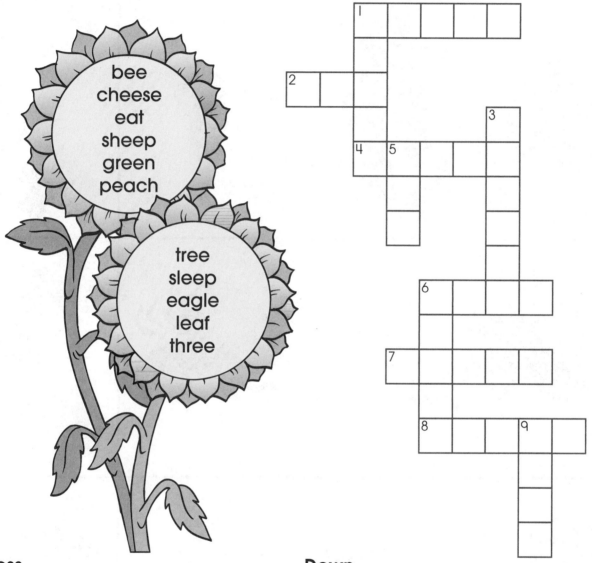

bee
cheese
eat
sheep
green
peach

tree
sleep
eagle
leaf
three

Across

1. A farm animal.
2. A buzzing bug.
4. A fruit.
6. A very tall plant.
7. The color of grass.
8. A big bird.

Down

1. At night you _____.
3. A mouse eats _____.
5. You _____ food.
6. 2 + 1 = _____.
9. A part of a plant.

Down by the Sea

Directions: Circle the animal that comes next in each row.

Holidays

Directions: Write the holidays from the word box in the puzzle. Then, find the secret word in the heavy boxes going down.

1. _ _ _ _ _ m _ _
2. _ _ _ _ _ `s ■ _ _
3. _ _ _ _ _ _ _ `s ■ _ _ _
4. _ _ _ _ n _ _ _ _ _ _
5. _ _ _ o ■ _ _
6. _ _ _ _
7. _ _ _ k _ _ _
8. _ _ _ _ _ s ■ _ _ _
9. M _ _ _ _ ■ _ _ _

| Mother's Day |
| Father's Day |
| Veterans Day |
| Independence Day |
| Arbor Day |
| Christmas |
| Easter |
| Valentine's Day |
| Hanukkah |

The secret word is _____.

Capitalization

The first word and all of the important words in a title begin with a capital letter.

Directions: Write the book titles on the lines below. Use capital letters.

1. _____

2. _____

3. _____

4. _____

5. _____

6. _____

Super Circus

Directions: Color each **v** green. Then, color the rest of the picture.

Fall

Directions: Read the clues and use the words in the word box to complete the puzzle.

leaves
pumpkin
apples
moon
yellow
squirrels
geese
rake

Across

3. They gather nuts.
5. Use this to gather fallen leaves.
6. These change color in the fall.
8. This looks big and bright in the sky.

Down

1. Pick a big, orange one.
2. They fly south in the fall.
4. Leaves turn red, brown, and this color.
7. Pick a basket of red, ripe ones.

Pronouns

Pronouns are words that can be used instead of nouns. **She**, **he**, **it**, and **they** are pronouns.

Directions: Read the sentence. Then, write the sentence again, using **she**, **he**, **it**, or **they** in the blank.

1. Dan likes funny jokes. _____ likes funny jokes.

2. Mei and Sam went to the zoo. _____ went to the zoo.

3. My dog likes to dig in the yard. _____ likes to dig in the yard.

4. Sara is a very good dancer. _____ is a very good dancer.

5. Levi and Leo are twins. _____ are twins.

Let's Play

Directions: Use the words in the word box to help you write the name of each picture.

1.

		l	

2.

	i		

3.

s					s

4.

		g		

5.

g			

6.

	w		n	

7.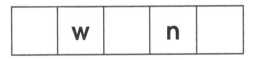

	r			

8.

			m

bike
skates
ball
swing
wagon
truck
swim
game

Name _____

Mystery Sentence

Directions: Color the following words in the puzzle green.

if	is	but	shoe	can	house	in

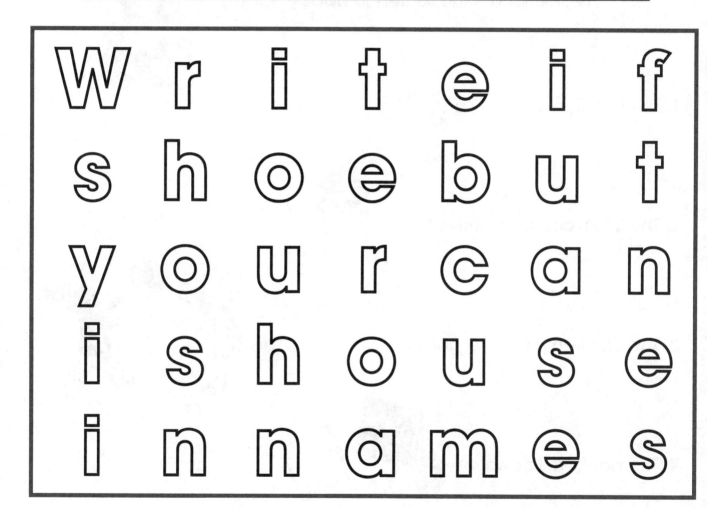

Directions: Write the words you did not color to make a sentence.

_____ _____ _____ .

Subjects

The **subject** of a sentence is the person, place, or thing the sentence is about.

Directions: Underline the subject in each sentence.

Example: Mom read a book.
(Think: Who is the sentence about? Mom)

1. The bird flew away.

2. The kite was high in the air.

3. The children played a game.

4. The books fell down.

5. The monkey climbed a tree.

Compound Subjects

Two similar sentences can be joined into one sentence if the predicate is the same. A **compound subject** is made of two subjects joined together by a conjunction, such as **and**.

Example: Jamie can sing
    Sofia can sing.

Jamie **and** Sofia can sing.

Directions: Combine the sentences. Write the new sentence on the line.

1. The cats are my pets.
   The dogs are my pets.

_____

2. Chairs are in the store.
   Tables are in the store.

_____

3. Myles can ride a bike.
   Jack can ride a bike.

_____

For the Birds

Directions: Write the bird names from the word box in the puzzle.

1. | | a | |
2. | | | |
3. | | g | |
4. | | | |
5. | | | | t | |
6. o | | | | |
7. | | e | | |
8. b | | | | |

buzzard   ostrich   eagle

jay   robin   owl

pigeons   parrots

The Calendar

Directions: Read the clues and use the words in the word box to complete the puzzle.

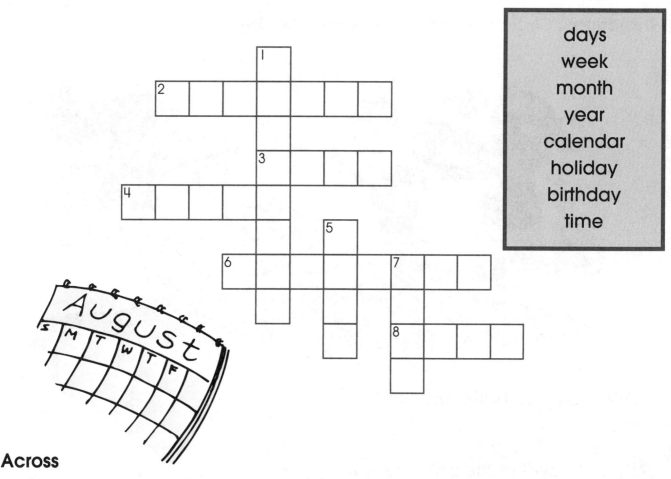

| days |
| week |
| month |
| year |
| calendar |
| holiday |
| birthday |
| time |

Across

2. It is a day for celebrating instead of working.
3. It can be measured in days, weeks, months, and years.
4. It can have 28 to 31 days.
6. You can hang it on a wall to keep track of the days.
8. This has twelve months.

Down

1. This is the day you were born.
5. It has seven days.
7. A year has 365 of these.

Verbs

A **verb** is the action word in a sentence. Verbs tell what something does.

Example: Run, **sleep**, and **jump** are verbs.

Directions: Circle the verbs in the sentences below.

1. We play baseball every day.

2. Maddy pitches the ball very well.

3. Marco swings the bat harder than anyone.

4. Chris slides into home base.

5. Laura hit a home run.

Verbs

Verbs tell when something happens. Add **ed** to verbs to tell that something has already happened.

Example: Today, we will **play**. Yesterday, we **played**.

Directions: Write the correct verb in the blank.

1. Today, I will _____ my dog, Fritz.
                    wash   washed

2. Last week, Fritz _____ when we said, "Bath time, Fritz."
                    cry   cried

3. My sister likes to _____ wash Fritz.
                    help   helped

4. One time she _____ Fritz by herself.
                    clean   cleaned

5. Fritz will _____ a lot better after his bath.
                    look   looked

What Can Hop?

Directions: Color the spaces with **S** green. Color the spaces with **T** yellow.

Unscramble Time

Directions: Unscramble each word. Be sure it goes with the meaning.

1. One who plays is called a

   lapeyr __ __ __ __ __ __.

2. A round thing you can kick is a

   lalb __ __ __ __.

3. A sweet treat to eat is

   danyc __ __ __ __ __.

4. Something you can win is a

   pzire __ __ __ __ __.

5. A person who wins is the

   rnnewi __ __ __ __ __ __.

6. One who sails a boat is a

   ailsor __ __ __ __ __ __.

| prize |
| winner |
| player |
| ball |
| sailor |
| candy |

Predicates

The **predicate** is the part of the sentence that tells about the action.

Directions: Circle the predicate in each sentence.

Example: The boys ran on the playground.

      (Think: The boys did what? ⟨ Ran ⟩)

1. The woman painted a picture.

2. The puppy chases his ball.

3. The students went to school.

4. Butterflies fly in the air.

5. The baby wants a drink.

Compound Predicates

A **compound predicate** is made by joining two sentences that have the same subject. The predicates are usually joined together by the word **and**.

Example: Evan can jump.
              Evan can run.

Evan can <u>run **and** jump</u>.

Directions: Combine the sentence. Write the new sentence on the line.

1. The dog can roll over.
   The dog can bark.

_____

2. My mom plays with me.
   My mom reads with me.

_____

3. Tara is tall.
   Tara is smart.

_____

Subjects and Predicates

The **subject** of the sentence is the person, place, or thing the sentence is about. The **predicate** is the part of the sentence that describes the subject or tells what the subject does.

Directions: Draw a line between the subject and the predicate. Underline the noun in the subject, and circle the verb in the predicate.

Example: The furry <u>cat</u> | (ate) food.

1. Hannah walks to school.

2. The bus driver drove the children.

3. The school bell rang very loudly.

4. The teacher spoke to the students.

5. The girls opened their books.

Around the World

Directions: Read the clues and use the words in the word box to complete the puzzle.

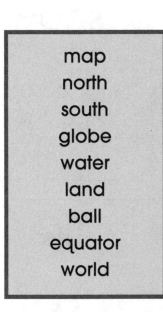

map
north
south
globe
water
land
ball
equator
world

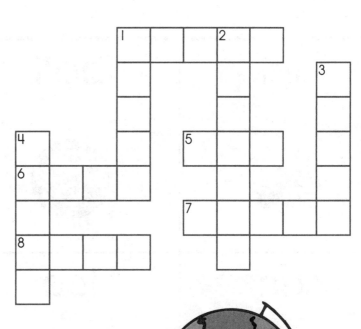

Across

1. It is blue on a globe.
5. It is a drawing of land and water on Earth.
6. It is green on a globe.
7. The direction moving toward the bottom of the globe.
8. A globe is shaped like a ____.

Down

1. A globe is a map of this.
2. It is an imaginary line around the middle of Earth.
3. The direction moving toward the top of the globe.
4. It is a model of Earth that is shaped like a ball.

Hot or Cold?

Directions: Draw straight lines to connect the words that name hot or cold things.

How many ways did you draw a line through three words in a row? _____

Fun in Art Class

Directions: Read the clues and use the words in the word box to complete the puzzle.

paintbrush
color
paper
clay
glue
paints
chalk
scissors
markers

Across
2. Use this to make paper stick together.
5. Remember to put the caps back on these.
7. Make a pot with this.
8. Use your brushes with these.
9. Draw a picture on this.

Down
1. Purple is one.
3. Use this to spread paint on paper.
4. Make sidewalk drawings with this.
6. Use this to cut scraps for a picture.

Parts of a Sentence

Directions: Draw a circle around the noun, the naming part of the sentence. Draw a line under the verb, the action part of the sentence.

Example: (John) drinks juice every morning.

1. Our class skates at the roller-skating rink.

2. Mason and Sadie go very fast.

3. Carson eats hot dogs.

4. Maya dances to the music.

5. Everyone likes the skating rink.

Name _____

A Space Trip

Directions: Color the letters **u** and **v** to find the path to the moon.

Adjectives

Adjectives are words that tell more about a person, place, or thing.

Examples: cold, fuzzy, dark

Directions: Circle the adjectives in the sentences.

1. The juicy apple is on the plate.

2. The furry dog is eating a bone.

3. It was a sunny day.

4. The kitten drinks warm milk.

5. The baby has a loud cry.

Adjectives

Directions: Choose an adjective from the box to fill in the blanks.

| hungry | sunny | busy | funny |
| fresh | deep | pretty | cloudy |

1. It is a _____ day on the Browns' farm.

2. Mr. Brown is a very _____ man.

3. Mrs. Brown likes to feed the _____ chickens.

4. Every day, she collects the _____ eggs.

5. The ducks swim in the _____ pond.

Ride It

Directions: Color the spaces with things you can ride in or on.

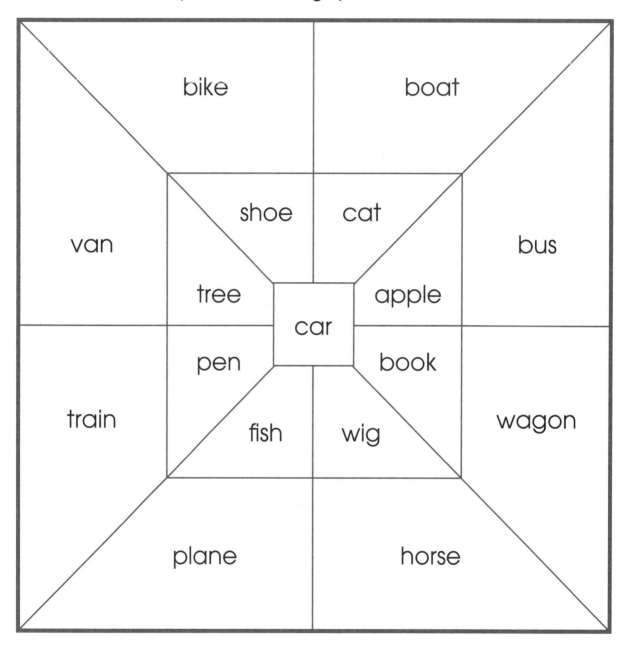

Articles

Articles are small words that help us to better understand nouns. **A** and **an** are articles. We use **an** before a word that begins with a vowel. We use **a** before a word that begins with a consonant.

Example: We looked in **a** nest. It had **an** eagle in it.

Directions: Read the sentences. Write **a** or **an** in the blank.

1. I found _____ book.

2. It had a story about _____ ant in it.

3. In the story, _____ lion gave three wishes to _____ ant.

4. The ant's first wish was to ride _____ elephant.

5. The second wish was to ride _____ alligator.

6. The last wish was _____ wish for three more wishes.

Mystery Picture

Directions: Read each sentence and cross out the picture. What picture is left?

1. It is not Earth.

2. It is not an astronaut.

3. It is not a shuttle.

4. It is not a helmet.

5. It is not a satellite.

6. It is not a rover.

7. It is not the moon.

The mystery picture is a _____ .

Sentences and Non-Sentences

A **sentence** tells a complete idea. It has a noun and a verb. It begins with a capital letter and has punctuation at the end.

Directions: Circle the group of words if it is a sentence.

1. Grass is a green plant.

2. Mowing the lawn.

3. Grass grows in fields and lawns.

4. Tickle the feet.

5. Sheep, cows, and horses eat grass.

6. We like to play in.

7. My sister likes to mow the lawn.

8. A picnic on the grass.

9. My dog likes to roll in the grass.

10. Plant flowers around.

Statements

Statements are sentences that tell us something. They begin with a capital letter and end with a period.

Directions: Write the sentences on the lines below. Begin each sentence with a capital letter, and end it with a period.

1. we like to ride our bikes

_____

2. we go down the hill very fast

_____

3. we keep our bikes shiny and clean

_____

4. we know how to change the tires

_____

Surprising Sentences

Surprising sentences tell a strong feeling and end with an exclamation point. A surprising sentence may be only one or two words showing fear, surprise, or pain. **Example: Oh, no!**

Directions: Put a period at the end of the sentences that tell something. Put an exclamation point at the end of the sentences that tell a strong feeling. Put a question mark at the end of the sentences that ask a question.

1. The cheetah can run very fast

2. Wow

3. Look at that cheetah go

4. Can you run fast

5. Oh, my

6. You're faster than I am

7. Let's run together

8. We can run as fast as a cheetah

9. What fun

10. Do you think cheetahs get tired

Commands

Commands tell someone to do something. **Example: Be careful.**
It can also be written as "Be careful!" if it tells a strong feeling.

Directions: Put a period at the end of the command sentences. Use an exclamation point if the sentence tells a strong feeling. Write your own commands on the lines below.

1. Clean your room

2. Now

3. Be careful with your goldfish

4. Watch out

5. Be a little more careful

_____

_____

Questions

Questions are sentences that ask something. They begin with a capital letter and end with a question mark.

Directions: Write the questions on the lines below. Begin each sentence with a capital letter, and end it with a question mark.

1. will you be my friend

_____

2. what is your name

_____

3. are you eight years old

_____

4. do you like rainbows

_____

Shining Bright

Directions: To find the mystery letter, color the spaces with the following letters **red**.

Q   F   V   P   G   O   M   N   U   S

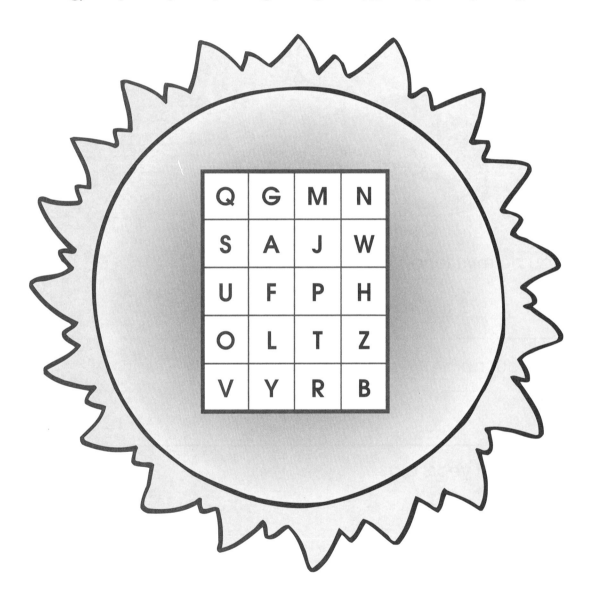

Circle the mystery letter.   E   F   P

Making Inferences: Writing Questions

Toban and Sean use many colors when they paint.

Directions: Write two questions for each answer.

Answer: It is red.

1. _____ ?

_____ ?

Answer: It is purple.

2. _____ ?

_____ ?

Answer: It is green.

3. _____ ?

_____ ?

Making Inferences: Point of View

Chelsea likes to pretend she is meeting famous people. She would like to ask them many questions.

Directions: Write a question you think Chelsea would ask if she met these people.

1. an actor in a popular new film _____

_____?

2. an Olympic gold medal winner _____

_____?

3. an alien from outer space _____

_____?

Directions: Now, write the answers these people might have given to Chelsea's questions.

4. an actor in a popular new film _____

_____

5. an Olympic gold medal winner _____

_____

6. an alien from outer space _____

_____

Making Inferences: Point of View

Ellen likes animals. Someday, she might want to be a veterinarian.

Directions: Write one question you think Ellen would ask each of these animals if she could speak their language.

1. a giraffe _____?

2. a mouse _____?

3. a shark _____?

4. a hippopotamus _____?

5. a penguin _____?

6. a gorilla _____?

7. an eagle _____?

Directions: Now, write the answers you think these animals might have given Ellen.

8. a giraffe _____

9. a mouse _____

10. a shark _____

11. a hippopotamus _____

12. a penguin _____

13. a gorilla _____

14. an eagle _____

Going Places

Directions: Read the clues and use the words in the word box to complete the puzzle.

airplane
train
bike
bus
car
truck
boat
horse
balloon

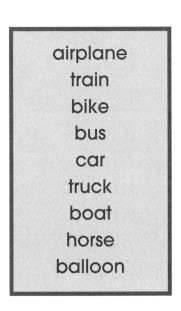
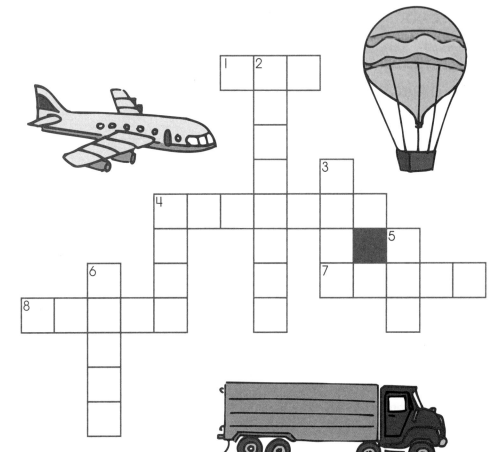

Across

1. It is an automobile.
4. Hot air makes it rise into the sky.
7. This can carry heavy loads on the road.
8. It has a saddle.

Down

2. This flies people from city to city.
3. This carries people and big loads on water.
4. It has two wheels and pedals.
5. This takes many people around the city.
6. It runs on tracks.

Ownership

Add **'s** to nouns (people, places, or things) to tell who or what owns something.

Directions: Read the sentences. Fill in the blanks to show ownership.

Example: The doll belongs to **Sara**.

It is **Sara's** doll.

1. Sparky has a red collar.

    _____ collar is red.

2. Jimmy has a blue coat.

    _____ coat is blue.

3. The tail of the cat is short.

    The _____ tail is short.

4. The name of my mother is Karen.

    My _____ name is Karen.

Ownership

Directions: Read the sentences. Choose the correct word and write it in each sentence below.

1. The _____ lunchbox is broken.   boys   boy's

2. The _____ played in the cage.   gerbil's   gerbils

3. _____ hair is brown.   Anns   Ann's

4. The _____ ran in the field.   horse's   horses

5. My _____ coat is torn.   sister's   sisters

6. The _____ fur is brown.   cats   cat's

7. Three _____ flew past our window.   birds   bird's

8. The _____ paws are muddy.   dogs   dog's

9. The _____ neck is long.   giraffes   giraffe's

10. The _____ are big and powerful.   lion's   lions

Word Triangles

Directions: Complete the word triangles by adding one letter in each row to form a new word. Use the sentence clues to help you.

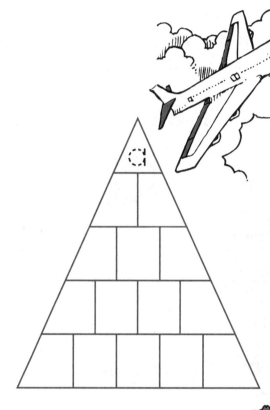

1. I got _____ new bike.

2. I saw _____ elephant at the zoo.

3. Sheila _____ I are friends.

4. The plane will _____ on time.

5. This food tastes _____ .

1. I have _____ dog.

2. Be there _____ noon.

3. Max _____ lunch at home.

4. At this _____, we'll be late.

5. I bought a _____ of oranges.

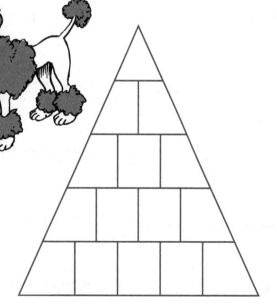

Is, Are, and Am

Is, **are**, and **am** are special action words that tell us something is happening now.

Use **am** with **I**. **Example: I am**.
Use **is** to tell about one person or thing. **Example: He is**.
Use **are** to tell about more than one. **Example: We are**.
Use **are** with **you**. **Example: You are**.

Directions: Write **is**, **are**, or **am** in the sentences below.

1. My friends _____ helping me build a tree house.

2. It _____ in my backyard.

3. We _____ using hammers, wood, and nails.

4. It _____ a very hard job.

5. I _____ lucky to have good friends.

Was and *Were*

Was and **were** tell about something that already happened.

Use **was** to tell about one person or thing. **Example:** I **was**, he **was**. Use **were** to tell about more than one person or thing or when using the word **you**. **Example:** We **were**, you **were**.

Directions: Write **was** or **were** in each sentence.

1. Lily _____ eight years old on her birthday.

2. Colin and Charley _____ happy to be at the party.

3. Megan _____ too shy to sing "Happy Birthday."

4. Ben _____ sorry he dropped his cake.

5. All of the children _____ happy to be invited.

Go, Going, and Went

Use **go** or **going** to tell about now or later. Sometimes, **going** is used with the words **am** or **are**. Use **went** to tell about something that already happened.

Directions: Write **go**, **going**, or **went** in the sentences below.

1. Today, I will _____ to the store.

2. Yesterday, we _____ shopping.

3. I am _____ to take Muffy to the vet.

4. Colin and Charley _____ to the party.

5. They are _____ to have a good day.

Have, Has, and Had

Use **have** and **has** to tell about now. Use **had** to tell about something that already happened.

Directions: Write **has**, **have**, or **had** in the sentences below.

I. We _____ three cats at home.

2. Ginger _____ brown fur.

3. Bucky and Charlie _____ gray fur.

4. My friend Antonio _____ one cat, but it ran away.

5. Antonio _____ a new cat now.

See, Saw, and Sees

Use **see** or **sees** to tell about now. Use **saw** to tell about something that already happened.

Directions: Write **see**, **sees**, or **saw** in the sentences below.

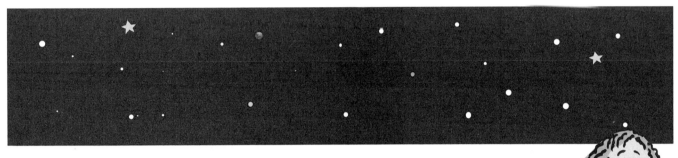

1. Last night, we _____ the stars.

2. John can _____ the stars from his window.

3. He _____ them every night.

4. Last week, he _____ the Big Dipper.

5. Can you _____ it in the night sky, too?

6. If you _____ it, you would remember it!

7. John _____ it often now.

8. How often do you _____ it?

Eat, *Eats*, and *Ate*

Use **eat** or **eats** to tell about now. Use **ate** to tell about what already happened.

Directions: Write **eat**, **eats**, or **ate** in the sentences below.

1. We like to _____ in the lunchroom.

2. Today, my teacher will _____ in a different room.

3. She _____ with the other teachers.

4. Yesterday, we _____ pizza, pears, and peas.

5. Today, we will _____ turkey and potatoes.

Leave, Leaves, and Left

Use **leave** and **leaves** to tell about now. Use **left** to tell about what already happened.

Directions: Write **leave**, **leaves**, or **left** in the sentences below.

1. Last winter, we _____ seeds in the bird feeder every day.

2. My mother likes to _____ food out for the squirrels.

3. When it rains, she _____ bread for the birds.

4. Yesterday, she _____ popcorn for the birds.

Spelling

Short *A* Words: Rhyming Words

Short a is the sound you hear in the word **math**.

Directions: Use the **short a** words in the box to write rhyming words.

lamp	fat	bat	van
path	can	cat	man
math	stamp	fan	sat

1. Write four words that rhyme with **mat**.

_____ _____

_____ _____

2. Write two words that rhyme with **bath**.

_____ _____

3. Write two words that rhyme with **damp**.

_____ _____

4. Write four words that rhyme with **pan**.

_____ _____

_____ _____

Short *A* Words: Sentences

Directions: Use a word from the box to complete each sentence.

fat	path	lamp	can
van	stamp	man	math
sat	cat	fan	bat

Example:

1. The _____ lamp _____ had a pink shade.

2. The bike _____ led us to the park.

3. I like to add in _____ class.

4. The cat is very _____.

5. The _____ of beans was hard to open.

6. The envelope needed a _____.

7. He swung the _____ and hit the ball.

8. The _____ blew air around.

9. My mom drives a blue _____.

10. I _____ in the backseat.

Long A Words

Long a is a vowel sound that says its own name. **Long a** can be spelled **ai**, as in the word **mail**, **ay**, as in the word **say**, and **a** with a **silent e** at the end of a word, as in the word **same**.

Directions: Say each word, and listen for the **long a** sound. Then, write each word, and underline the letters that make the **long a** vowel sound.

mail	bake	train
game	day	sale
paint	play	name
made	gray	tray

1. _____

2. _____

3. _____

4. _____

5. _____

6. _____

7. _____

8. _____

9. _____

10. _____

11. _____

12. _____

Long *A* Words: Rhyming Words

Long a is the vowel sound that you hear in the word **cake**.

Directions: Use the **long a** words in the box to write rhyming words.

paint	gray	train	tray
mail	day	sale	play
game	made	name	bake

1. Write the word that rhymes with **make**.

_____

2. Write the words that rhyme with **hail**.

_____   _____

3. Write the words that rhyme with **say**.

_____   _____

_____   _____

4. Write the word that rhymes with **shade**.

_____

5. Write the words that rhyme with **same**.

_____   _____

Long *A* Words

Directions: Write the words in order so that each sentence tells a complete idea. Begin each sentence with a capital letter, and end it with a period or a question mark.

1. plate was on the cake a

_____

2. like you would to play a game

_____

3. gray around the a corner train came

_____

4. was on mail Bob's name the

_____

5. sail for on day we went a nice a

_____

Can You Find It?

Directions: Help the detective find the magnifying glass.

Break the Code

Directions: Use the code to reveal the words. Draw lines to match rhyming words.

✕	⇨	✓	⚑	☆	❖	🎧	○	■	✴	★	☺	❄	✧	💧	❀	✐	◎	▢	✳	▤
e	k	m	w	s	d	c	i	q	r	h	g	u	f	o	l	a	p	n	j	t

1. ____ ____ ____ ____ ____ ____   ____ ____ ____ ____
   ☆   ■   ❄   ✕   ✐   ⇨   ✧   ✕   ✕   ▤

2. ____ ____ ____ ____ ____   ____ ____ ____ ____ ____
   🎧   ★   ✐   ☆   ✕   ☆   ⚑   ✕   ❀   ❀

3. ____ ____ ____ ____   ____ ____ ____ ____ ____
   ▤   ✕   ❀   ❀   ❀   ✕   ✐   ✴   ▢

4. ____ ____ ____ ____   ____ ____ ____ ____
   ✴   💧   ✐   ✴   ❖   💧   ▢   ✕

5. ____ ____ ____   ____ ____ ____ ____
   ✕   ✐   ▤   ❀   ✕   ✐   ⇨

6. ____ ____ ____   ____ ____ ____ ____
   ✴   ❄   ▢   ❀   ✐   🎧   ✕

7. ____ ____ ____ ____   ____ ____ ____ ____
   ▤   ❄   ✴   ▢   ❖   💧   💧   ✴

Name _____

Find the Path

Directions: Color the path to the circus tent.

Out and About

Directions: Help the family get from the bank to the library. Change two letters in each word to make a new word. Write the new word in the next step. Use the words in the word box.

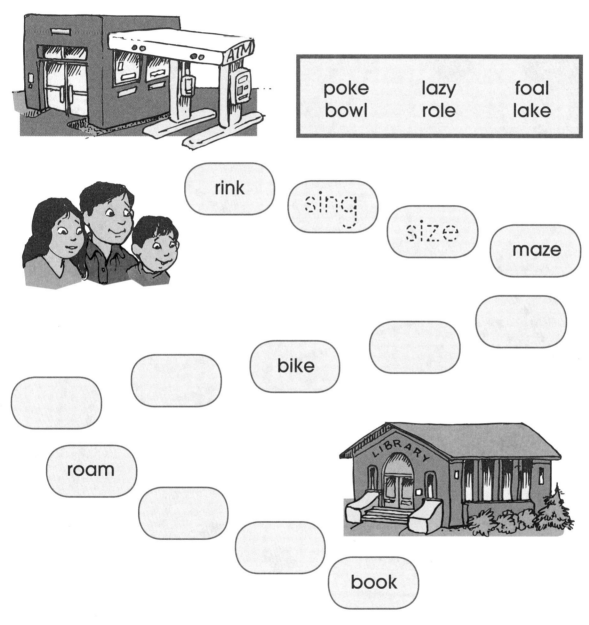

| poke | lazy | foal |
| bowl | role | lake |

rink

sing

size

maze

bike

roam

book

Around the World

Directions: Read the clues and use the words in the word box to complete the puzzle.

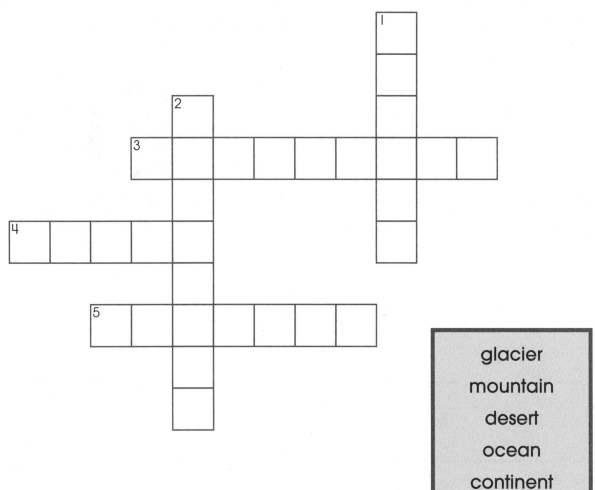

glacier
mountain
desert
ocean
continent

Across

3. A very large area of land.
4. A very large body of water.
5. A river of ice that seems to stand still.

Down

1. A hot, dry area.
2. A very high hill.

Short *O* Words

Short o is the vowel sound you hear in the word **pot**.

Directions: Say each word, and listen for the **short o** sound. Then, write each word, and underline the letter that makes the **short o** sound.

hot	box	sock	mop
stop	not	fox	cot
rob	rock	clock	lock

1. _____

2. _____

3. _____

4. _____

5. _____

6. _____

7. _____

8. _____

9. _____

10. _____

11. _____

12. _____

Short *O* Words: Rhyming Words

Short o is the vowel sound you hear in the word **got**.

Directions: Use the **short o** words in the box to write rhyming words.

hot	rock	lock	cot
stop	sock	fox	mop
box	mob	clock	rob

1. Write the words that rhyme with **dot**.

_____   _____

2. Write the words that rhyme with **socks**.

_____   _____

3. Write the words that rhyme with **hop**.

_____   _____

4. Write the words that rhyme with **dock**.

_____   _____

_____   _____

5. Write the words that rhyme with **cob**.

_____   _____

Long *O* Words

Long o is a vowel sound that says its own name. **Long o** can be spelled **oa**, as in the word **float**, or **o** with a **silent e** at the end, as in **cone**.

Directions: Say each word, and listen for the **long o** sound. Then, write each word, and underline the letters that make the **long o** sound.

rope	coat	soap	wrote
note	hope	boat	cone
bone	pole	phone	hole

1. _____

2. _____

3. _____

4. _____

5. _____

6. _____

7. _____

8. _____

9. _____

10. _____

11. _____

12. _____

Long *O* Words: Rhyming Words

Long o is the vowel sound you hear in the word **home**.

Directions: Use the **long o** words in the box to write rhyming words.

rope	soap	coat	wrote
note	boat	hope	cone
bone	phone	pole	hole

1. Write the words that rhyme with **mope**.

_____   _____   _____

2. Write the words that rhyme with **tote**.

_____   _____

_____   _____

3. Write the words that rhyme with **lone**.

_____   _____   _____

4. Write the words that rhyme with **goal**.

_____   _____

Name _____

Long *O* Words: Sentences

Directions: Draw a line from the first part of the sentence to the part that completes the sentence.

1. Do you know

in the water.

2. The dog

was in the tree.

3. The boat floats

who wrote the note?

4. I hope the phone

has a bone.

5. Ebony's ice-cream cone

rings soon for me!

6. The rope swing

a coat in the cold.

7. I had to wear

was melting.

Giddyup!

Directions: Help the horse find the pasture.

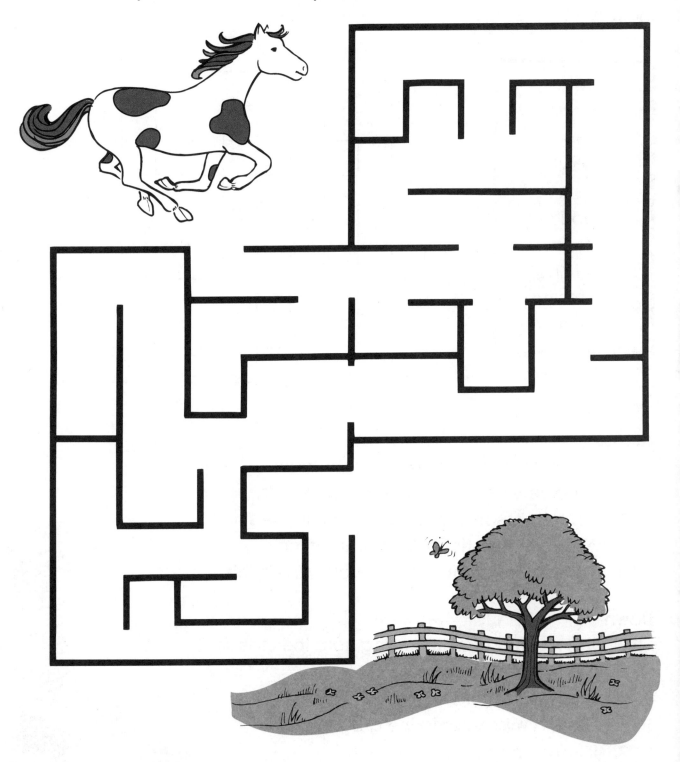

Weather Watch

Directions: Read the clues and use the words in the word box to complete the puzzle.

Word Box:
rain
thunder
tornado
wind
sunshine
cloud
storm
lightning
hurricane
fog

Across
1. This is a strong wind with rain or snow.
5. It is a very strong storm with high winds.
7. You might see a puffy white one in the sky.
8. A loud noise after a flash of lightning.
10. When there are no clouds, you will see this.

Down
2. This is drops of water falling from the clouds.
3. It is a twisting whirlwind.
4. This is a flash of electricity in the sky.
6. This is a mist close to the ground.
9. It is moving air.

Where's Teddy?

Directions: Help the girl find the teddy bear.

Fishes

Directions: Read the sentences and use the words in the word box to complete the puzzle.

colors

ocean

lakes

fins

mouths

gills

Across

1. Saltwater fish live in the ____.
3. Fish open and close their ____ as they swim to get air from the water.
4. The water comes out of their ____.
6. Fish have tails and ____.

Down

2. Fish are many different sizes, shapes, and ____.
5. Freshwater fish live in ponds, rivers, or ____.

Q Words

Directions: Write the word from the word box that means the same thing. Then, color the spaces with **q** words green. Color the other words orange.

1. bed cover _____	**2.** sick _____	**3.** silent _____
4. flower _____	**5.** fast _____	**6.** shoe _____
7. stop _____	**8.** present _____	**9.** bird _____

quit   quiet   ill   quilt   blossom

quick   sneaker   quail   gift

Name _____

Animal Words

Directions: Write the animal names twice beside each picture.

| fox | rabbit | bear | squirrel | mouse | fox |

Example:

 squirrel   squirrel

Animal Words

Directions: Circle the word in each sentence that is not spelled correctly. Then, write it correctly.

squirrel	bears	rabbit	deer	fox	mouse

Example:

Animals like to live in (threes.)

trees

1. Bares do not eat people

_____

2. The squirel found a nut.

_____

3. Sometimes, a little moose might get into your house.

_____

4. Dear eat leaves and grass.

_____

5. A focks has a bushy tail.

_____

6. One day, a rabbitt came into our yard.

_____

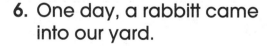

Animal Words: More Than One

To show more than one of something, add **s** to most words.

Example: one dog – **two dogs**   one book – **two books**

But some words are different. For words that end with **x**, use **es** to show two.

Example: one fox – **two foxes**   one box – **two boxes**

The spelling of some words changes a lot when there are two.

Example: one mouse – **two mice**

Some words stay the same, even when you mean two of something.

Example: one deer – **two deer**   one fish – **two fish**

Directions: Complete the sentences below with the correct word.

1. The  run fast.   _____

2. The  are eating.   _____

3. Have you seen any today?   _____

4. Where do the  live?   _____

5. Did you ever have  for pets?   _____

Animal Words: More Than One

Directions: Write the two sentences below as one sentence. Remember the special spelling of **fox**, **mouse**, and **deer** when there are more than one.

Example:

I saw a mouse. You saw a mouse.

We saw two mice.

1. Julie petted a deer.
   Matt petted a deer.

_____

_____

2. Avi colored a fox.
   Nora colored a fox.

_____

_____

Animal Words: Kinds of Sentences

Another name for an asking sentence is a **question**.

Directions: Use the words in the box to write a telling sentence.
Then, use the words to write a question.

Example:

a	mouse	I	see
the	bed	under	do

Telling sentence:

I see a mouse under the bed.

Question:

Do I see a mouse under the bed?

in	live
these	woods
bears	do

Telling sentence:

_____

Question:

_____

Pet Time

Directions: Look in the bone for the things you might need for a new pet. Then, write the words in the puzzle.

leash   food   collar   treats

bones   bed   blanket

Name _____

Rain, Rain, Go Away

Directions: Find these things that begin with **m**. Color them **brown**. Then, color the rest of the picture.

mouse   monkey   mop   milk   mask

Ready for Rain

Directions: Color the spaces with **S** red. Color the spaces with **t** blue.

Short *E* Words

Short e is the vowel sound you hear in the word **pet**.

Directions: Say each word, and listen for the **short e** sound. Then, write each word, and underline the letter that makes the **short e** sound.

get	beg	rest	tent
red	spent	test	help
bed	pet	when	best

1. _____

2. _____

3. _____

4. _____

5. _____

6. _____

7. _____

8. _____

9. _____

10. _____

11. _____

12. _____

Name _____

Short *E* Words: Rhyming Words

Short e is the vowel sound you hear in the word **egg**.

Directions: Use the **short e** words in the box to write rhyming words.

get	test	pet	help
let	head	spent	red
best	tent	rest	bed

1. Write the words that rhyme with **fed**.

_____   _____   _____

2. Write the words that rhyme with **bent**.

_____   _____

3. Write the words that rhyme with **west**.

_____   _____   _____

4. Write the words that rhyme with **bet**.

_____   _____   _____

Short *E* Words: Sentences

Directions: Write the correct **short e** word in each sentence.

get	beg	rest	bed	spent	best
test	help	head	pet	red	tent

1. Of all my crayons, I like the color _____

the _____ !

2. I always make my _____ when I _____ up.

3. My new hat keeps my _____ warm.

4. _____ your mom for a _____ dog.

5. When we go camping, my job is to _____ put up

the _____ .

6. I have a _____ in math tomorrow, so I want to get

a good night's _____ .

Name _____

Long *E* Words

Long e is the vowel sound that says its own name. **Long e** can be spelled **ee**, as in the word **teeth**, **ea**, as in the word **meat**, or **e**, as in the word **me**.

Directions: Say each word, and listen for the **long e** sound. Then, write the words, and underline the letters that make the **long e** sound.

street	neat	treat	feet
sleep	keep	deal	meal
mean	clean	beast	feast

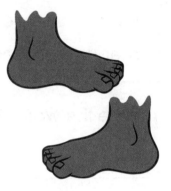

1. _____

2. _____

3. _____

4. _____

5. _____

6. _____

7. _____

8. _____

9. _____

10. _____

11. _____

12. _____

Long *E* Words: Rhyming Words

Long e is the vowel sound you hear in the word **meet**.

Directions: Use the **long e** words in the box to write rhyming words.

street	feet	neat	treat
keep	deal	sleep	meal
mean	beast	clean	feast

1. Write the words that rhyme with **beat**.

_____   _____

_____   _____

2. Write the words that rhyme with **deep**.

_____   _____

3. Write the words that rhyme with **feel**.

_____   _____

4. Write the words that rhyme with **bean**.

_____   _____

5. Write the words that rhyme with **least**.

_____   _____

Long *E* Words: Sentences

Directions: Write a word from the box to complete each sentence.

street	feet	neat	treat
keep	deal	sleep	meal
mean	beast	clean	feast

1. I went to _____ late last night.

2. One of my favorite stories is "Beauty and

    the _____ ."

3. Look both ways when you cross the _____ .

4. It would be _____ to kick someone.

5. I wear socks and shoes on my _____ .

6. The most important _____ of the day

    is breakfast.

Morse Code

Directions: Use the code box to decode the messages by substituting the correct letters for the dots and dashes. Then, try to write your own message in Morse code. Ask a friend to solve it.

1. --/---/•-•/•••/•   -•-•/---/-••/•   •--/•-/•••

   _____ _____ _____

   -••/•/•••-/•/•-••/---/•--•/•/-••   -•••/-•--

   _____ _____

   •••/•-/--/••-/•/•--••   --/---/•-•/•••/•

   _____ _____ .

2. ••/-   ••/•••   •-   •••/•/•-•/••/•••/   ---/•--

   __ ____ __ _____ _____

   -••/---/-/•••   •-/-•/•••   -••/•-/•••/•••/•/•/•/••

   _____ _____ _____

   ••-/•••/•/-••   -/---   •••/•/-•/-••

   _____ ____ _____

   --/•/•••/•••/•-/--•/•/•••   ---/-   -/••••/•

   _____ _____ _____

   -/•/•-••/•/--•/•-•/•-/--•/•••

   _____ .

A	• —
B	— • • •
C	— • — •
D	— • •
E	•
F	• • — •
G	— — •
H	• • • •
I	• •
J	• — — —
K	— • —
L	• — • •
M	— —
N	— •
O	— — —
P	• — — •
Q	— — • —
R	• — •
S	• • •
T	—
U	• • —
V	• • • —
W	• — —
X	— • • —
Y	— • — —
Z	— — • •

Find It

Directions: Look at the two closets. Find and circle **5** objects in the top picture that are not in the bottom picture.

Name _____

Parts of a Book

Directions: Read the clues and use the words in the word box to complete the puzzle.

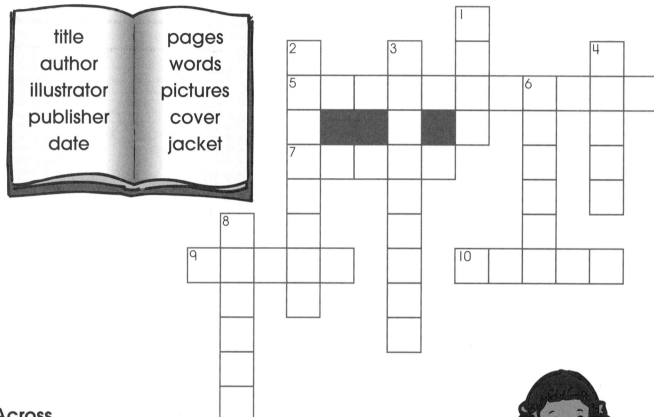

title pages
author words
illustrator pictures
publisher cover
date jacket

Across

5. This is a person who draws the pictures.
7. This is the name of the book.
9. The pieces of paper in a book.
10. The writing in a book.

Down

1. The year the book was made.
2. The drawings or photos in a book.
3. The company that made the book.
4. The outside front and back of the book.
6. The person who wrote the book.
8. A paper cover on the outside of a book.

What Might You See?

Directions: When you ride on the highway, what do you see? Draw what you think you might see. Then, color.

Name _____

Camping Out

Directions: Color the letters **R** and **r** to find the path to the tent.

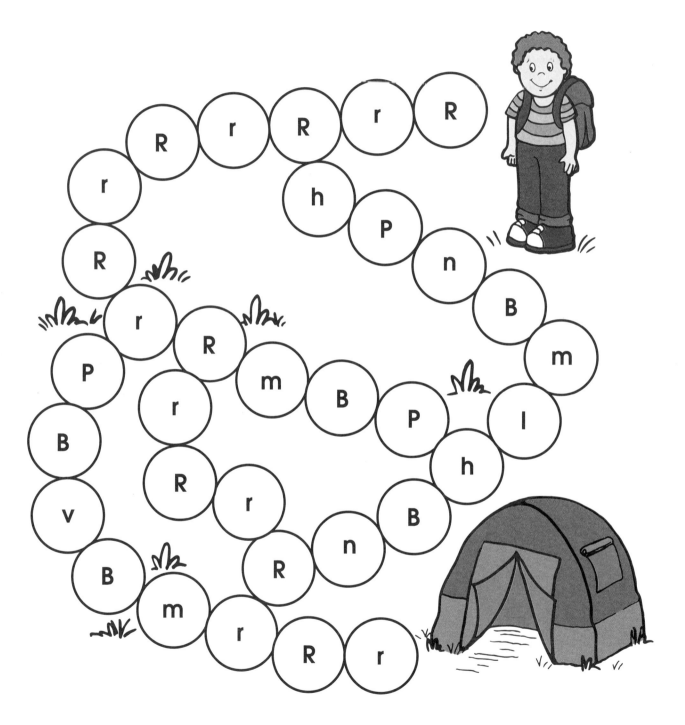

What Shines?

Directions: Color the spaces with **N** orange. Color the spaces with **n** yellow.

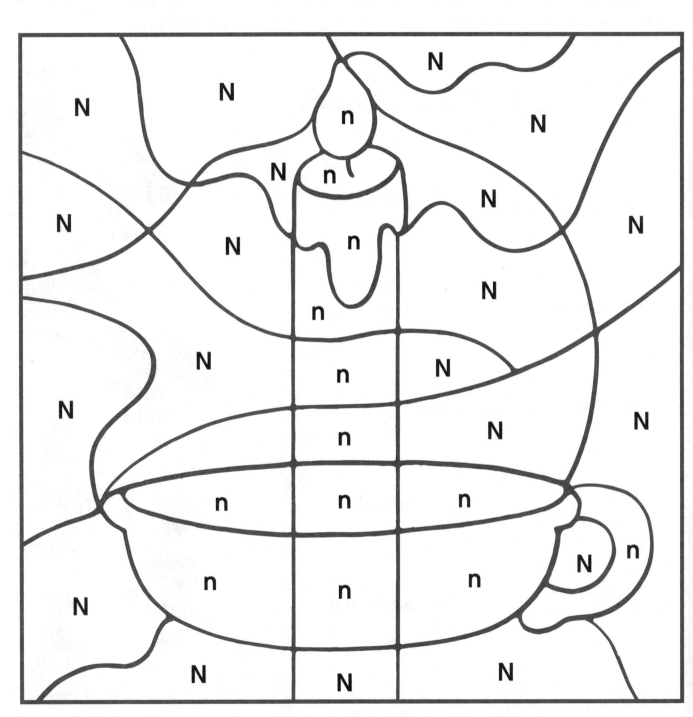

Verbs

Verbs are words that tell the action in the sentence.

Directions: Draw a line from each sentence to its picture. Then, finish the sentence with the verb or action word that is under each picture.

Example:
He will _____help_____ the baby.

carry

help

1. I can _____ my book.

cut

2. It is time to _____ up.

build

3. That chair might _____.

4. They _____ houses.

clean

5. I _____ this out myself.

fix

6. Is that too heavy to _____?

break

Verbs: Sentences

Directions: Read the two sentences in each story below. Then, write one more sentence to tell what happened next. Use the verbs from the box.

break	build	fix	clean	cut	carry

 Today is Nate's birthday.

Nate asked four friends to come.

_____

 Audrey's dog walked in the mud.

He got mud in the house.

_____

Verbs: Sentences

Directions: Join each pair of sentences to make one longer sentence. Use one of the **joining** words: **and**, **but**, or **or**. In the second part of the sentence, use **he**, **she**, or **they** in place of the person's name.

Example: I asked Tim to help me. Tim wanted to play.

<u>I asked Tim to help me, but he wanted to play.</u>

1. Kelly dropped a glass. Kelly cut her finger.

_____

_____

2. Linda and Allen got a new dog. Linda and Allen named it Baby.

_____

_____

Verbs: Word Endings

Most **verbs** end with **s** when the sentence tells about one thing. The **s** is taken away when the sentence tells about more than one thing.

Example:

One dog walks.   One boy runs.
Two dogs **walk**.   Three boys **run**.

The spelling of some **verbs** changes when the sentence tells about only one thing.

Example:

One girl carries her lunch.   The boy fixes his car.
Two girls **carry** their lunches.   Two boys **fix** their cars.

Directions: Write the missing verbs in the sentences.

Example:

Alma works hard. She and Peter ___work___ all day.

1. The father bird builds a nest

   The mother and father _____ it together.

2. The girls clean their room. Jenny _____ under her bed.

3. The children cut out their pictures. Henry _____ his slowly.

4. These workers fix things. This man _____ televisions.

5. Two trucks carry horses. One truck _____ pigs.

Verbs: Completing a Story

Directions: Write a sentence that tells what happens in each picture. Use the **verb** under the picture.

Example:

fall　　　　　　　　**break**　　　　　　　　**clean**

A glass falls off the table.

_____

_____

fix　　　　　　　　**cut**　　　　　　　　**carry**

_____

_____

_____

Verbs

Directions: Circle the words in each sentence that are not spelled correctly. Then, write the sentence correctly.

Example:

I need to (klean) the cage my (mouses) live in.

I need to clean the cage
my mice live in.

1. The chair will brake if tree of us sit on it.

_____

_____

2. A muther bare carries her baby in hir mouth.

_____

_____

Jump With J

Directions: Write the j words in the puzzles. Find the mystery words by reading the letters in the boxes going down.

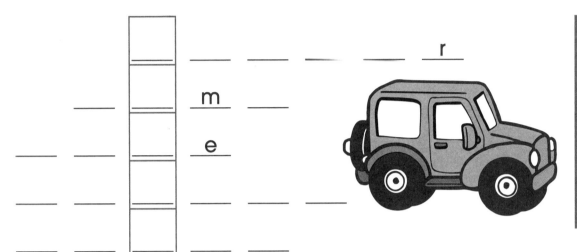

_ _ _ _ _ r _

_ _ m _

_ _ _ e _

_ _ _ _

_ _ _ _ _

_ e _

Word box:
jump
jaguar
June
jelly
juggle
jeep

The mystery word is

_____ .

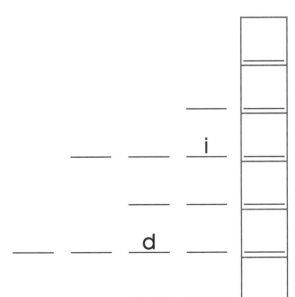

_ o _

_ _ m _

_ i _

_ _ _

_ d _ _

_ _ _

Word box:
jet
joke
juice
judge
jog
jam

The mystery word is

_____ .

Mouse House

Directions: Help the mouse get to its hole by following words in ABC order.

apple	bone	eagle	map
eggs	dollar	color	pie	igloo
finger	gate	note	on	dog
van	ham	ice	pen	red
ax	queen	jet	kite	lion

Name _____

What Floats?

Directions: Color the spaces with **Q** yellow. Color the spaces with **q** blue.

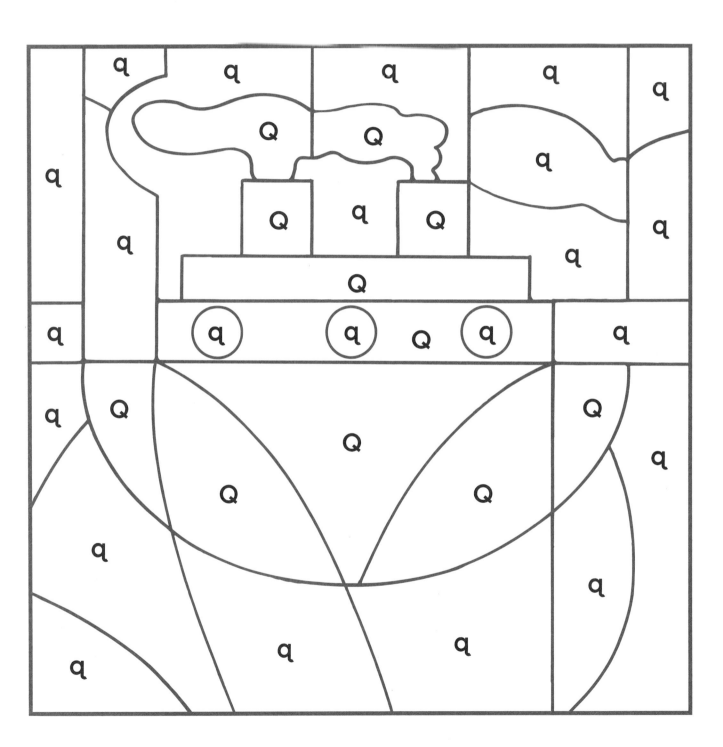

Name _____

Fire Safety

Directions: Read the sentences and use the words in the word box to complete the puzzle.

breathe

shout

opening

roll

call

calm

Across

2. Feel the door first before _____ it.
3. Stay low, close to the floor, to _____ the cleaner air.
6. _____ 9-1-1 immediately.

Down

1. _____ loudly to let people know there's a fire.
4. Stop, drop, and _____ if your clothing is on fire.
5. Stay _____.

Name _____

Secret Word

Directions: Use the clues to help you fill in the puzzles.

1. It means large. ◯ _ _

2. You can chew it. ___ ◯ ___

3. You can eat it. ◯ ___ ___

4. It can keep you cool. ___ ___ ◯ ___

5. It can melt. ◯ ___ ___

6. You sleep in it. ___ ◯ ___

7. It keeps Earth warm. ◯ ___ ___

fan

ice

bed

nut

big

sun

gum

Directions: Find the secret word by writing the circled letters in order.

___ ___ ___ ___ ___ ___ ___

Land and Water

Directions: Read the clues and use the words in the word box to complete the puzzle.

| mountain |
| valley |
| plain |
| ocean |
| lake |
| river |

Across

2. This is a body of fresh water surrounded by land.
4. This is a very high hill.
6. This is low land between mountains or hills.

Down

1. This is a very flat stretch of land.
3. This is a flowing stream of water.
5. This is a large body of salt water.

Short *I* Words

Short i is the vowel sound you hear in the word **pig**.

Directions: Say each word, and listen for the **short i** sound. Then, write each word, and underline the letter that makes the **short i** sound.

pin	fin	dip	dish
kick	rich	ship	wish
win	fish	sick	pitch

1. _____

2. _____

3. _____

4. _____

5. _____

6. _____

7. _____

8. _____

9. _____

10. _____

11. _____

12. _____

Short *I* Words: Rhyming Words

Short i is the vowel sound you hear in the word **pin**.

Directions: Use the **short i** words in the box to write rhyming words.

pin	fin	win	fish
pitch	wish	rich	kick
ship	dip	dish	sick

1. Write the words that rhyme with **spin**.

_____ _____ _____

2. Write the words that rhyme with **ditch**.

_____ _____

3. Write the words that rhyme with **rip**.

_____ _____

4. Write the words that rhyme with **squish**.

_____ _____ _____

5. Write the words that rhyme with **lick**.

_____ _____

Name _____

Short *I* Words: Sentences

Directions: Complete each sentence by drawing a line to the correct **short i** word.

1. I made a _____ on a star.

    fin

2. All we could see was the shark's _____ above the water.

    fish

3. I like to eat vegetables with _____ .

    kick

4. We saw lots of _____ in the water.

    win

5. The soccer player will _____ the ball and score a goal.

    dish

6. If you feel _____ , see a doctor.

    dip

7. Did Kenji _____ the race?

    wish

8. The _____ was full of candy.

    sick

Long *I* Words

Long i is the vowel sound that says its own name. **Long i** can be spelled **igh**, as in **sight**, **i** with a **silent e** at the end, as in **mine**, and **y** at the end, as in **fly**.

Directions: Say each word, and listen for the **long i** sound. Then, write each word, and underline the letters that make the **long i** sound.

bike	fry	ride	line
glide	ripe	nine	pipe
fight	high	light	sigh

1. _____

2. _____

3. _____

4. _____

5. _____

6. _____

7. _____

8. _____

9. _____

10. _____

11. _____

12. _____

Long *I* Words: Rhyming Words

Long i is the sound you hear in the word **fight**.

Directions: Use the **long i** words in the box to write rhyming words.

hide	ride	line	my
by	nine	high	light
sight	fly		

1. Write the words that rhyme with **sigh**.

_____ _____ _____ _____

2. Write the words that rhyme with **side**.

_____ _____

3. Write the words that rhyme with **fine**.

_____ _____

4. Write the words that rhyme with **fight**.

_____ _____

Figure It Out

Directions: Write the beginning letter of each word in the boxes to make a new word.

1.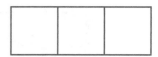

2.

3.

4.

Name _____

Plants We Eat

Directions: Read the sentences and use the words in the word box to complete the puzzle.

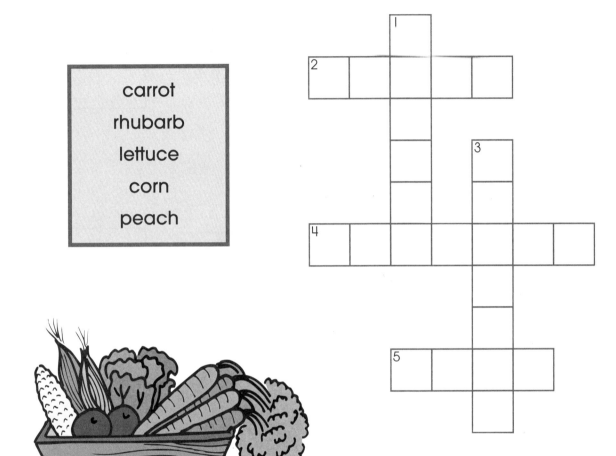

carrot

rhubarb

lettuce

corn

peach

Across

2. When we eat a ____, we are eating the fruit of a plant.
4. When we eat ____, we are eating the leaves of a plant.
5. When we eat ____, we are eating the seeds of a plant.

Down

1. When we eat a ____, we are eating the root of a plant.
3. When we eat ____, we are eating the stem of a plant.

Picnic

Directions: Find these things that begin with **c**. Color them yellow. Then, color the rest of the picture.

cat   can   cap   cloud   cake

In Space

Directions: Read the clues and use the words in the word box to complete the puzzle.

Earth
planets
stars
sun
moon
space
astronaut
orbit

Across

2. It is the planet we live on.
4. It is the path Earth takes around the sun.
5. This warms Earth and gives it light.
6. It goes around Earth and we see it at night.
7. Astronauts ride shuttles to get to outer _____.
8. Eight of these go around the sun.

Down

1. There are many of these in the night sky.
3. Someone who travels in space.

Up, Up, and Away

Directions: Color the spaces with things that we eat **blue**. Color the spaces with things that we wear yellow. Color the spaces with things that we ride in green.

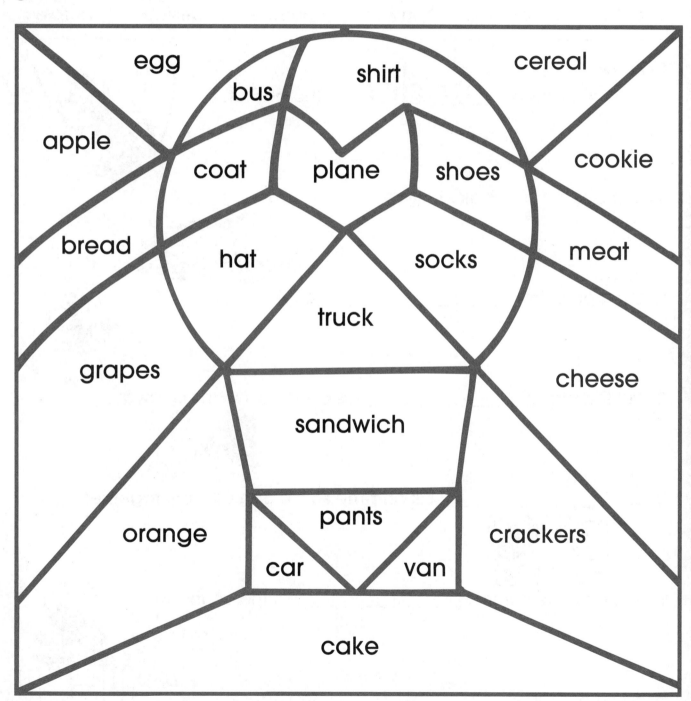

Location Words

Directions: Use one of the location words from the box to complete each sentence.

between	around	Inside	outside	beside	across

Example:

She will hide ___under___ the basket.

1. In the summer, we like to play _____.

2. She can swim _____ the lake.

3. Put the bird _____ its cage so it won't fly away.

4. Sit _____ Bill and me so we can all work together.

5. Your picture is right _____ mine on the wall.

6. The fence goes _____ the house.

Location Words

Directions: Draw a line from each sentence to its picture. Then, complete each sentence with the word under the picture.

Example:

He is walking ___**behind**___ the tree.

outside

1. We stay _____ when it rains.

behind

2. She drew a dog _____ his house.

between

3. She stands _____ her friends.

across

4. They walked _____ the bridge.

around

5. Let the cat go _____.

beside

6. Draw a circle _____ the fish.

inside

Location Words

Directions: Write the location words that answer the questions.

between	around	inside	outside	beside	across

1. Write all the smaller words you find In the location words.

   _____

   _____

2. Which two words begin with the same sound as ?

   _____   _____

3. Put these clues together to write a location word.

   a + ◯   _____

   a + ✝   _____

4. Write three words that rhyme with **hide**.

   _____   _____   _____

At the Pond

Directions: Read the sentences and use the words in the word box to complete the puzzle.

| cattails |
| fish |
| lily pad |
| willow |
| turtle |
| pond |

Across

4. A bullfrog sits on a ____ and croaks a loud song.
5. A family of ducks waddle into the ____ for a swim.
6. A raccoon tries to catch a ____ as it swims by.

Down

1. A ____ sits on a rock in the morning sun.
2. The weeping ____ gives shade to the animals.
3. Birds fly over the many ____ sticking out of the water.

A-maze-ing

Directions: Find your way through the maze by following the words in ABC order.

START

ant	ball	ten	off	sun
van	car	dot	eat	top
wig	six	rug	fan	on
jump	ice	hat	gum	can
king	bed	cup	five	big
lion	map	nut	off	pen

FINISH

Name _____

J, K, L Words

Directions: Look at the picture clues. Then, complete the puzzle using the words from the word box.

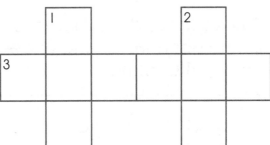

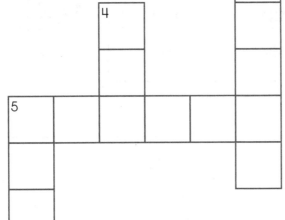

jaguar	
leaves	
letters	
key	
jet	
log	

Across

 3.

5.

Down

1.

2.

4.

5.

Short *U* Words

Short u is the sound you hear in the word **bug**.

Directions: Say each word, and listen for the **short u** sound. Then, write each word, and underline the letter that makes the **short u** sound.

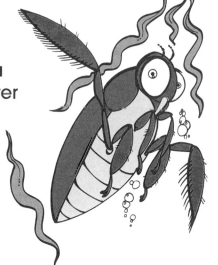

dust	must	nut	bug
bump	pump	tub	jump
cut	hug	rug	cub

1. _____

2. _____

3. _____

4. _____

5. _____

6. _____

7. _____

8. _____

9. _____

10. _____

11. _____

12. _____

Name _____

Short *U* Words: Sentences

Directions: Circle the words in each sentence that are not correct. Then, write the correct **short u** words from the box on the lines.

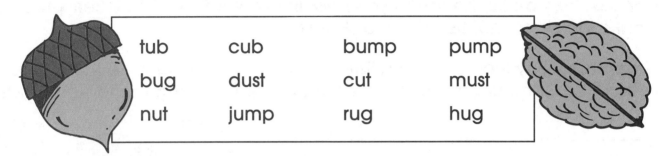

tub	cub	bump	pump
bug	dust	cut	must
nut	jump	rug	hug

1. The crust made me sneeze.   _____

2. I need to take a bath in the cub.   _____

3. The mug bite left a big pump on my arm.

_____   _____

4. It is time to get my hair hut.   _____

5. The mother bear took care of her shrub.   _____

6. We need to jump more gas into the car.   _____

Long *U* Words

Long u is a vowel sound that says its own name. **Long u** is spelled **u** with a silent **e** at the end, as in **cute**. The letters **oo** make a sound very much like **long u**. They make the sound you hear in the word **zoo**. The letters **ew** also make the **oo** sound, as in the word **grew**.

Directions: Say the words, and listen for the **u** and **oo** sounds. Then, write each word, and underline the letters that make the **long u** and **oo** sounds.

choose	blew	moon	fuse
cube	rude	tooth	use
flew	loose	goose	noon

1. _____

2. _____

3. _____

4. _____

5. _____

6. _____

7. _____

8. _____

9. _____

10. _____

11. _____

12. _____

Long *U* Words: Rhyming Words

Long u is a vowel sound you hear in the word **cube**. Another vowel sound that is very much like the **long u** sound is the **oo** sound you hear in the word **boot**.

Directions: Use the **long u** and **oo** words in the box to write rhyming words

moon	tooth	use	choose
flew	loose	goose	
fuse	noon	blew	

1. Write the words that rhyme with **soon**.

_____ _____

2. Write the words that rhyme with **lose**.

_____ _____ _____

3. Write the words that rhyme with **grew**.

_____ _____

4. Write the words that rhyme with **moose**.

_____ _____

5. Write the word that rhymes with **booth**.

_____

Long *U* Words: Sentences

Directions: Write the words in the sentences below in the correct order. Begin each sentence with a capital letter, and end it with a period or a question mark.

1. the pulled dentist tooth my loose

_____

2. ice cubes I choose in my drink to put

_____

3. a rude fuse the blew yesterday boy

_____

4. loose the got in garden goose the

_____

5. flew the goose winter for the south

_____

6. is full there a moon tonight

_____

Funny Fish

Directions: Can you help Fred Fish find Frieda Fish? Color the pictures that start with **f** to go through the maze.

Directions: Write two words that begin with **f**.

f

_____   _____

Safety

Directions: Read the clues and use the words in the word box to complete the puzzle.

seat belt
helmet
life jacket
stop sign
traffic light

Across

4. I tell cars when to stop and go.
5. I help you keep afloat when you are in the water.

Down

1. I am red with white letters. I sit on a post.
2. You wear me on your head when you ride a bike.
3. You wear me when you ride in a car.

Word Ladders

Directions: On each ladder, change one letter in each word to make a new word beneath. Use the words in the word box. You should end up with the word at the bottom.

tame	tail	dime	mail	role
roll	pool	cool	time	lime

Example:

	1.	2.
like	tile	rule
lake		
lace		
race	name	doll

3.	4.	5.
main	dice	cook
tall	limp	poor

Name _____

In a City

Directions: Read the clues and use the words in the word box to complete the puzzle.

subway
taxi
skyscraper
mall
hospital
bus
museum
zoo

Across

2. This is a place with many stores in one building.
3. This is a place where many animals live.
4. This is a very tall building.
6. Many people ride in this on city streets.
7. People whistle, yell, or wave to get a ride in this thing.

Down

1. This is a place where people go when they are very sick.
2. People visit this place to see very old things.
5. This train goes underground and many people ride on it.

Name _____

Picture Clues

Directions: Letters, numbers, and pictures take the place of words in each sentence below. Write each sentence correctly.

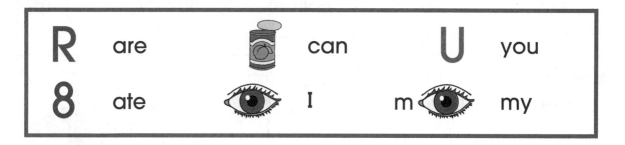

1. 👁 **8** an apple.

   _____

2. **R U** happy?

   _____

3. 🥫 **U** see m👁 dog?

   _____

4. 👁 🥫 see **U** .

   _____

Opposite Words

Directions: Opposites are words that are different in every way. Use the opposite words from the box to complete these sentences.

hard	hot	bottom	quickly	happy
sad	slowly	cold	soft	top

Example:

My new coat is blue on _____top_____ and

red on the ___bottom___.

1. Snow is _____, but fire is _____.

2. A rabbit runs _____, but a turtle

   moves _____.

3. A bed is _____, but a floor is _____.

4. I feel _____ when my friends come

   and _____ when they leave.

Opposite Words

Directions: Draw a line from each sentence to its picture. Then, complete each sentence with the word under the picture.

Example:

She bought a ___*new*___ bat.

hard

1. I like my _____ pillow.

new

2. Birthdays make me _____.

top

3. Put that book on _____.

sad

4. Sydney runs _____.

slowly

5. A rock makes a _____ seat.

quickly

6. I feel _____ when it rains.

happy

7. He eats _____.

soft

What a Great Place!

Directions: Fill in the puzzle with words that name the pictures below. Use the word box to help you.

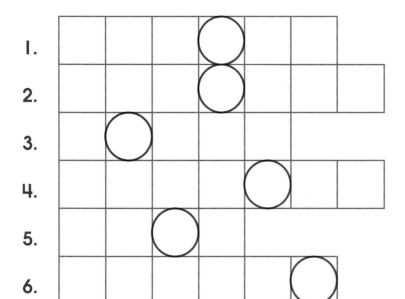

1.
2.
3.
4.
5.
6.

teacher

pencil

book

crayons

eraser

chalk

1.

2.

3.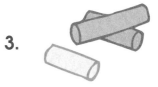

4.

5.

6.

Directions: The letters in the circles going down spell a mystery word. The word names a place where all these things can be found. Write the mystery word.

_____

Let's Picnic

Directions: Color the spaces with foods yellow. Color the spaces with drinks red. Color the spaces with other things green.

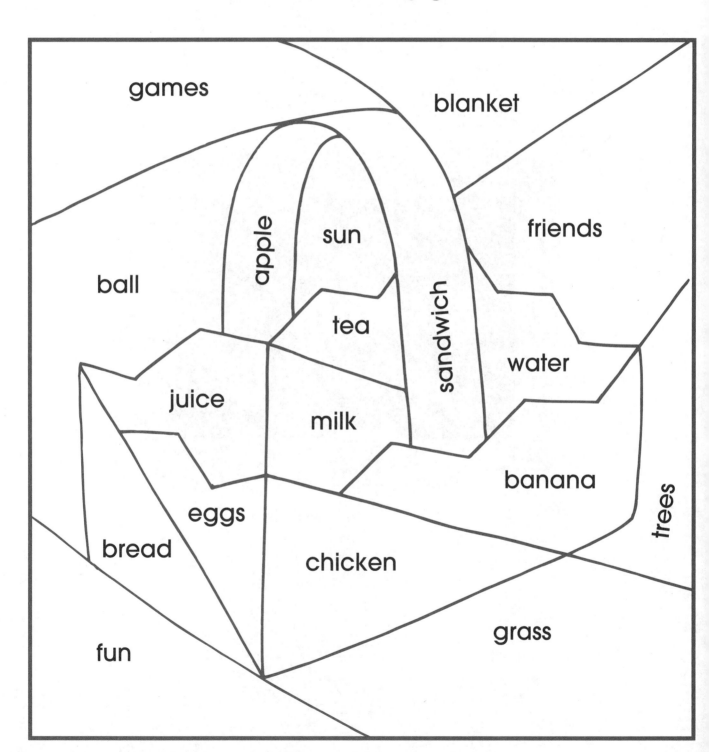

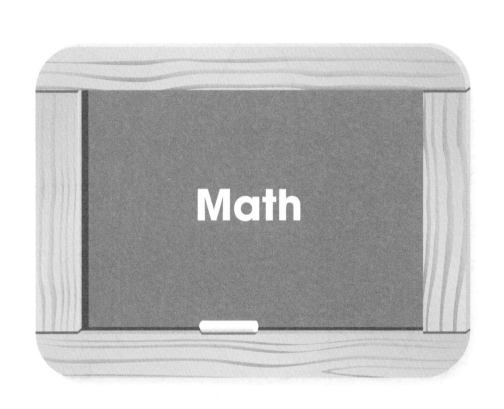

Math

Less Than, Greater Than

Directions: The open mouth points to the larger number. The small point goes to the smaller number. Draw the symbol **<** or **>** to compare the numbers.

Example:

5 3

This means that 5 is greater than 3, and 3 is less than 5.

12 ◯ 2   16 ◯ 6

16 ◯ 15   1 ◯ 2

7 ◯ 1   19 ◯ 5

9 ◯ 6   11 ◯ 13

The Coral Reef

Directions: Find the differences to complete the paths. Start at the top and go down.

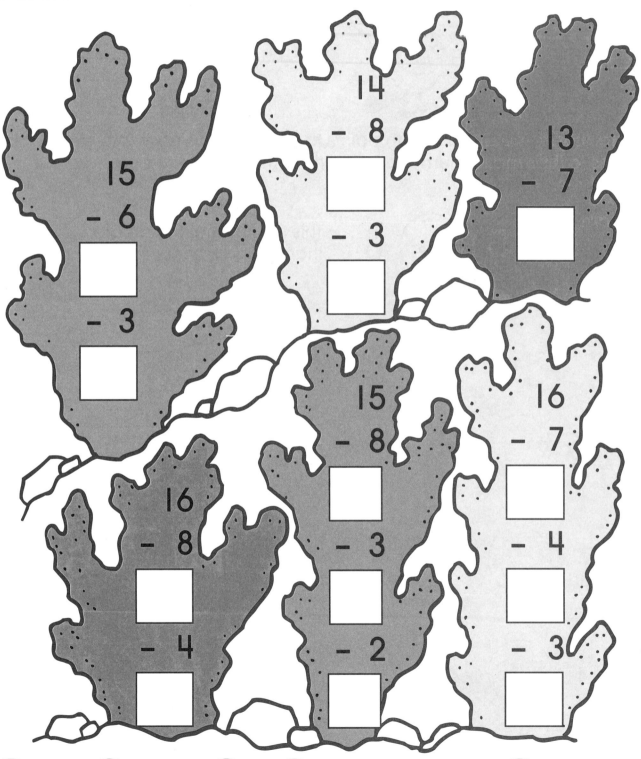

A Garden Helper

Directions: This insect helps flowers grow. Connect the dots from **1** to **25**. Then, color to finish the picture.

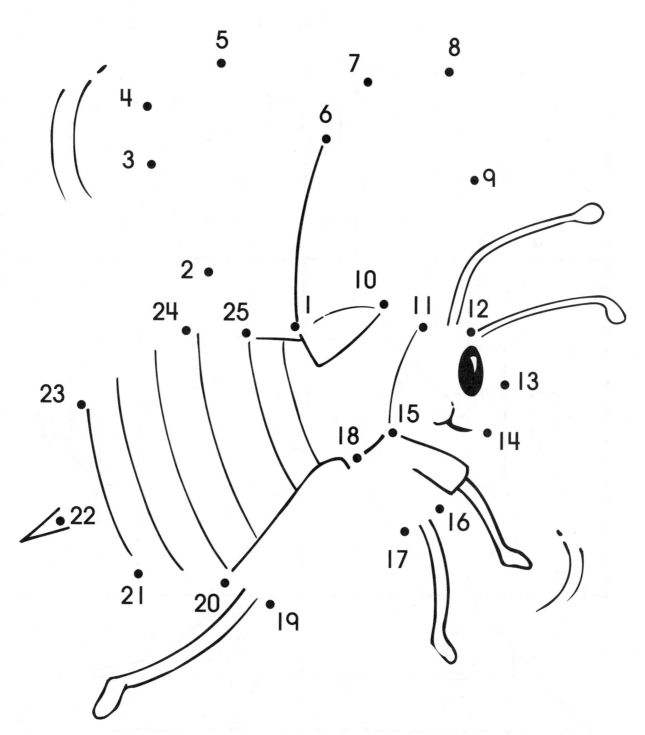

Water Spout

Directions: Color to find the hidden picture. Use the number key to help you.

1 = yellow   2 = red   3 = blue

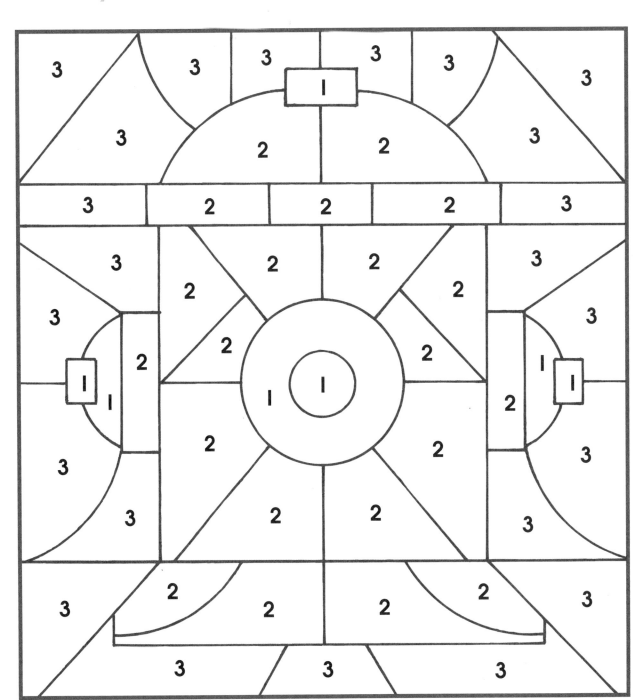

Taylor the Treehopper

Directions: Connect the dots from **0** to **65**. Then, color to finish the picture.

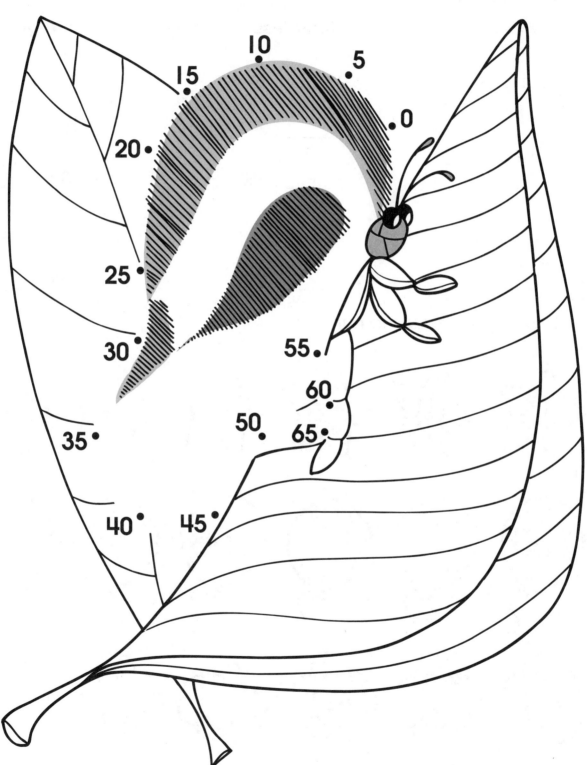

Counting

Directions: Write numbers that are:

next in order	one less	one greater
22, 23, _____ , _____	_____ , 16	6, _____
674, _____ , _____	_____ , 247	125, _____
227, _____ , _____	_____ , 550	499, _____
199, _____ , _____	_____ , 333	750, _____
329, _____ , _____	_____ , 862	933, _____

Directions: Write the missing numbers.

Counting by Twos

Directions: Each basket the players make is worth 2 points. Help your team win by counting by twos to beat the other team's score.

2

___

___

8

___

___

16

___

20

___

Final Score	
Home	Visitor
	30

___

28

___

32

Winner!

___

Counting: Twos, Fives, Tens

Directions: Write the missing numbers.

Count by twos:

Count by fives:

Count by tens:

The Genie

Directions: Connect the dots from **8** to **36**. Then, color to finish the picture.

Autumn Search

Directions: Find **10** pumpkins below. Color them orange. Then, color the rest of the picture.

At School

Directions: Find books and crayons and color them **purple**. Then, color the rest of the picture.

Directions: Circle to show how many.

          6   7      6   7

Vera the Velvet Ant

Directions: Connect the dots from **5** to **65**. Then, color to finish the picture.

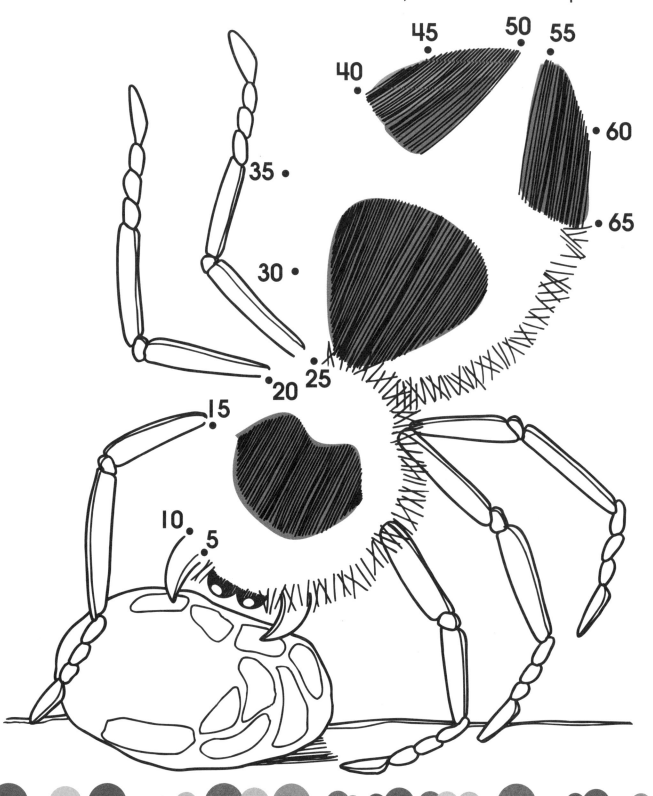

Name _____

Aladdin and the Lamp

Directions: Connect the dots from **4** to **40**. Then, color to finish the picture.

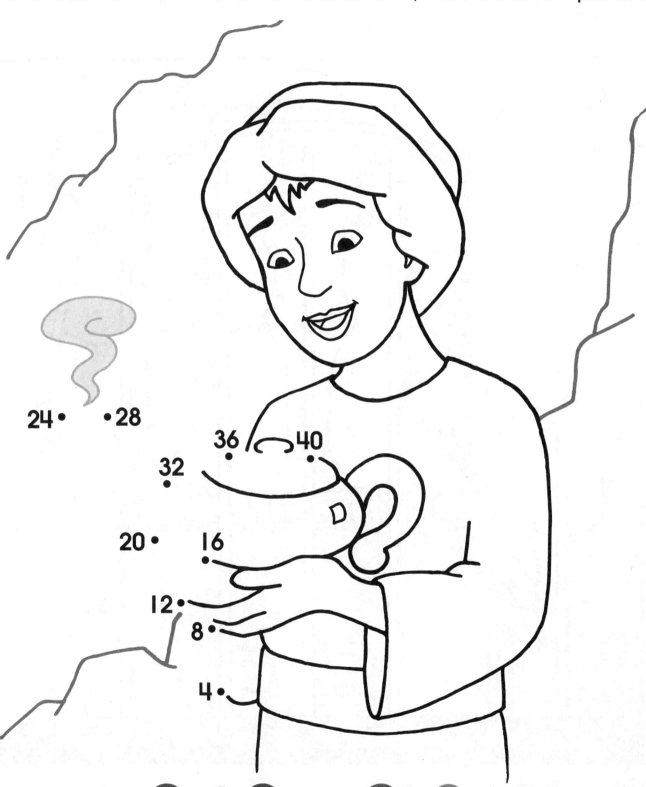

Bird Buddies

Directions: Find the numbers **1** to **10**. Color them. Then, color the rest of the picture.

Patterns

Directions: Write or draw what comes next in the pattern.

Example: 1, 2, 3, 4, ___5___

---

1.    _____

2. A, 1, B, 2, C, _____

3. 2, 4, 6, 8, _____

4. A, C, E, G, _____

5. 5, 10, 15, 20, _____

Finding Patterns: Numbers

Mia likes to count by twos, threes, fours, fives, tens, and hundreds.

Directions: Complete the number patterns.

1. 5, ____, ____, 20, ____, ____, 35, ____, ____, 50

2. 100, ____, ____, 400, ____, ____, ____, 800, ____

3. ____, 4, 6, ____, ____, 12, ____, 16, ____, ____

4. 10, ____, ____, 40, ____, ____, 70, ____, 90

5. 4, ____, 12, ____, ____, 24, ____, 32, ____, 40

6. ____, 6, 9, ____, ____, 18, ____, 24, ____, 30

Directions: Make up two of your own number patterns.

____, ____, ____, ____, ____, ____, ____, ____

____, ____, ____, ____, ____, ____, ____, ____

Finding Patterns: Shapes

Directions: Complete each row by drawing the correct shape.

_____

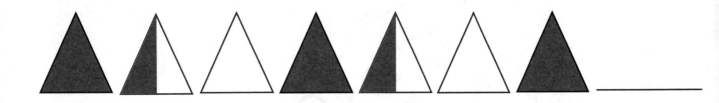

_____

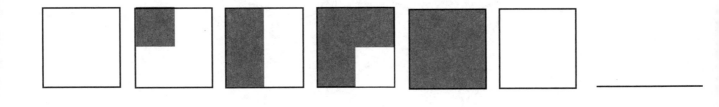

_____

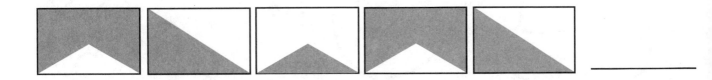

_____

The Gingerbread Man

Directions: Connect the dots from **0** to **24**. Then, color to finish the picture.

Counting Clothes

Directions: Count the clothing. Write the number words in the puzzle. Use the word box to help you.

Across

2.

4.

Down

1.

2.

3.

eleven	
twelve	
thirteen	
fourteen	
fifteen	

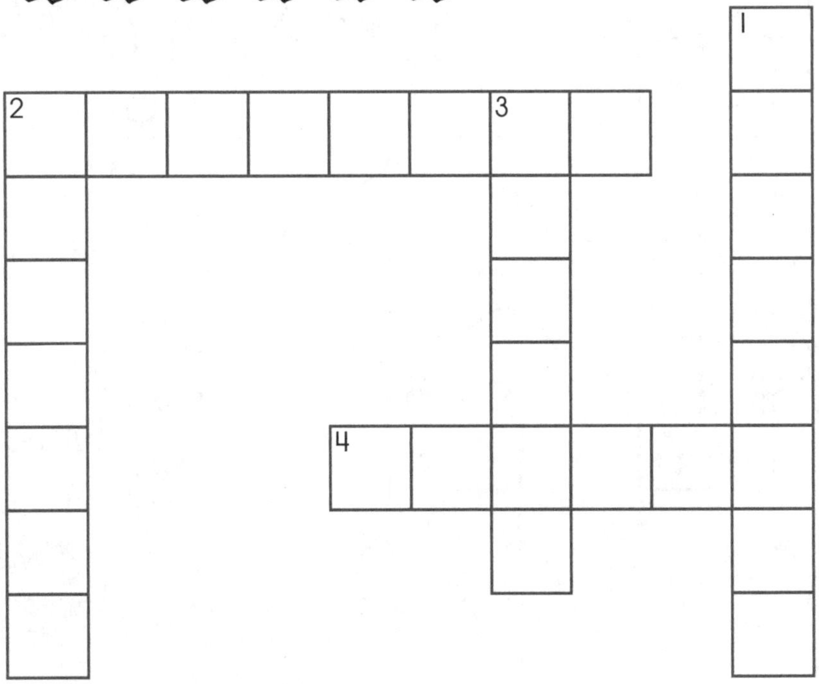

In the Doghouse!

Directions: Find the differences. Color the bones with answers that are odd numbers to help Dugan get back to her house.

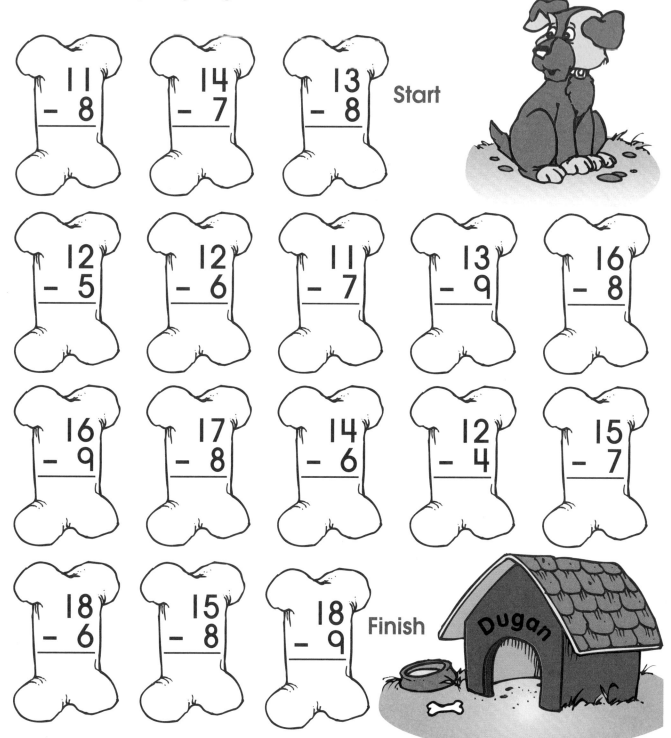

11
− 8

14
− 7

13
− 8   Start

12
− 5

12
− 6

11
− 7

13
− 9

16
− 8

16
− 9

17
− 8

14
− 6

12
− 4

15
− 7

18
− 6

15
− 8

18
− 9   Finish

Dugan

A Friendly Sea Lion

Directions: Connect the dots from **0** to **90**. Then, color to finish the picture.

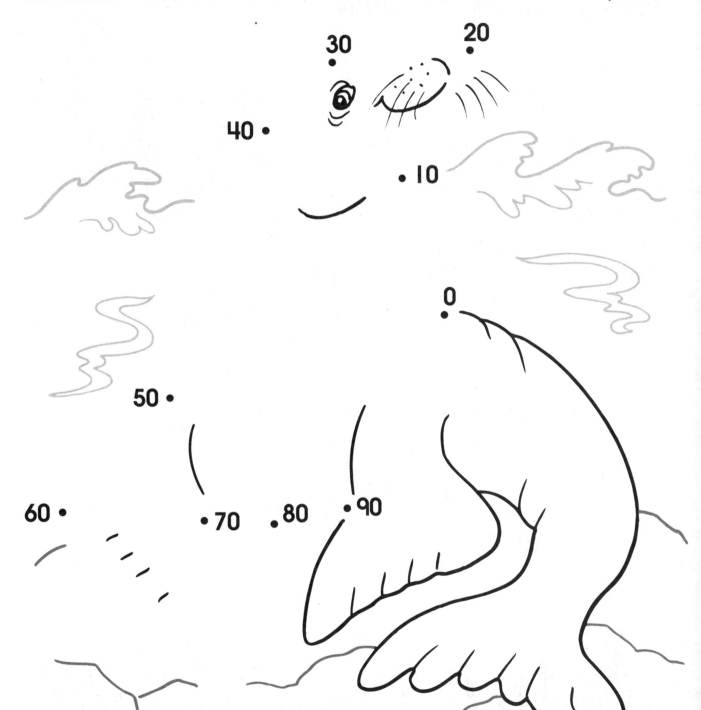

Great in the Garden

Directions: This adds so much color to nature! Connect the dots from **1** to **25**. Then, color to finish the picture.

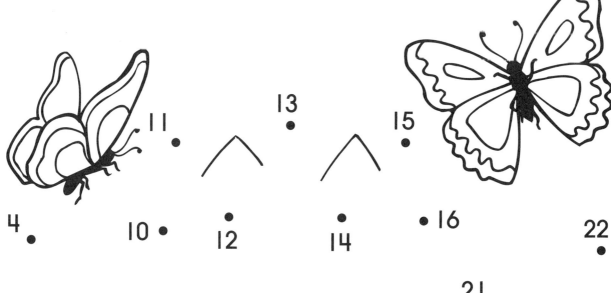

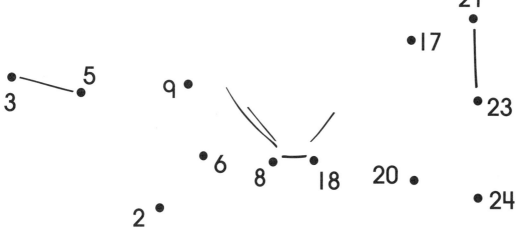

Name _____

Lining Them Up

Directions: Unscramble and write the number words.

1. nnei ____ ____ ____ ____

2. neves ____ ____ ____ ____ ____

3. wetlev ____ ____ ____ ____ ____ ____

4. etreh ____ ____ ____ ____ ____

5. xis ____ ____ ____

6. etn ____ ____ ____

7. neo ____ ____ ____

8. efvi ____ ____ ____ ____

9. eeenlv ____ ____ ____ ____ ____ ____

10. wot ____ ____ ____

11. theig ____ ____ ____ ____ ____

12. rufo ____ ____ ____ ____

one
two
three
four
five
six
seven
eight
nine
ten
eleven
twelve

The Frog Prince

Directions: Connect the dots from **4** to **28**. Then, color to finish the picture.

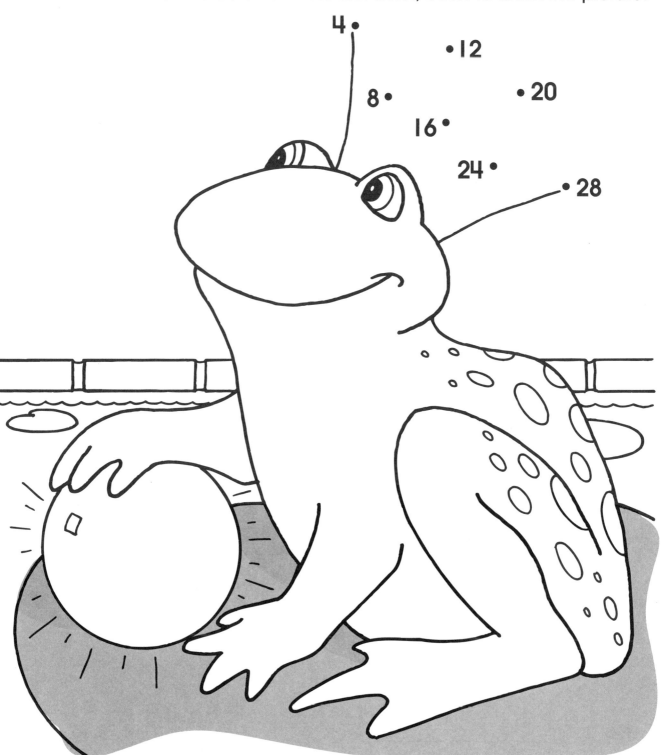

Name _____

Ordinal Numbers

Ordinal numbers indicate order in a series, such as **first**, **second**, or **third**.

Directions: Follow the instructions to color the train cars. The first car is the engine.

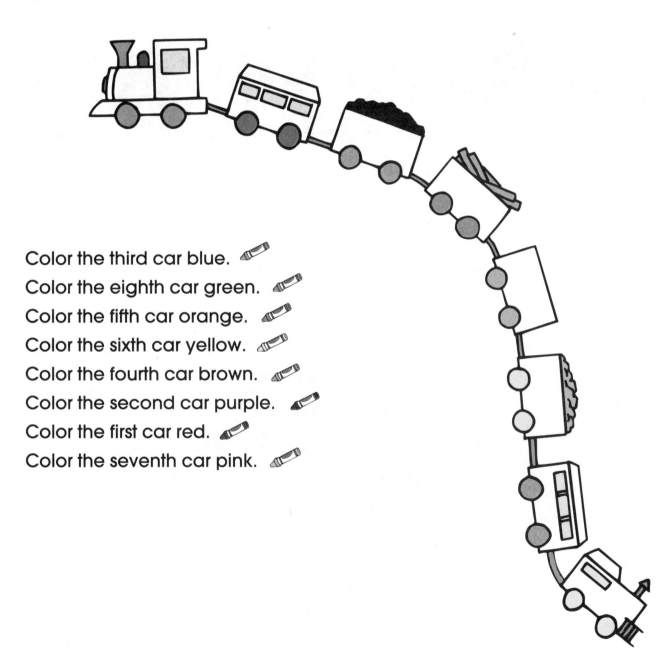

Color the third car blue.

Color the eighth car green.

Color the fifth car orange.

Color the sixth car yellow.

Color the fourth car brown.

Color the second car purple.

Color the first car red.

Color the seventh car pink.

Ordinal Numbers

Directions: Follow the instructions.

Draw glasses on the second child.

Put a hat on the fourth child.

Color blonde hair on the third child.

Draw a tie on the first child.

Draw ears on the fifth child.

Draw black hair on the seventh child.

Put a bow on the head of the sixth child.

Duck or a Dino?

Directions: Connect the dots from **4** to **40**. Then, color to finish the picture.

Who Is Bigger?

Directions: Help the bear get home. Color numbers greater than **10**.

A Hungry Dino

Directions: Find the numbers **7**, **8**, **9**, and **10**. Color them. Then, color the rest of the picture.

Hansel and Gretel

Directions: Connect the dots from **4** to **32**. Then, color to finish the picture.

Addition

Addition is "putting together" or adding two or more numbers to find the sum.

Directions: Add.

Example:

$$\begin{array}{r} 2 \\ +5 \\ \hline 7 \end{array}$$

$$\begin{array}{r} 3 \\ +4 \\ \hline \end{array} \qquad \begin{array}{r} 6 \\ +2 \\ \hline \end{array} \qquad \begin{array}{r} 7 \\ +1 \\ \hline \end{array} \qquad \begin{array}{r} 8 \\ +2 \\ \hline \end{array} \qquad \begin{array}{r} 5 \\ +4 \\ \hline \end{array} \qquad \begin{array}{r} 3 \\ +1 \\ \hline \end{array}$$

$$\begin{array}{r} 8 \\ +2 \\ \hline \end{array} \qquad \begin{array}{r} 9 \\ +5 \\ \hline \end{array} \qquad \begin{array}{r} 10 \\ +3 \\ \hline \end{array} \qquad \begin{array}{r} 6 \\ +6 \\ \hline \end{array} \qquad \begin{array}{r} 4 \\ +9 \\ \hline \end{array} \qquad \begin{array}{r} 7 \\ +7 \\ \hline \end{array}$$

$$\begin{array}{r} 9 \\ +3 \\ \hline \end{array} \qquad \begin{array}{r} 8 \\ +7 \\ \hline \end{array} \qquad \begin{array}{r} 6 \\ +5 \\ \hline \end{array} \qquad \begin{array}{r} 7 \\ +9 \\ \hline \end{array} \qquad \begin{array}{r} 7 \\ +6 \\ \hline \end{array} \qquad \begin{array}{r} 9 \\ +9 \\ \hline \end{array}$$

Addition: Commutative Property

The **commutative property** of addition states that even if the order of the numbers is changed in an addition sentence, the sum will stay the same.

Example: 2 + 3 = 5
             3 + 2 = 5

Directions: Look at the addition sentences below. Complete the addition sentences by writing the missing numerals.

5 + 4 = 9   3 + 1 = 4   2 + 6 = 8
4 + __ = 9   1 + __ = 4   6 + __ = 8

6 + 1 = 7   4 + 3 = 7   1 + 9 = 10
1 + __ = 7   3 + __ = 7   9 + __ = 10

Now, try these:

6 + 3 = 9   10 + 2 = 12   8 + 3 = 11
__ + __ = 9   __ + __ = 12   __ + __ = 11

Look at these sums. Can you think of two number sentences that would show the commutative property of addition?

__ + __ = 7   __ + __ = 11   __ + __ = 9

__ + __ = 7   __ + __ = 11   __ + __ = 9

Adding 3 or More Numbers

Directions: Add all the numbers to find the sum. Draw pictures or add two numbers together to break up the problem into two smaller problems.

Example:

$$
\begin{array}{r}
1 \\
2 \\
+3 \\
\hline
6
\end{array}
\quad
\bigcirc \\
\bigcirc\bigcirc \\
\bigcirc\bigcirc\bigcirc
$$

$$
\begin{array}{r}
+\,2 \\
5
\end{array}
\Big\rangle\ 7
\qquad
\begin{array}{r}
+\,2 \\
4
\end{array}
\Big\rangle\ +6
$$

$$13$$

$$
\begin{array}{r}
3 \\
6 \\
+2 \\
\hline
\end{array}
\qquad
\begin{array}{r}
8 \\
5 \\
+4 \\
\hline
\end{array}
\qquad
\begin{array}{r}
3 \\
1 \\
+5 \\
\hline
\end{array}
\qquad
\begin{array}{r}
8 \\
2 \\
+9 \\
\hline
\end{array}
$$

$$
\begin{array}{r}
2 \\
8 \\
4 \\
+3 \\
\hline
\end{array}
\qquad
\begin{array}{r}
3 \\
6 \\
5 \\
+2 \\
\hline
\end{array}
\qquad
\begin{array}{r}
4 \\
1 \\
2 \\
+5 \\
\hline
\end{array}
\qquad
\begin{array}{r}
6 \\
7 \\
3 \\
+1 \\
\hline
\end{array}
$$

Marty the Mantis

Directions: Connect the dots from **10** to **80**. Then, color to finish the picture.

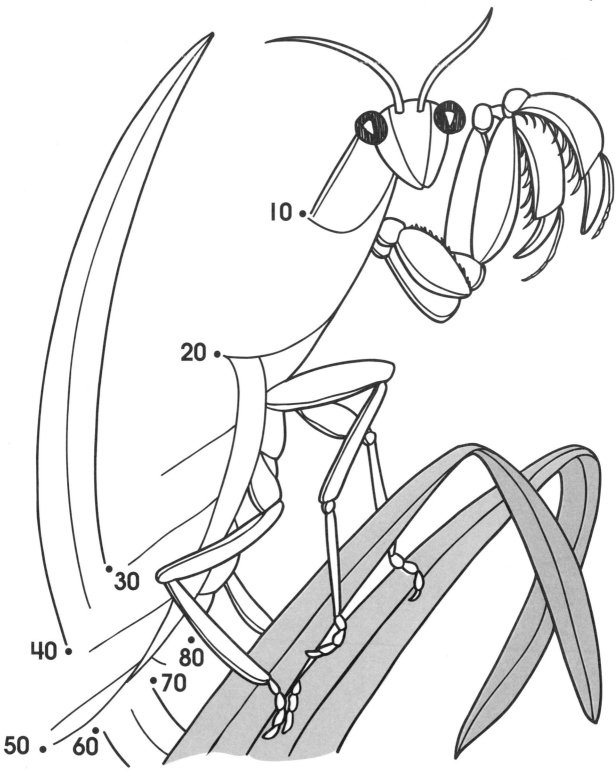

Hot Stuff

Directions: Color to find the hidden picture. Use the number key to help you.

16 = orange   17 = red   18 = black

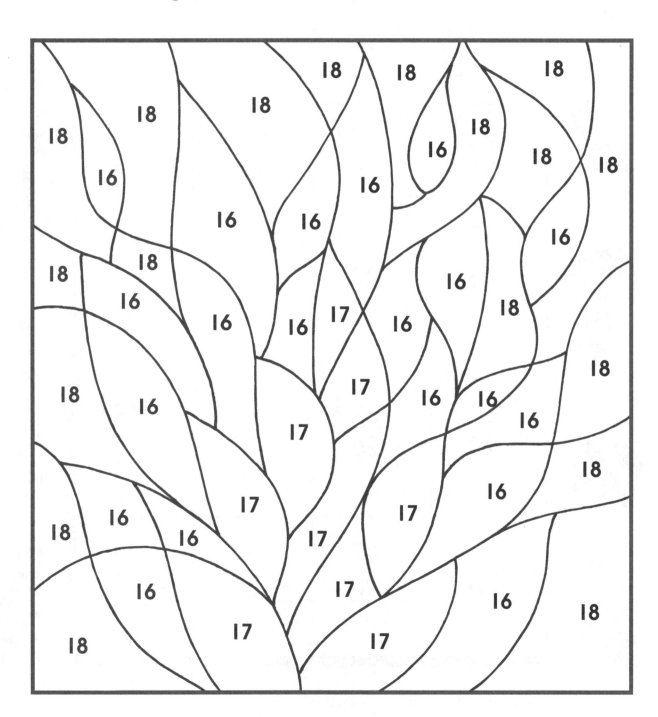

I Spy Something Flying!

Directions: To find out what I spy, color the boxes with differences from **60** to **72**. Then, write the letters from the colored boxes in the blanks, working left to right.

I spy a ____ ____ ____ ____ ____

____ ____ ____ ____ ____ ____ ____ ____ ____ !

90 S − 30	87 P − 26	86 F − 42	78 A − 16
96 Y − 53	99 C − 36	69 E − 5	87 Z − 54
87 S − 22	69 L − 25	79 H − 13	68 U − 1
98 T − 30	89 T − 20	90 L − 20	88 E − 17

Lily the Ladybug

Directions: Connect the dots from **10** to **100**. Then, color to finish the picture.

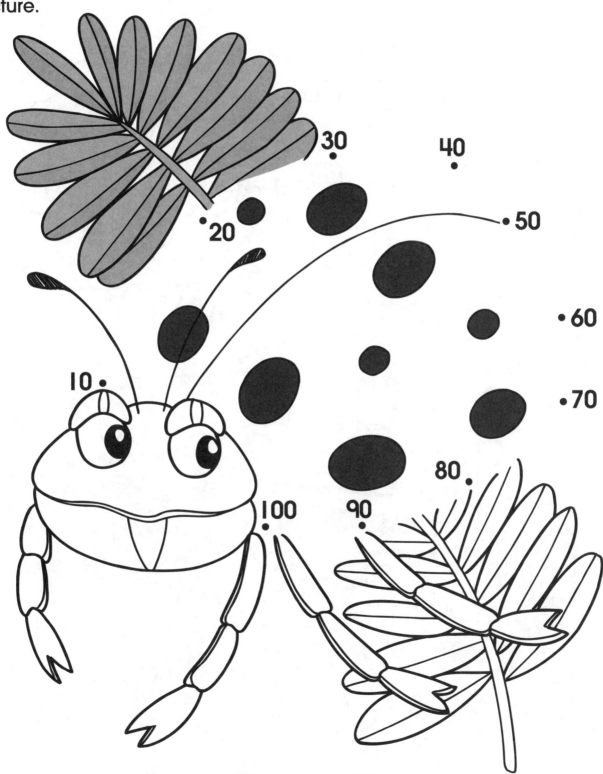

Name _____

Busy Builders

Directions: Find the numbers **1** to **20**. Color them. Then, color the rest of the picture.

Subtraction

Subtraction is "taking away" or subtracting one number from another to find the difference.

Directions: Subtract.

Example:

$$\begin{array}{r} 4 \\ -3 \\ \hline \end{array}$$

$\begin{array}{r} 5 \\ -3 \\ \hline \end{array}$	$\begin{array}{r} 6 \\ -1 \\ \hline \end{array}$	$\begin{array}{r} 4 \\ -3 \\ \hline \end{array}$	$\begin{array}{r} 3 \\ -1 \\ \hline \end{array}$	$\begin{array}{r} 2 \\ -0 \\ \hline \end{array}$	$\begin{array}{r} 1 \\ -1 \\ \hline \end{array}$
$\begin{array}{r} 9 \\ -2 \\ \hline \end{array}$	$\begin{array}{r} 7 \\ -4 \\ \hline \end{array}$	$\begin{array}{r} 10 \\ -5 \\ \hline \end{array}$	$\begin{array}{r} 14 \\ -6 \\ \hline \end{array}$	$\begin{array}{r} 15 \\ -9 \\ \hline \end{array}$	$\begin{array}{r} 12 \\ -3 \\ \hline \end{array}$
$\begin{array}{r} 18 \\ -8 \\ \hline \end{array}$	$\begin{array}{r} 13 \\ -5 \\ \hline \end{array}$	$\begin{array}{r} 14 \\ -7 \\ \hline \end{array}$	$\begin{array}{r} 11 \\ -4 \\ \hline \end{array}$	$\begin{array}{r} 17 \\ -9 \\ \hline \end{array}$	$\begin{array}{r} 16 \\ -8 \\ \hline \end{array}$

Addition and Subtraction

Addition is "putting together" or adding two or more numbers to find the sum. Subtraction is "taking away" or subtracting one number from another to find the difference.

Directions: Add or subtract. Circle the answers that are less than 10.

Examples:

$$\begin{array}{r} 3 \\ +1 \\ \hline (4) \end{array}$$

$$\begin{array}{r} 3 \\ -1 \\ \hline (2) \end{array}$$

9 +3	6 −2	12 − 1	18 +1	15 −6
7 + 6	16 − 9	10 − 3	14 + 5	16 − 8
8 +7	12 + 2	13 − 4	17 + 2	9 +9

Name _____

Manny the Mosquito

Directions: Connect the dots from **0** to **110**. Then, color to finish the picture.

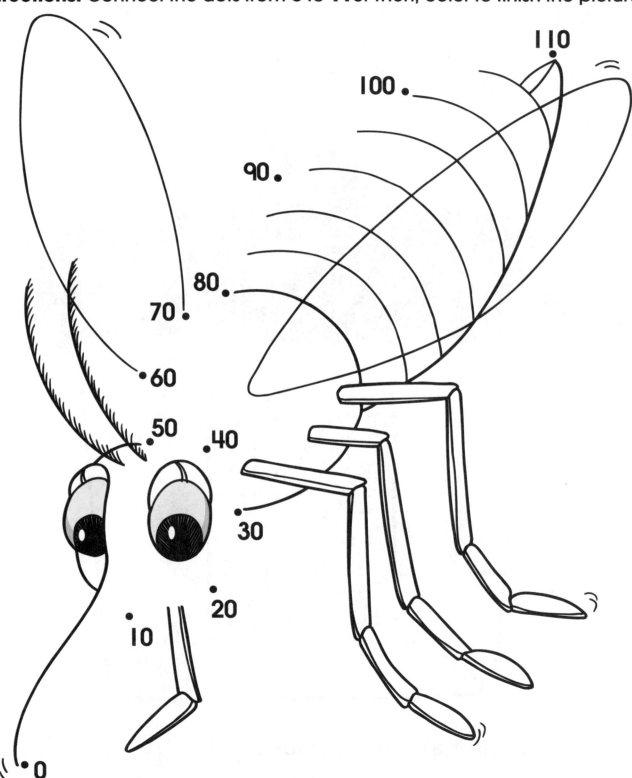

A Yummy Number

Directions: To find the mystery number, color the spaces with the following numbers **purple**.

9   5   8   7   10   13   18   17   20   19   11

8	10	7	15
18	6	16	1
17	5	9	4
2	14	19	12
11	13	20	3

Circle the mystery number.   5   10   18

The Emperor's New Clothes

Directions: Connect the dots from **12** to **48**. Then, color to finish the picture.

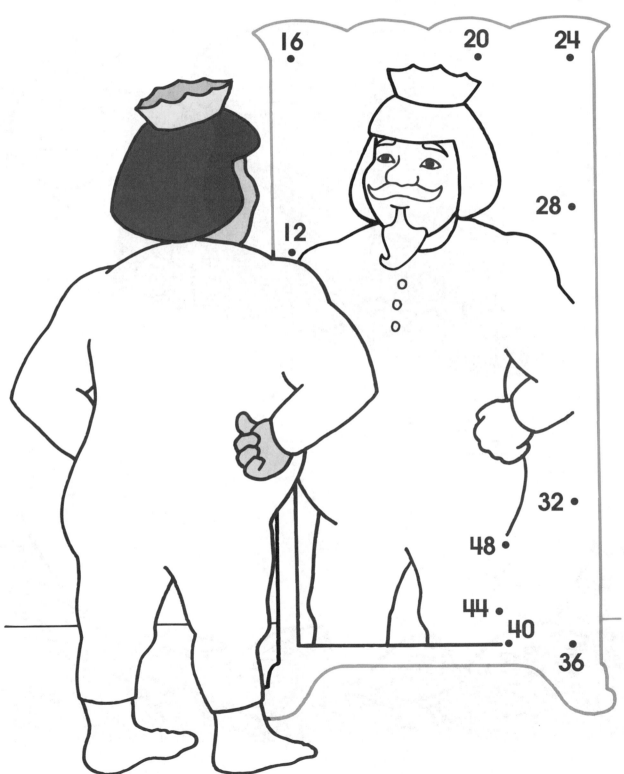

Ahoy There!

Directions: Subtract.

15
− 7

16
− 7

14
− 7

15
− 9

13
− 4

13
− 8

12
− 9

15
− 6

16
− 9

15
− 8

14
− 9

13
− 7

12
− 8

14
− 5

16
− 8

13
− 6

11
− 5

14
− 5

Place Value: Ones, Tens

The **place value** of a digit or numeral is shown by where it is in the number. For example, in the number **23**, **2** has the place value of **tens**, and **3** is **ones**.

Directions: Add the tens and ones, and write your answers in the blanks.

Example:

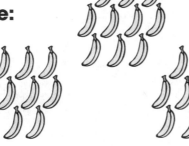

+ 🍌🍌🍌 = _33_

3 tens + 3 ones = _33_

	tens ones			tens ones
7 tens + 5 ones	= _____		4 tens + 0 ones	= _____
2 tens + 3 ones	= _____		8 tens + 1 one	= _____
5 tens + 2 ones	= _____		1 ten + 1 one	= _____
5 tens + 4 ones	= _____		6 tens + 3 ones	= _____
9 tens + 5 ones	= _____			

Directions: Draw a line to the correct number.

6 tens + 7 ones	73
4 tens + 2 ones	67
8 tens + 0 ones	51
7 tens + 3 ones	80
5 tens + 1 one	42

Place Value: Ones, Tens

Directions: Write the numbers for the **tens** and **ones**. Then, add.

Example:

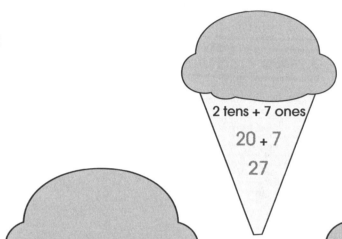

2 tens + 7 ones

20 + 7

27

6 tens + 2 ones

____ + ____

____

3 tens + 4 ones

____ + ____

____

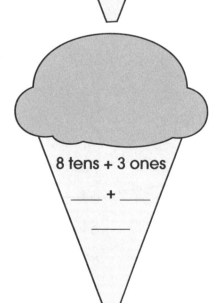

8 tens + 3 ones

____ + ____

____

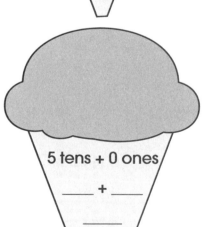

5 tens + 0 ones

____ + ____

____

Walter the Water Bug

Directions: Connect the dots from **0** to **70**. Then, color to finish the picture.

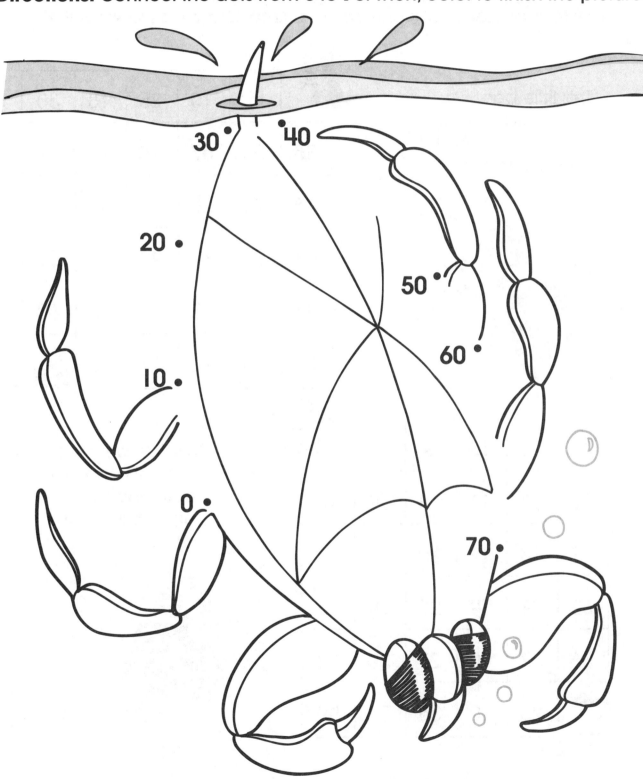

Mystery Mazes

Directions: Help the bees travel through the mazes. They can move up, down, across, or diagonally one box at a time. Draw lines to show their paths.

This little bee
   Counts by fives
Through the maze
   And to the hive.

5	10	25	18	30
35	56	57	15	75	12
16	25	20	6	45	50
43	30	80	40	95	55
85	19	35	14	6	60
29	70	21	37	90	

11	23	12	8	4
62	15	16	14	34	18
17	38	19	20	43	21
52	48	44	22	24	53
56	37	40	27	30	28
	25	10	36	32	49

This little bee
   Counts by fours,
Searching for
   the apple core.

What Big Teeth You Have!

Directions: Subtract. Use the differences to answer the riddle.

What do you get from an alligator in a bad mood?

____ ____ ____　　____ ____ ____ ____!
　5　　7　　8　　　　7　　9　　7　　6

Y	A
15 – 9 = _____	15 – 8 = _____
T	**S**
11 – 9 = _____	12 – 9 = _____
F	**R**
13 – 8 = _____	16 – 8 = _____
W	**P**
16 – 7 = _____	13 – 9 = _____

Katie the Katydid

Directions: Connect the dots from **10** to **120**. Then, color to finish the picture.

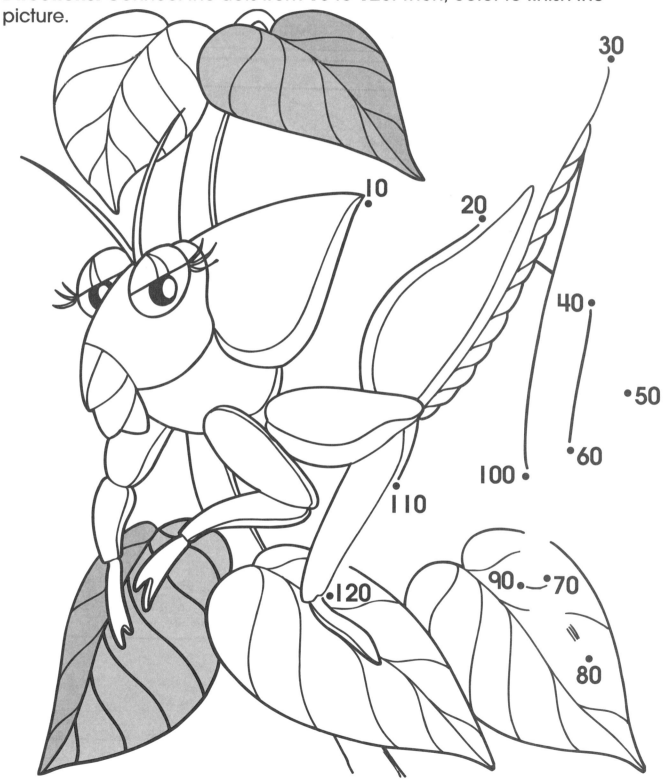

2-Digit Addition

Directions: Study the example. Follow the steps to add.

Example: 33
               +41

Step 1: Add the ones.

tens	ones
3	3
+4	1
	4

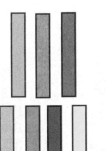

Step 2: Add the tens.

tens	ones
3	3
+4	1
7	4

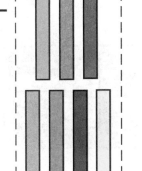

tens	ones
4	2
+2	4
6	6

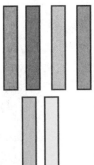

tens	ones
5	0
+4	7
9	7

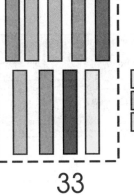

24	15	38	11	37	72	33	10
+62	+23	+61	+26	+42	+11	+51	+30

25	62	32	25	82	91	16	55
+42	+14	+44	+13	+ 6	+ 5	+71	+ 3

2-Digit Addition

Directions: Add the total points scored in each game. Remember to add **ones** first and **tens** second.

Example:

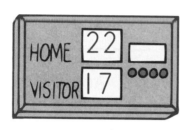

Total ___39___

Total _____

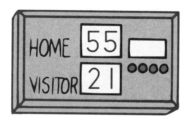

Total _____

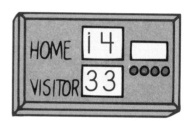

Total _____

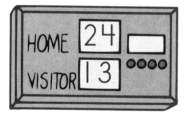

Total _____

Total _____

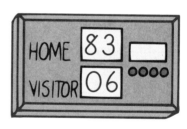

Total _____

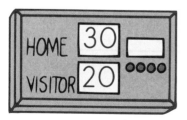

Total _____

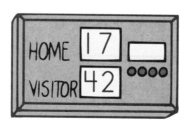

Total _____

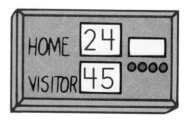

Total _____

Irene the Moth

Directions: Connect the dots from **25** to **100**. Then, color to finish the picture.

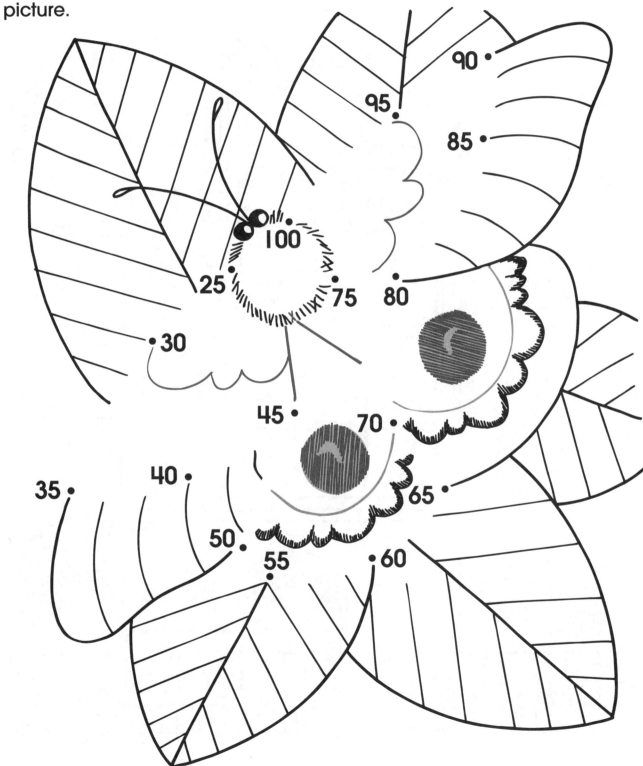

The Sky Is the Limit

Directions: Find the numbers **17**, **18**, **19**, and **20**. Color them. Then, color the rest of the picture.

2-Digit Addition: Regrouping

Addition is "putting together" or adding two or more numbers to find the sum. Regrouping is using **ten ones** to form **one ten**, **ten tens** to form **one 100**, **fifteen ones** to form **one ten** and **five ones**, and so on.

Directions: Study the examples. Follow the steps to add.

Example: 14
              + 8

Step 1: Add the ones.   **Step 2:** Regroup the tens.   **Step 3:** Add the tens.

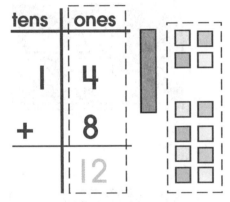

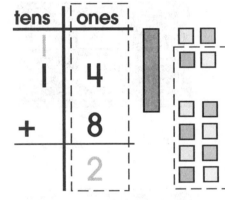

tens	ones
1	6
+3	7
5	3

tens	ones
1	
3	8
+5	3
9	1

tens	ones
1	
2	4
+4	7
7	1

28	32	54	19	44	25	29	79
+17	+38	+25	+55	+48	+64	+33	+15

2-Digit Addition: Regrouping

Directions: Add the total points scored in each game. Remember to add ones, regroup, and then add the tens.

Example:

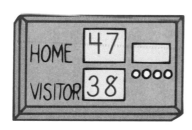

Total __85__

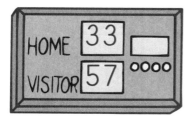

Total _____

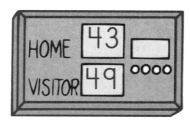

Total _____

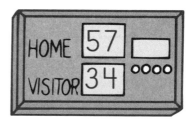

Total _____

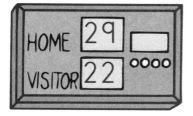

Total _____

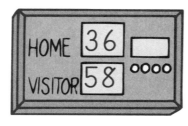

Total _____

Total _____

Total _____

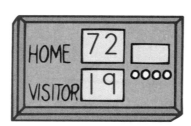

Total _____

Total _____

Name _____

2-Digit Subtraction

Directions: Study the example. Follow the steps to subtract.

Example:
$$\begin{array}{r} 28 \\ -14 \\ \hline \end{array}$$

Step 1: Subtract the ones.

tens	ones
2	8
-1	4
	4

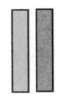 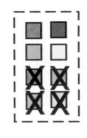

Step 2: Subtract the tens.

tens	ones
2	8
-1	4
1	4

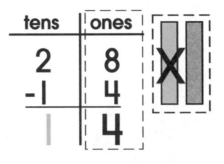 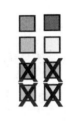

tens	ones
2	4
-1	2
1	2

tens	ones
3	8
-1	5
2	3

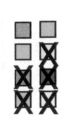

$$\begin{array}{r} 24 \\ -12 \\ \hline \end{array} \qquad \begin{array}{r} 61 \\ -30 \\ \hline \end{array} \qquad \begin{array}{r} 77 \\ -44 \\ \hline \end{array} \qquad \begin{array}{r} 85 \\ -24 \\ \hline \end{array} \qquad \begin{array}{r} 57 \\ -23 \\ \hline \end{array} \qquad \begin{array}{r} 87 \\ -33 \\ \hline \end{array} \qquad \begin{array}{r} 59 \\ -34 \\ \hline \end{array} \qquad \begin{array}{r} 96 \\ -16 \\ \hline \end{array}$$

$$\begin{array}{r} 29 \\ -15 \\ \hline \end{array} \qquad \begin{array}{r} 74 \\ -51 \\ \hline \end{array} \qquad \begin{array}{r} 46 \\ -32 \\ \hline \end{array} \qquad \begin{array}{r} 69 \\ -35 \\ \hline \end{array} \qquad \begin{array}{r} 95 \\ -32 \\ \hline \end{array} \qquad \begin{array}{r} 33 \\ -33 \\ \hline \end{array} \qquad \begin{array}{r} 78 \\ -26 \\ \hline \end{array} \qquad \begin{array}{r} 22 \\ -11 \\ \hline \end{array}$$

2-Digit Addition: Regrouping

Subtraction is "taking away" or subtracting one number from another to find the difference. Regrouping is using **one ten** to form **ten ones**, **one 100** to form **ten tens**, and so on.

Directions: Study the examples. Follow the steps to subtract.

Example: 37
                −19

Step 1: Regroup.   **Step 2:** Subtract the ones.   **Step 3:** Subtract the tens.

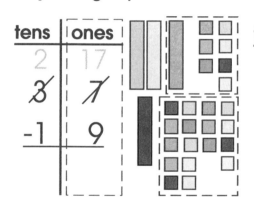

tens	ones
2	17
3̷	7̷
−1	9

tens	ones
2	17
3̷	7̷
−1	9
	8

tens	ones
2	17
3̷	7̷
−1	9
1	8

tens	ones
0	12
1̷	2̷
−	9
	3

tens	ones
2	14
3̷	4̷
−1	6
1	8

tens	ones
3	15
4̷	5̷
−2	9
1	6

28	46	12	30	52	47	21	45
− 19	− 18	− 8	− 12	− 25	− 35	− 13	− 25

2-Digit Addition: Regrouping

Directions: Study the steps for subtracting. Solve the problems using the steps.

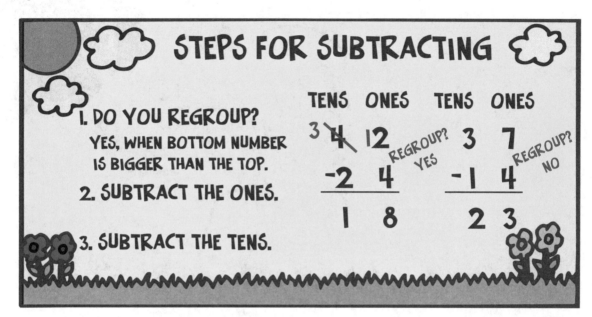

STEPS FOR SUBTRACTING

1. DO YOU REGROUP?
   YES, WHEN BOTTOM NUMBER
   IS BIGGER THAN THE TOP.
2. SUBTRACT THE ONES.
3. SUBTRACT THE TENS.

TENS	ONES		TENS	ONES	
3 4̸	12	REGROUP? YES	3	7	REGROUP? NO
-2	4		-1	4	
1	8		2	3	

tens	ones		tens	ones		tens	ones
4	7		6	4		5	3
- 2	8		- 3	4		- 3	9

56	83	43	75	91
- 27	- 47	- 39	- 53	- 18

73	35	67	26	68
- 66	- 14	- 58	- 7	- 45

Beauty

Directions: Connect the dots from **4** to **48**. Then, color to finish the picture.

Fourth of July

Directions: Answer each problem by regrouping. Use the sums to answer the riddle.

Where was the Declaration of Independence signed?

___ ___   ___ ___ ___   ___ ___ ___ ___ ___ ___!
35 70   70 94 88   61 83 70 70 83 91

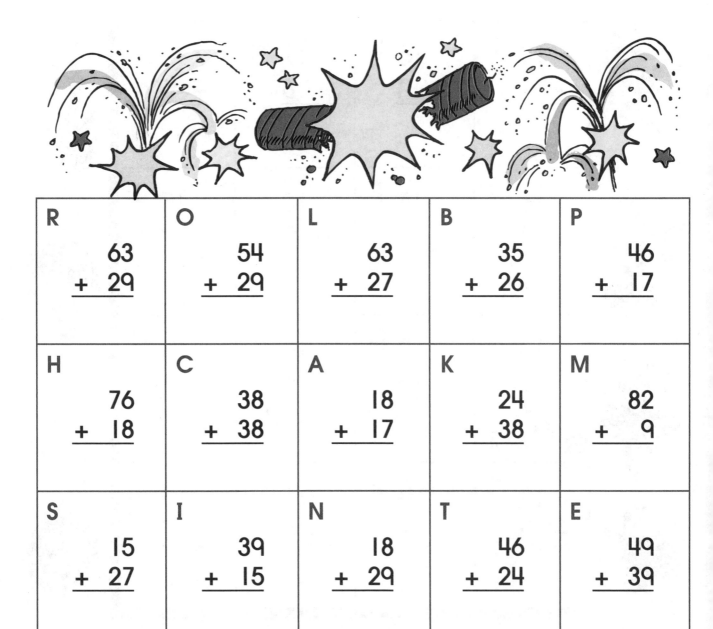

R	O	L	B	P
63 + 29	54 + 29	63 + 27	35 + 26	46 + 17

H	C	A	K	M
76 + 18	38 + 38	18 + 17	24 + 38	82 + 9

S	I	N	T	E
15 + 27	39 + 15	18 + 29	46 + 24	49 + 39

I Spy Something in the Spring

Directions: To find out what I spy, color the boxes with differences of 8 or 9. Then, write the letters from the colored boxes in the blanks, working left to right.

I spy a ____ ____ ____ ____ ____ ____ ____ !

14 L − 7	16 P − 9	17 G − 8	13 W − 6
16 R − 7	15 F − 8	18 O − 9	15 U − 7
13 H − 7	17 N − 9	14 D − 6	16 H − 8
18 O − 9	14 R − 7	15 G − 6	12 P − 5

The Beast

Directions: Connect the dots from **8** to **52**. Then, color to finish the picture.

How Many Toys?

Directions: Count the objects. Write the number words in the puzzle. Use the word box to help you.

Across

2.

3.

4.

6.

7. ✳ ✳ ✳ ✳ ✳ ✳ ✳ ✳

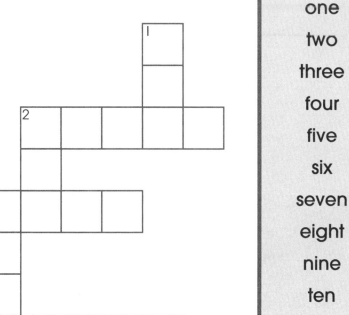

| one |
| two |
| three |
| four |
| five |
| six |
| seven |
| eight |
| nine |
| ten |

Down

1.

2. (two balls)

3.

5.

6.

Oscar the Owlet Moth

Directions: Connect the dots from **0** to **90**. Then, color to finish the picture.

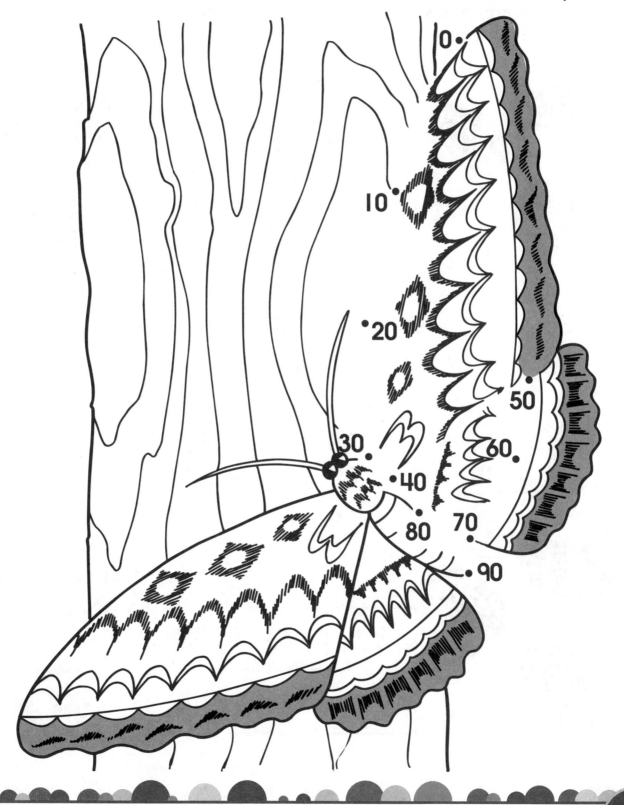

Bingo!

Directions: Find the differences. Color the answers on the bingo cards. Be careful! Some answers are on both. The first board to be completely covered is the winner!

 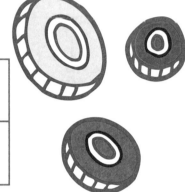

50	35	43
21	65	32

86 − 43	92 − 71	85 − 52	76 − 41	67 − 35

74 − 30	98 − 33	83 − 60	79 − 38

 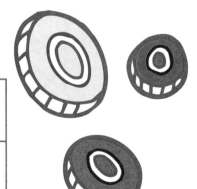

32	23	33
41	43	44

Willy the Walkingstick

Directions: Connect the dots from **0** to **50**. Then, color to finish the picture.

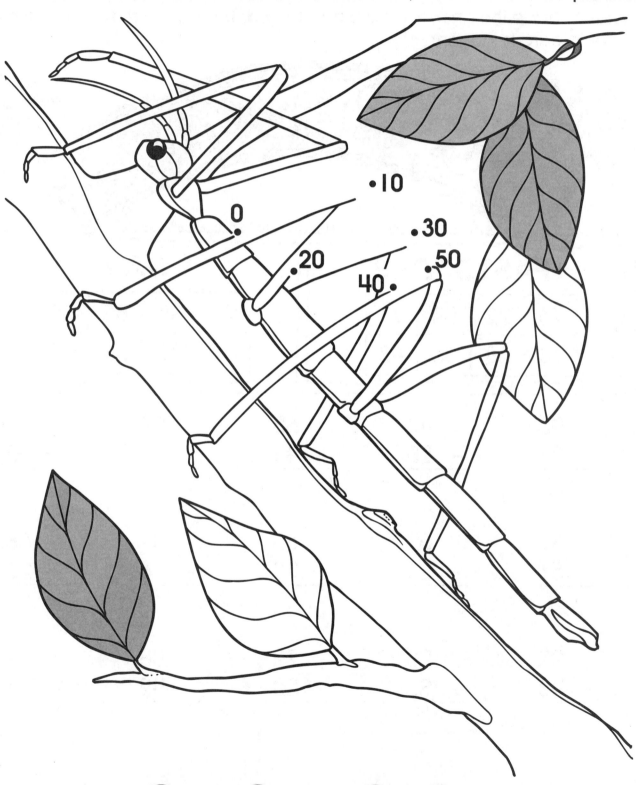

The Ball Game

Directions: Which team will win? Find each difference, working from left to right. Shade the answer on a bingo board. The first team to completely cover its card is the winner!

FASTBACKS

46	22	59	71
73	68	35	43

SWANS

21	34	62	32
51	78	23	30

96	43	65	98	74
− 25	− 20	− 44	− 63	− 52

81	57	66	89	68
− 51	− 23	− 34	− 16	− 25

99	98	79	88	99
− 48	− 36	− 20	− 42	− 31

Snail Garden

Directions: Color **25** snails **brown** . Circle to show how many snails are left over.

③   4   5

Ocean Friend

Directions: This sea animal has eight arms! Connect the dots from **1** to **25**. Then, color to finish the picture.

Back in Time

Directions: Find the numbers **17**, **18**, **19**, and **20**. Color them. Then, color the rest of the picture.

The Three Bears

Directions: Connect the dots from **16** to **68**. Then, color to finish the picture.

Let's Go!

Directions: Kitty says, "Take me for a ride." Connect the dots from **1** to **25**. Then, color to finish the picture.

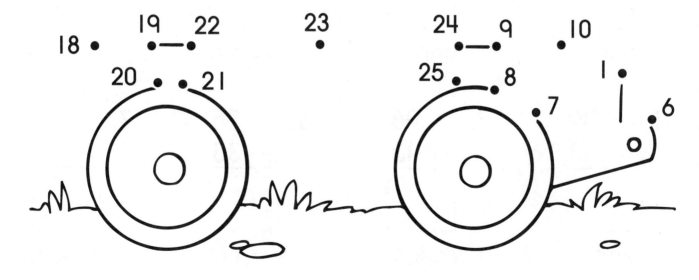

Tic-Tac-Toe

Directions: Find the differences. Then, mark **X** or **O** over the answers on the tic-tac-toe game to find the winner!

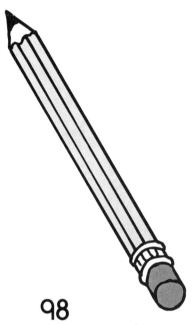

22	64	55
68	46	42
32	72	31

1. 74
  – 52
  [ ]
  Mark X.

2. 85
  – 53
  [ ]
  Mark O.

3. 98
  – 67
  [ ]
  Mark X.

4. 89
  – 43
  [ ]
  Mark O.

5. 98
  – 43
  [ ]
  Mark X.

6. 75
  – 33
  [ ]
  Mark O.

7. 96
  – 32
  [ ]
  Mark X.

The Elves and the Shoemaker

Directions: Connect the dots from **4** to **56**. Then, color to finish the picture.

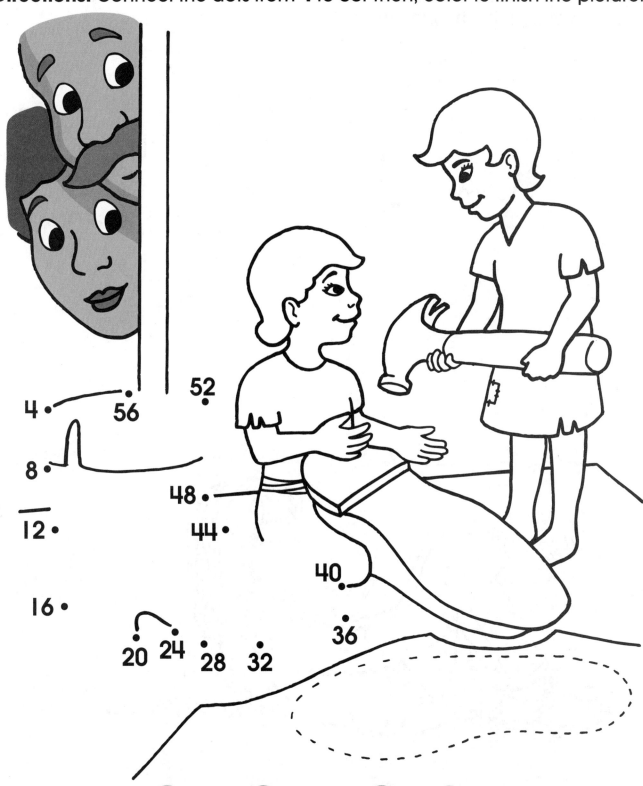

So Peaceful

Directions: Grace loves to sit in the shade. Connect the dots from **1** to **25**. Then, color to finish the picture.

Add or Subtract

Directions: Add or subtract. Use regrouping when needed. Always do ones first and tens last.

tens	ones		tens	ones		tens	ones		tens	ones
9	3		3	0		6	5		7	1
−2	5		+2	7		+1	7		−3	6

tens	ones		tens	ones		tens	ones		tens	ones
7	6		8	2		5	6		2	5
−2	8		+1	9		−2	8		−1	6

tens	ones		tens	ones		tens	ones		tens	ones
4	3		5	3		2	4		4	8
−1	4		−1	5		+5	7		+2	8

33	52	46	97
+47	+29	−37	−68

2-Digit Addition and Subtraction

Addition is "putting together" or adding two or more numbers to find the sum. Subtraction is "taking away" or subtracting one number from another to find the difference. Regrouping is using **one ten** to form **ten ones**, **one 100** to form **ten tens**, and so on.

Directions: Add or subtract using regrouping.

Example:

tens	ones
2	15
3̸	5̸
-2	7
	8

$$
\begin{array}{r} 56 \\ -27 \\ \hline \end{array}
\quad
\begin{array}{r} 40 \\ -16 \\ \hline \end{array}
\quad
\begin{array}{r} 35 \\ +27 \\ \hline \end{array}
\quad
\begin{array}{r} 42 \\ -14 \\ \hline \end{array}
\quad
\begin{array}{r} 53 \\ +38 \\ \hline \end{array}
\quad
\begin{array}{r} 97 \\ -48 \\ \hline \end{array}
\quad
\begin{array}{r} 44 \\ +27 \\ \hline \end{array}
\quad
\begin{array}{r} 93 \\ -39 \\ \hline \end{array}
$$

$$
\begin{array}{r} 56 \\ -17 \\ \hline \end{array}
\quad
\begin{array}{r} 44 \\ +28 \\ \hline \end{array}
\quad
\begin{array}{r} 68 \\ -49 \\ \hline \end{array}
\quad
\begin{array}{r} 73 \\ -24 \\ \hline \end{array}
\quad
\begin{array}{r} 33 \\ +18 \\ \hline \end{array}
\quad
\begin{array}{r} 49 \\ +32 \\ \hline \end{array}
\quad
\begin{array}{r} 77 \\ -68 \\ \hline \end{array}
\quad
\begin{array}{r} 27 \\ +19 \\ \hline \end{array}
$$

2-Digit Addition and Subtraction

Directions: Add or subtract using regrouping.

```
  23          84          69          41
 +48         -56         +29         -17
____        ____        ____        ____


  52          73          84          57
 -28         +18         -27         -39
____        ____        ____        ____


  33          64          37          36
 -15         +17         +58         -19
____        ____        ____        ____


  65          48          33          25
 -28         -30         +18         +35
____        ____        ____        ____
```

Goldilocks

Directions: Connect the dots from **36** to **80**. Then, color to finish the picture.

40

44

48

36

80

76

56

52

72

60

68

64

On a Roll

Directions: Color to find the hidden picture. Use the number key to help you.

16 = green   **17 = red**   **18 = black**   **19 = brown**

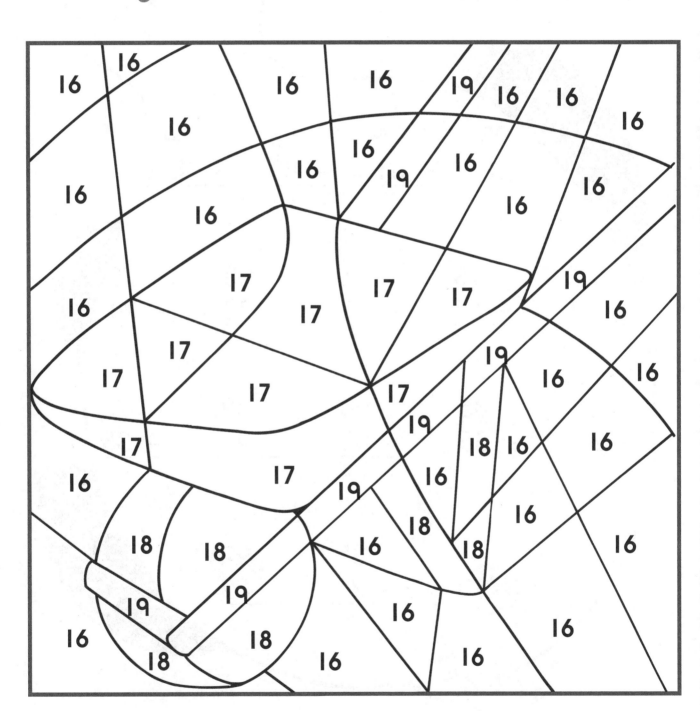

Go Fish!

Directions: Subtract.

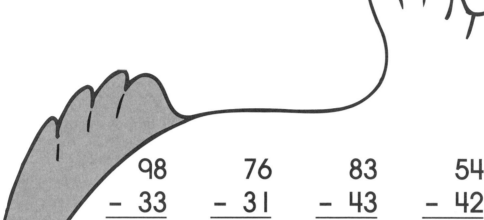

$$\begin{array}{r} 98 \\ -\ 33 \\ \hline \end{array} \qquad \begin{array}{r} 76 \\ -\ 31 \\ \hline \end{array} \qquad \begin{array}{r} 83 \\ -\ 43 \\ \hline \end{array} \qquad \begin{array}{r} 54 \\ -\ 42 \\ \hline \end{array}$$

$$\begin{array}{r} 37 \\ -\ 21 \\ \hline \end{array} \quad \begin{array}{r} 78 \\ -\ 57 \\ \hline \end{array} \quad \begin{array}{r} 65 \\ -\ 13 \\ \hline \end{array} \quad \begin{array}{r} 93 \\ -\ 30 \\ \hline \end{array} \quad \begin{array}{r} 75 \\ -\ 24 \\ \hline \end{array}$$

$$\begin{array}{r} 94 \\ -\ 21 \\ \hline \end{array} \quad \begin{array}{r} 86 \\ -\ 35 \\ \hline \end{array} \quad \begin{array}{r} 98 \\ -\ 45 \\ \hline \end{array} \quad \begin{array}{r} 82 \\ -\ 41 \\ \hline \end{array} \quad \begin{array}{r} 76 \\ -\ 33 \\ \hline \end{array}$$

$$\begin{array}{r} 85 \\ -\ 21 \\ \hline \end{array} \qquad \begin{array}{r} 99 \\ -\ 52 \\ \hline \end{array}$$

Place Value: Hundreds

The place value of a digit or numeral is shown by where it is in the number. For example, in the number **123**, **1** has the place value of **hundreds**, **2** is **tens**, and **3** is **ones**.

Directions: Study the examples. Then, write the missing numbers in the blanks.

Examples:

2 hundreds + 3 tens + 6 ones =

hundreds	tens	ones
2	3	6 = _236_

1 hundred + 4 tens + 9 ones =

hundreds	tens	ones
1	4	9 = _149_

	hundreds	tens	ones	total
3 hundreds + 4 tens + 8 ones =	3	4	8	= _____
_ hundreds + _ ten + _ ones =	2	1	7	= _____
_ hundreds + _ tens + _ ones =	6	3	5	= _____
_ hundreds + _ tens + _ ones =	4	7	9	= _____
_ hundreds + _ tens + _ ones =	2	9	4	= _____
_ hundreds + 5 tens + 6 ones =	4	____	____	= _____
3 hundreds + 1 ten + 3 ones =	____	____	____	= _____
3 hundreds + _ tens + 7 ones =	____	5	____	= _____
6 hundreds + 2 tens + _ ones =	____	____	8	= _____

Place Value: Hundreds

Directions: Write the numbers for hundreds, tens, and ones. Then, add.

Example:

1 hundred + 4 tens + 6 ones
100 + 40 + 6
146

7 hundreds + 3 tens + 5 ones
_____ + _____ + _____
_____

3 hundreds + 1 ten + 9 ones
_____ + _____ + _____
_____

5 hundreds + 8 tens + 0 ones
_____ + _____ + _____
_____

9 hundreds + 0 tens + 7 ones
_____ + _____ + _____
_____

The Magic Coach

Directions: Connect the dots from **4** to **80**. Then, color to finish the picture.

I Spy Something Shiny!

Directions: To find out what I spy, color the boxes with differences of **7**, **8**, or **9**. Then, write the letters from the colored boxes in the blanks, working left to right.

I spy a ___ ___ ___ ___ ___ ___ ___

___ ___ ___ ___ ___ ___ ___ ___ !

15 P − 7	16 I − 9	14 L − 8	14 R − 7
13 A − 6	12 T − 5	16 E − 8	13 T − 5
14 R − 6	14 E − 5	13 T − 8	15 A − 6
16 S − 7	12 U − 4	13 R − 4	15 E − 8

Let's Swing

Directions: Find the hidden numbers. Color them. Then, color the rest of the picture.

3-Digit Addition: Regrouping

Directions: Study the examples. Follow the steps to add.

Example:

Step 1: Add the ones.   **Step 2:** Add the tens.   **Step 3:** Add the hundreds.

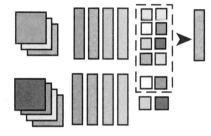   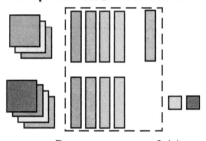   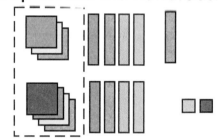

Do you regroup? Yes   Do you regroup? No

hundreds	tens	ones	hundreds	tens	ones	hundreds	tens	ones
	1			1			1	
3	4	8	3	4	8	3	4	8
+4	4	4	+4	4	4	+4	4	4
		2		9	2	7	9	2

hundreds	tens	ones	hundreds	tens	ones	hundreds	tens	ones
	1			1			1	
2	1	4	3	6	8	1	1	9
+2	3	8	+2	1	3	+5	6	5
4	5	2		8	1			4

$$
\begin{array}{cccccccc}
418 & 471 & 334 & 659 & 736 & 426 & 567 & 327 \\
+323 & +319 & +528 & +127 & +145 & +165 & +228 & +354
\end{array}
$$

3-Digit Addition: Regrouping

Directions: Study the example. Follow the steps to add. Regroup when needed.

Step 1: Add the ones.
Step 2: Add the tens.
Step 3: Add the hundreds.

$$10 = 1 \text{ ten} + 0 \text{ ones}$$

hundreds	tens	ones
1	1	
3	4	8
+4	5	4
8	0	2

$$
\begin{array}{r}
348 \\
+214 \\
\hline
\end{array}
\qquad
\begin{array}{r}
172 \\
+418 \\
\hline
\end{array}
\qquad
\begin{array}{r}
575 \\
+329 \\
\hline
\end{array}
\qquad
\begin{array}{r}
623 \\
+268 \\
\hline
\end{array}
\qquad
\begin{array}{r}
369 \\
+533 \\
\hline
\end{array}
\qquad
\begin{array}{r}
733 \\
+229 \\
\hline
\end{array}
$$

$$
\begin{array}{r}
411 \\
+299 \\
\hline
\end{array}
\qquad
\begin{array}{r}
423 \\
+169 \\
\hline
\end{array}
\qquad
\begin{array}{r}
639 \\
+177 \\
\hline
\end{array}
\qquad
\begin{array}{r}
624 \\
+368 \\
\hline
\end{array}
\qquad
\begin{array}{r}
272 \\
+469 \\
\hline
\end{array}
\qquad
\begin{array}{r}
393 \\
+418 \\
\hline
\end{array}
$$

3-Digit Subtraction: Regrouping

Directions: Study the example. Follow the steps to subtract.

Step 1: Regroup ones.
Step 2: Subtract ones.
Step 3: Subtract tens.
Step 4: Subtract hundreds.

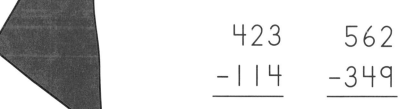

$$\begin{array}{r} 423 \\ -114 \\ \hline \end{array} \qquad \begin{array}{r} 562 \\ -349 \\ \hline \end{array}$$

Example:

hundreds	tens	ones
	5	12
4	6̸	2̸
−2	5	3
2	0	9

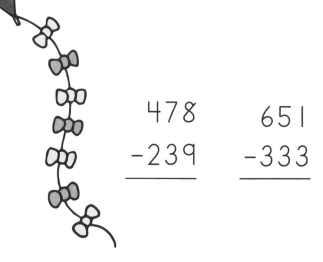

$$\begin{array}{r} 478 \\ -239 \\ \hline \end{array} \qquad \begin{array}{r} 651 \\ -333 \\ \hline \end{array}$$

Directions: Draw a line to the correct answer. Color the kites.

$$\begin{array}{r} 347 \\ -218 \\ \hline \end{array} \quad \begin{array}{r} 144 \\ -135 \\ \hline \end{array} \quad \begin{array}{r} 963 \\ -748 \\ \hline \end{array} \quad \begin{array}{r} 762 \\ -553 \\ \hline \end{array} \quad \begin{array}{r} 287 \\ -179 \\ \hline \end{array} \quad \begin{array}{r} 427 \\ -398 \\ \hline \end{array}$$

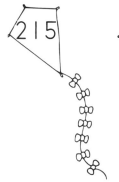
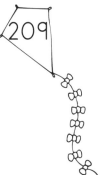
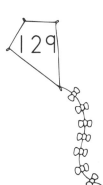
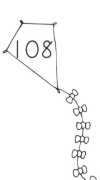
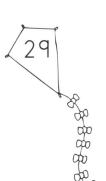
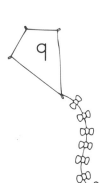

215   209   129   108   29   9

3-Digit Subtraction: Regrouping

Directions: Subtract. Circle the **7**s that appear in the **tens** place.

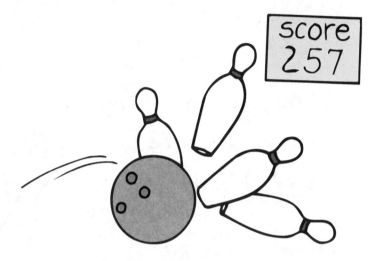

score
257

```
  492          184
 -221         -129
 -----        -----
 2(7)1
```

```
  358          765          584          693          921
 -238         -326         -435         -314         -362
 -----        -----        -----        -----        -----
```

```
  128          744          835          248          635
 -109         -674         -217         -199         -428
 -----        -----        -----        -----        -----
```

Cinderella

Directions: Connect the dots from **28** to **92**. Then, color to finish the picture.

Back in Time

Directions: Connect the dots from **12** to **51**. Then, color to finish the picture.

Out for the Count

Directions: Find the numbers **1** to **10**. Color them. Then, color the rest of the picture.

Place Value: Thousands

Directions: Study the example. Write the missing numbers.

Example:

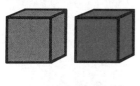

1,000   100   10 |
1,000   10 |
               10

2 thousands + 1 hundred + ___3___ tens + 2 ones = __2,132__

5,286 = ____ thousands + ____ hundreds + ____ tens + ____ ones

1,831 = ____ thousands + ____ hundreds + ____ tens + ____ ones

8,972 = ____ thousands + ____ hundreds + ____ tens + ____ ones

4,528 = ____ thousands + ____ hundreds + ____ tens + ____ ones

3,177 = ____ thousands + ____ hundreds + ____ tens + ____ ones

Directions: Draw a line to the number that has:

8 hundreds	7,103
5 ones	2,862
9 tens	5,996
7 thousands	1,485

Place Value: Thousands

6 , 4 3 1

thousands | hundreds | tens | ones

Directions: Tell which number is in each place.

 Thousands place:

2,456   4,621   3,456

_____   _____   _____

 Tens place:

4,286   1,234   5,678

_____   _____   _____

 Hundreds place:

6,321   3,210   7,871

_____   _____   _____

☆ **Ones place:**

5,432   6,531   9,980

_____   _____   _____

Place Value: Thousands

Directions: Use the code to color the fan.

If the answer has:
9 thousands, color it **pink**.   8 tens, color it **red**.
6 thousands, color it **green**.   3 ones, color it **blue**.
5 hundreds, color it **orange**.

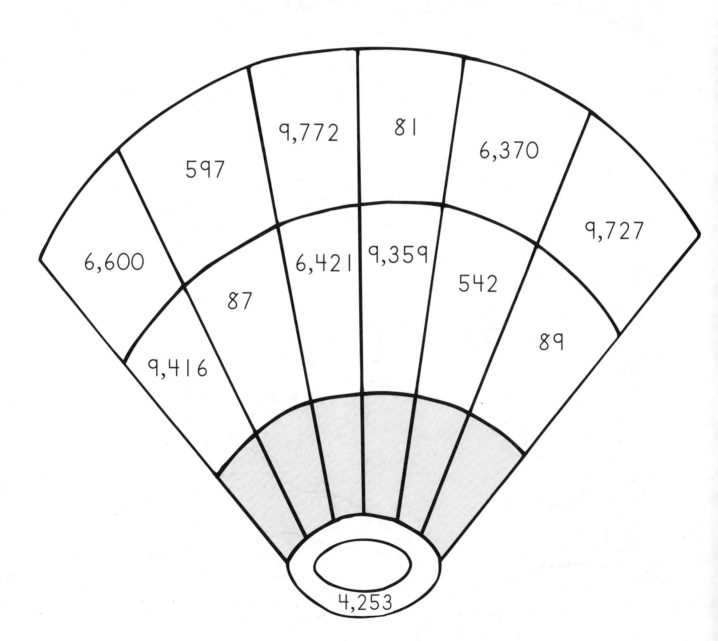

A Pointy Fish

Directions: Connect the dots from **0** to **50**. Then, color to finish the picture.

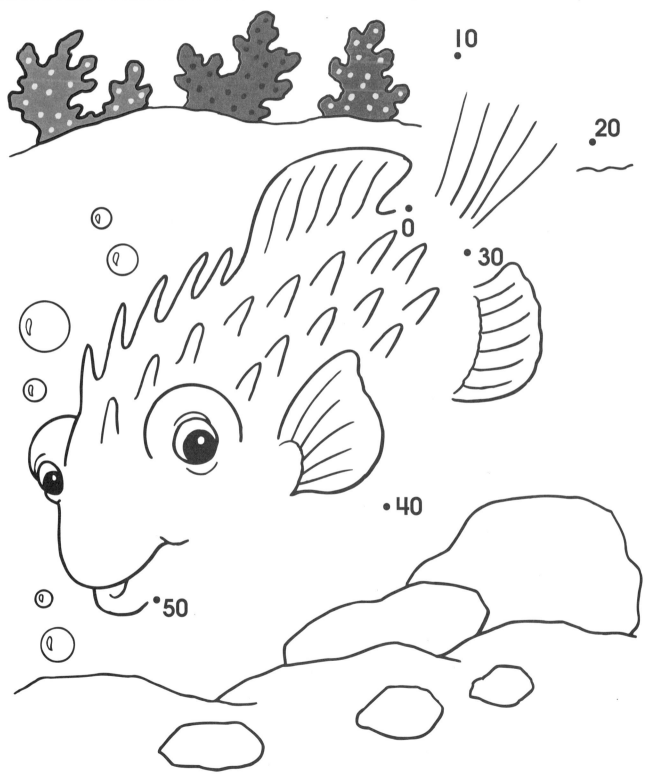

Rip Van Winkle

Directions: Connect the dots from **4** to **32**. Then, color to finish the picture.

A Smart Coral

Directions: Connect the dots from **9** to **54**. Then, color to finish the picture.

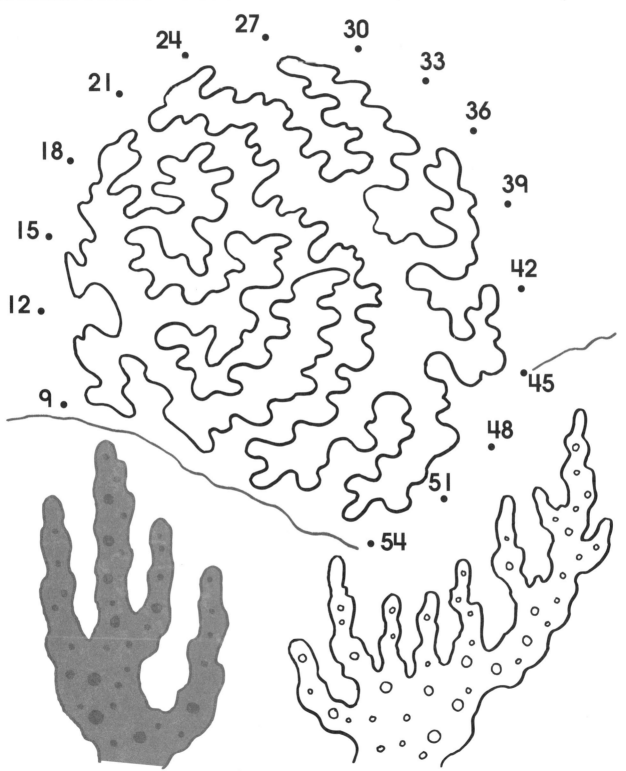

Graphs

A graph is a drawing that shows information about numbers.

Directions: Count the apples in each row. Color the boxes to show how many apples have bites taken out of them.

Example:

1	2	3	4	5	6	7	8

Graphs

Directions: Count the bananas in each row. Color the boxes to show how many have been eaten by the monkeys.

Graphs

Directions: Count the fish. Color the bowls to make a graph that shows the number of fish.

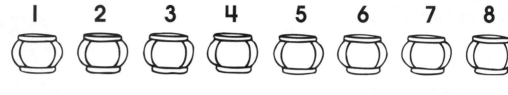

Directions: Use your fishbowl graphs to find the answers to the following questions. Draw a line to the correct bowl.

The most fish

The fewest fish

A What?

Directions: Add. Use the sums to answer the riddle.

What do you call a hamburger
bun in a rocking chair?

,

59	68	54	78	86	92

59	68	73	73	!

21 C + 33	60 N + 32	63 W + 20
43 I + 43	42 R + 17	54 S + 43
34 O + 34	53 K + 25	42 L + 31

Sharpy Swordfish

Directions: Connect the dots from **3** to **27**. Then, color to finish the picture.

Multiplication

Multiplication is a short way to find the sum of adding the same number a certain amount of times. For example, **4 x 7 = 28** instead of **7 + 7 + 7 + 7 = 28.**

Directions: Study the example. Solve the problems.

Example:

3 + 3 + 3 = 9
3 threes = 9
3 x 3 = 9

7 + 7 = __14__
2 sevens = __14__
2 x 7 = __14__

4 + 4 + 4 + 4 = ____
4 fours = ____
4 x ____ = ____

5 + 5 = ____
2 fives = ____
2 x ____ = ____

2 + 2 + 2 + 2 = ____
4 twos = ____
4 x ____ = ____

6 + 6 = ____
2 sixes = ____
2 x ____ = ____

Multiplication

Multiplication is repeated addition.

Directions: Draw a picture for each problem. Then, write the missing numbers.

Example:
Draw 2 groups of 3 apples.

$$3 + 3 = 6$$
$$\text{or } 2 \times 3 = 6$$

Draw 3 groups of 4 hearts.	Draw 2 groups of 5 boxes.

4 + 4 + 4 = _____	5 + _____ = _____
or 3 x _____ = _____	or 2 x _____ = _____

Draw 6 groups of 2 circles.

2 + ____ + ____ + ____ + ____ + ____ = ____

or   6 x ____ = ____

Draw 7 groups of 3 triangles.

3 + ____ + ____ + ____ + ____ + ____ + ____ = ____

or   ____ x ____ = ____

Multiplication

Directions: Study the example. Draw the groups, and write the total.

Example: 3 x 2
　　　　　 2 + 2 + 2   =   → 6 _____
　　　　　 (●● ●● ●●)

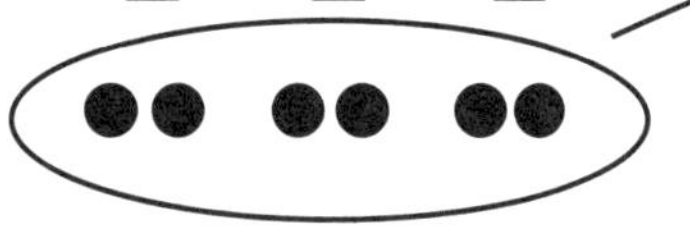

3 x 4

___ + ___ + ___ = _____

2 x 5

____ + ____ = _____

5 x 3

___ + ___ + ___ + ___ + ___ = _____

Multiplication

Directions: Solve the problems.

$9 + 9 =$ __18__

2 nines = ____

$2 \times 9 =$ ____

$7 + 7 =$ ____

2 sevens = ____

$2 \times$ __7__ $=$ ____

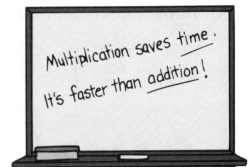

Multiplication saves time. It's faster than addition!

$4 + 4 + 4 + 4 =$ ____

__4__ fours = ____

____ $\times 4 =$ ____

$8 + 8 + 8 + 8 + 8 =$ ____

____ eights = ____

____ $\times 8 =$ ____

$5 + 5 + 5 =$ ____

____ fives = ____

____ $\times 5 =$ ____

$9 + 9 =$ ____

____ nines = ____

____ $\times 9 =$ ____

$6 + 6 + 6 =$ ____

____ sixes = ____

____ $\times 6 =$ ____

$3 + 3 =$ ____

____ threes = ____

____ $\times 3 =$ ____

$7 + 7 + 7 + 7 =$ ____

____ sevens = ____

____ $\times 7 =$ ____

$2 + 2 =$ ____

____ twos = ____

____ $\times 2 =$ ____

Lynn the Luna Moth

Directions: Connect the dots from **0** to **190**. Then, color to finish the picture.

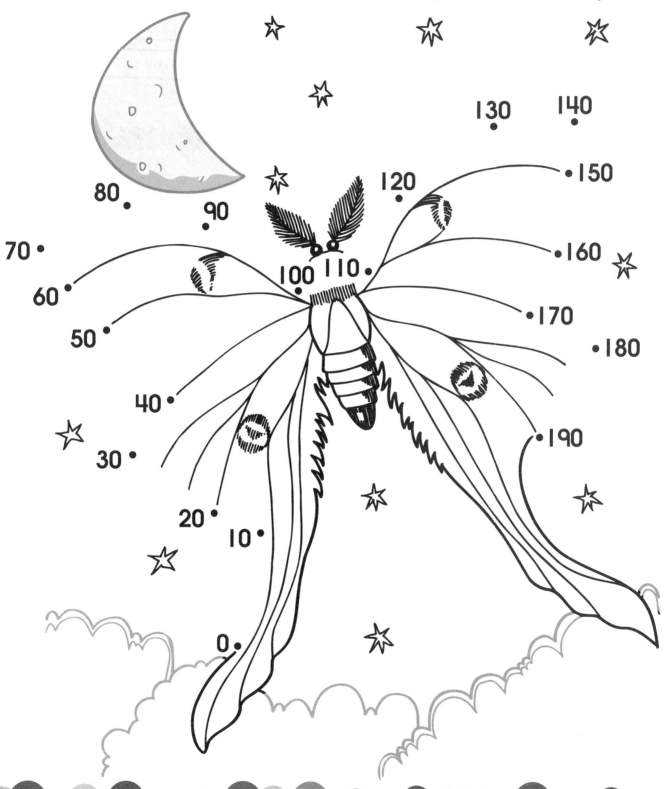

Name _____

All Coiled Up

Directions: Color to find the hidden picture. Use the number key to help you.

4 = black   **5 = red**   **6 = yellow**

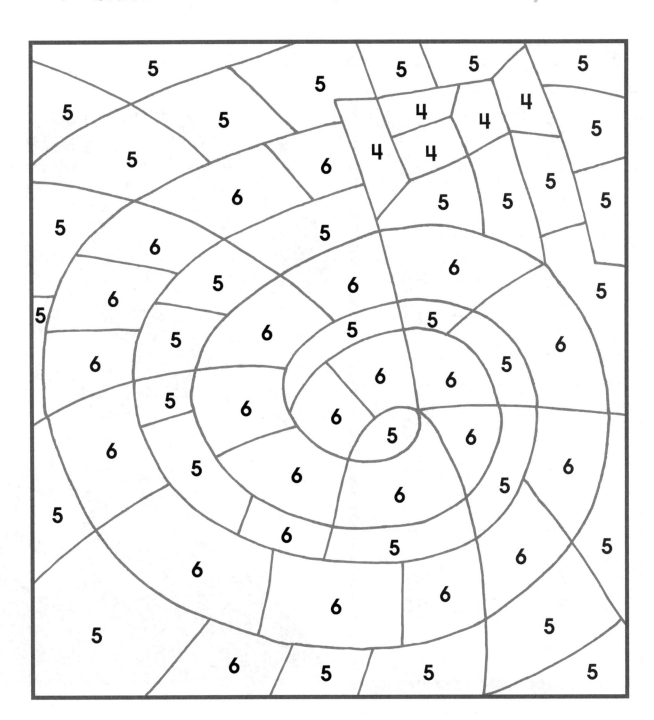

Out of This World

Directions: Subtract. Use the differences to answer the riddle.

What game do astronauts like to play?

___ ___ ___ ___ ___ ___ ___ ___ ___**!**
53   36   36   82   36   27   36   41   60

P 38 − 11	**O** 59 − 23
R 96 − 71	**F** 88 − 17
M 96 − 43	**N** 93 − 11
L 77 − 36	**Y** 99 − 39

Carrie the Caterpillar

Directions: Connect the dots from **20** to **190**. Then, color to finish the picture.

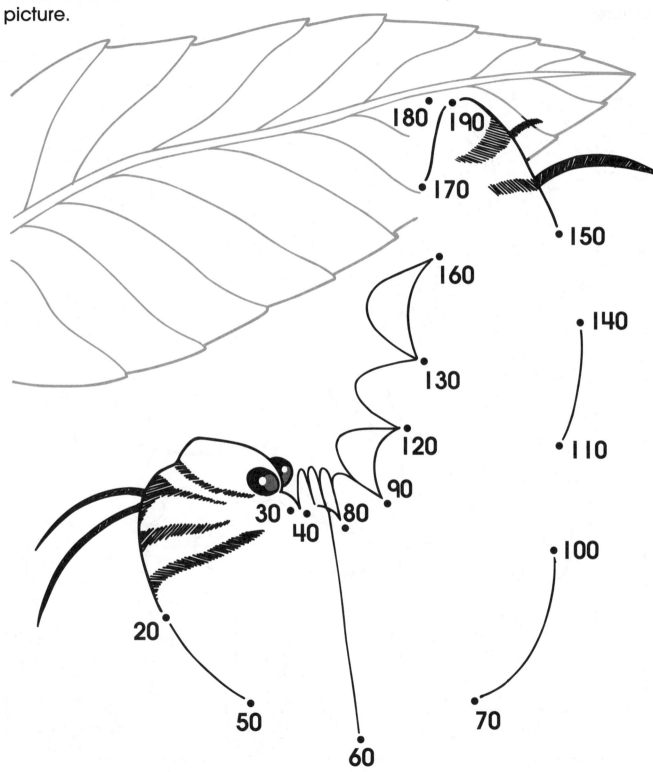

Life on the Farm

Directions: Find the numbers **1** to **6**. Color them. Then, color the rest of the picture.

A Long Fish

Directions: Connect the dots from **12** to **38**. Then, color to finish the picture.

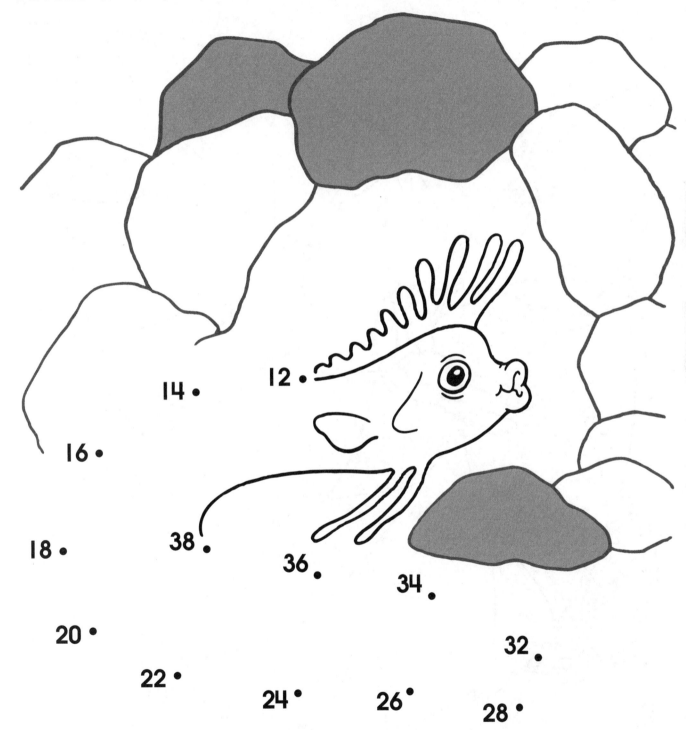

Gary Glowworm

Directions: Connect the dots from **0** to **25**. Then, color to finish the picture.

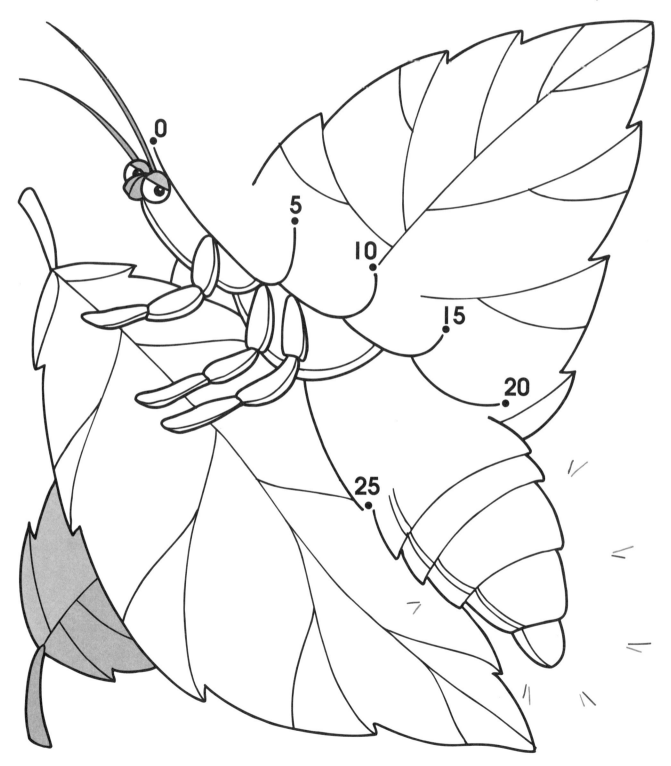

Sail Away

Directions: Color to find the hidden picture. Use the number key to help you.

1 = brown   2 = yellow   3 = red   4 = green   5 = blue

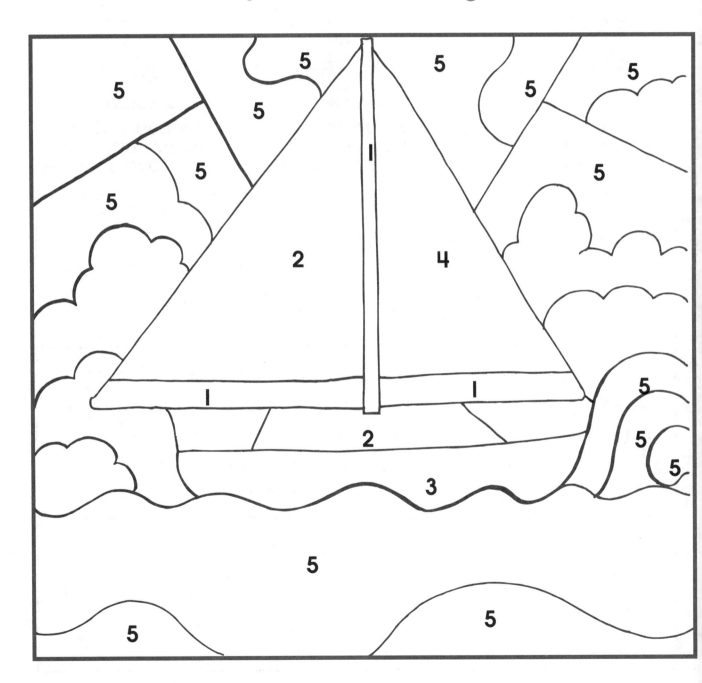

Fractions: Half, Third, Fourth

A **fraction** is a number that names part of a whole, such as $\frac{1}{2}$ or $\frac{1}{3}$.

Directions: Study the examples. Color the correct fraction of each shape.

Examples:

shaded part   1
equal parts   2
$\frac{1}{2}$ (one-half) shaded

shaded part   1
equal parts   3
$\frac{1}{3}$ (one-third) shaded

shaded part   1
equal parts   4
$\frac{1}{4}$ (one-fourth) shaded

Color: $\frac{1}{3}$ red	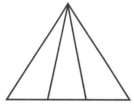 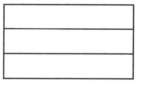 
Color: $\frac{1}{4}$ blue	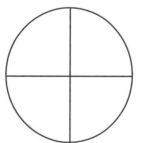  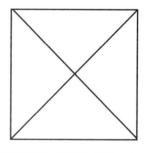
Color: $\frac{1}{2}$ orange	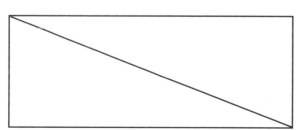 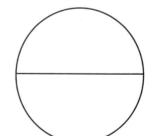

Name _____

Fractions: Half, Third, Fourth

Directions: Study the examples. Circle the fraction that shows the shaded part. Then, circle the fraction that shows the whole part.

Examples:

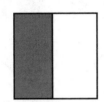

shaded
$\frac{1}{4}$ $\frac{1}{3}$ $\boxed{\frac{1}{2}}$

white
$\frac{1}{3}$ $\boxed{\frac{1}{2}}$ $\frac{1}{4}$

shaded
$\frac{1}{2}$ $\boxed{\frac{2}{3}}$ $\frac{3}{4}$

white
$\frac{2}{3}$ $\frac{1}{2}$ $\boxed{\frac{1}{3}}$

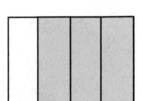

shaded
$\frac{1}{4}$ $\frac{1}{2}$ $\boxed{\frac{3}{4}}$

white
$\boxed{\frac{1}{4}}$ $\frac{2}{3}$ $\frac{1}{2}$

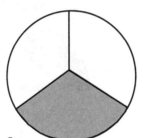

shaded
$\frac{1}{4}$ $\frac{1}{3}$ $\frac{1}{2}$

white
$\frac{2}{4}$ $\frac{2}{3}$ $\frac{2}{2}$

shaded
$\frac{3}{4}$ $\frac{1}{3}$ $\frac{3}{2}$

white
$\frac{1}{2}$ $\frac{1}{4}$ $\frac{1}{3}$

shaded
$\frac{2}{3}$ $\frac{2}{4}$ $\frac{2}{2}$

white
$\frac{1}{3}$ $\frac{2}{4}$ $\frac{2}{2}$

shaded
$\frac{2}{4}$ $\frac{2}{3}$ $\frac{2}{2}$

white
$\frac{1}{2}$ $\frac{1}{4}$ $\frac{1}{3}$

Fractions: Half, Third, Fourth

Directions: Draw a line from the fraction to the correct shape.

$\frac{1}{4}$ shaded

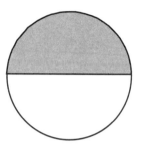

$\frac{2}{4}$ shaded

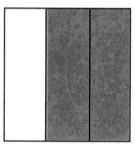

$\frac{1}{2}$ shaded

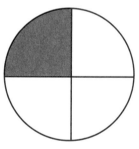

$\frac{1}{3}$ shaded

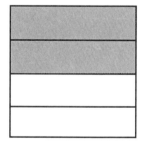

$\frac{2}{3}$ shaded

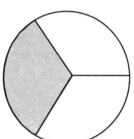

Angie the Ant

Directions: Connect the dots from **0** to **30**. Then, color to finish the picture.

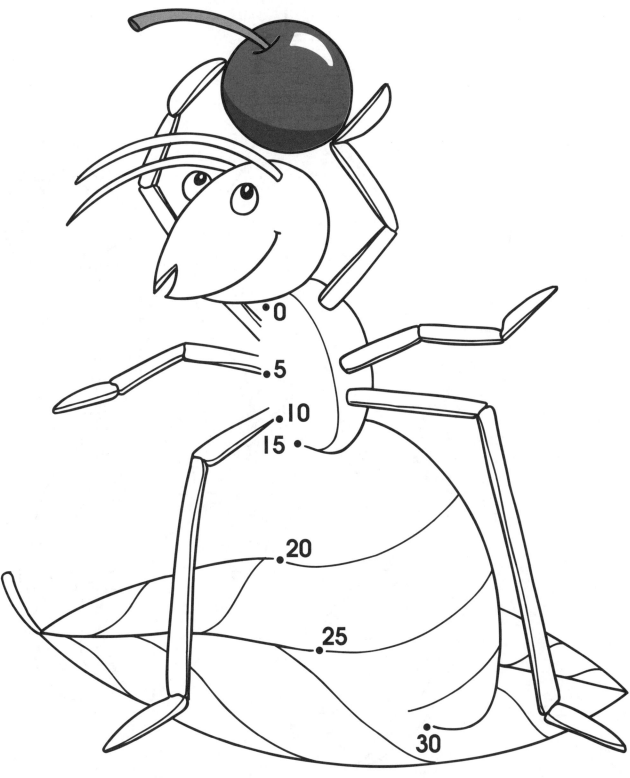

Name _____

Amy the Atlas Moth

Directions: Connect the dots from **0** to **60**. Then, color to finish the picture.

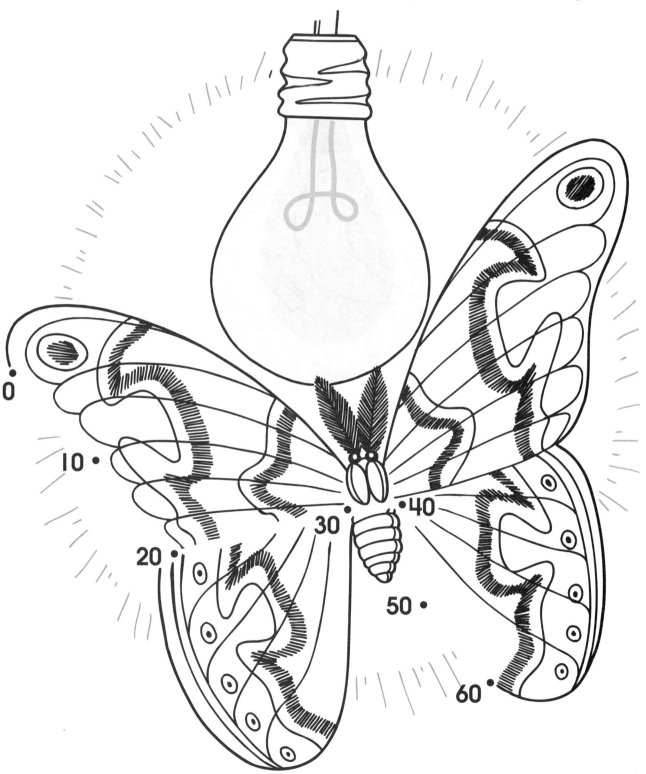

Treetop Friends

Directions: Find the animals and color them **brown**. Then, color the rest of the picture.

Directions: Circle to show how many.

   5   6      5   6

T-rex's Tooth

Directions: Connect the dots from **0** to **30**. Then, color to finish the picture.

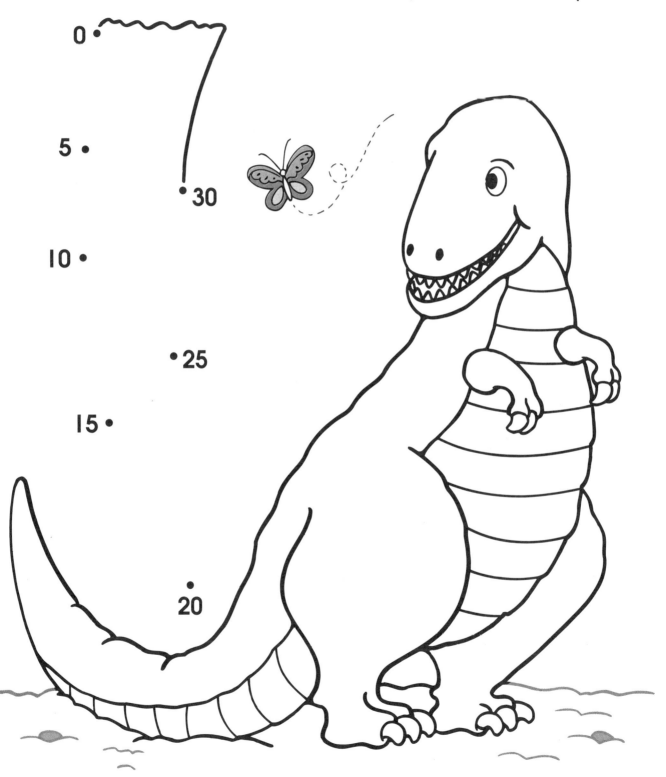

0

5

30

10

25

15

20

Geometry

Geometry is mathematics that has to do with lines and shapes.

Directions: Color the shapes.

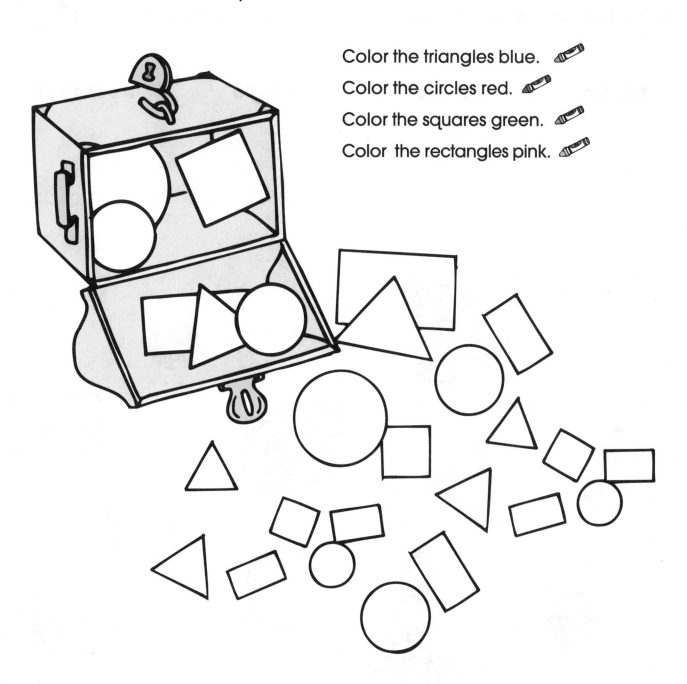

Color the triangles blue.

Color the circles red.

Color the squares green.

Color the rectangles pink.

Name _____

Geometry

Directions: Draw a line from the word to the shape.

Use a red line for circles. ✏️
Use a blue line for squares. ✏️

Use a yellow line for rectangles. ✏️
Use a green line for triangles. ✏️

Circle   **Square**   **Triangle**   **Rectangle**

Numbers 1-10

Directions: Find and circle the words in the puzzle.

```
w  t  t  o  n  e  r  s
n  w  t  h  r  e  e  f
i  o  u  s  i  x  q  i
n  v  e  i  g  h  t  v
e  f  o  u  r  b  e  e
x  s  e  v  e  n  n  o
```

1 one

2 two

3 three

4 four

5 five

6 six

7 seven

8 eight

9 nine

10 ten

Gardening Counting

Directions: Count the objects. Write the number. Circle the smaller number.

Swim On!

Directions: Connect the dots from **5** to **30**. Then, color to finish the picture.

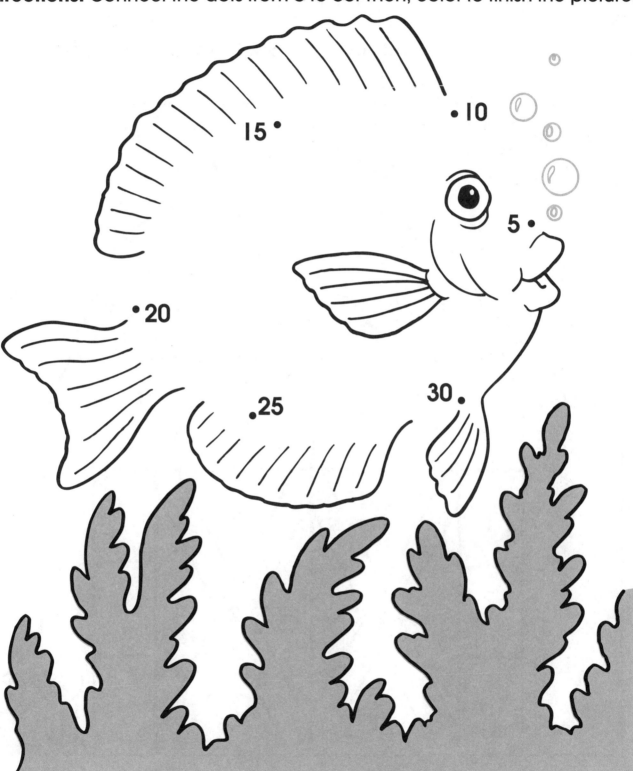

The Big Red Barn

Directions: Color to find the hidden picture. Use the number key to help you.

l = red   2 = yellow   3 = blue   4 = brown

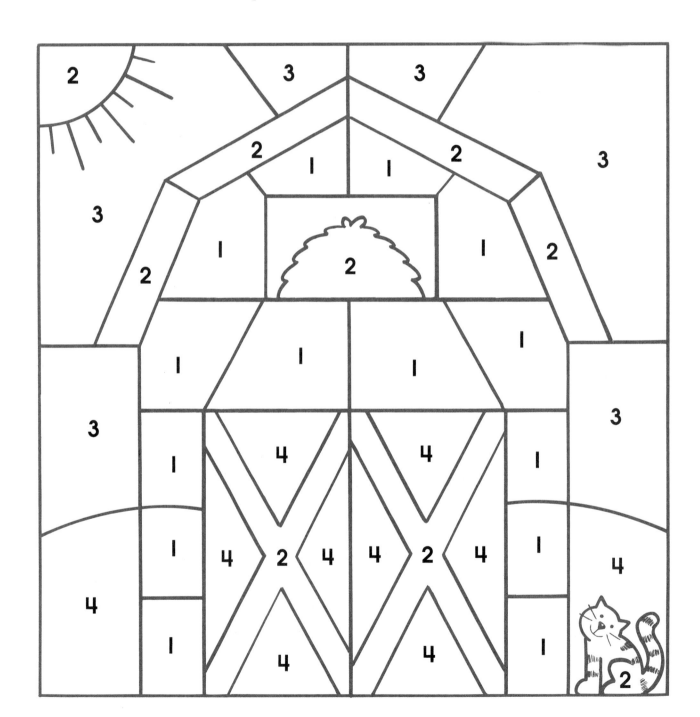

Measurement: Inches

An **inch** is a unit of length in the standard measurement system.

Directions: Use a ruler to measure each object to the nearest inch.

I inch

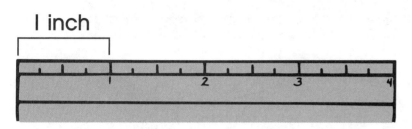

about __I__ inch

about _____ inch

about _____ inches

about _____ inches

about _____ inches

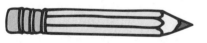
about _____ inches

about _____ inches

about _____ inches

Measurement: Inches

Directions: Use the ruler to measure the fish to the nearest inch.

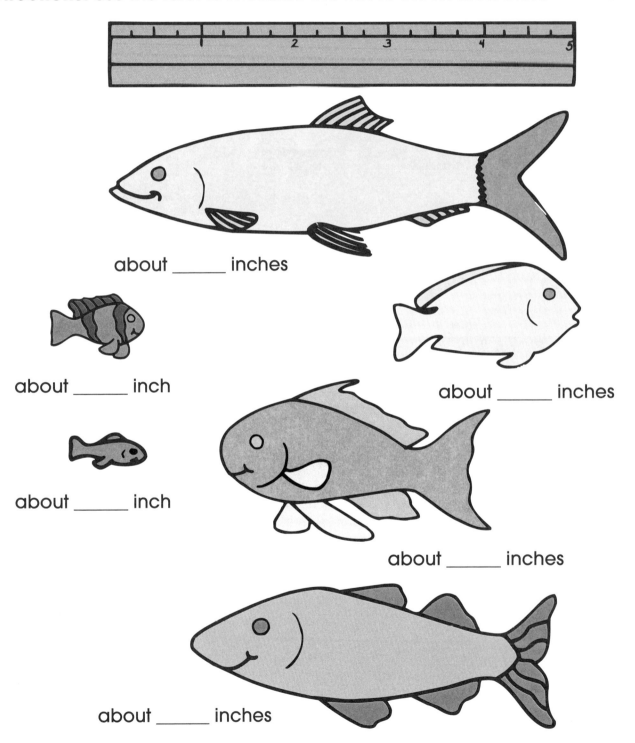

about _____ inches

about _____ inch

about _____ inches

about _____ inch

about _____ inches

about _____ inches

Measurement: Centimeters

A **centimeter** is a unit of length in the metric system. There are 2.54 centimeters in an inch

Directions: Use a centimeter ruler to measure the crayons to the nearest centimeter.

Example: The first crayon is about 7 centimeters long.

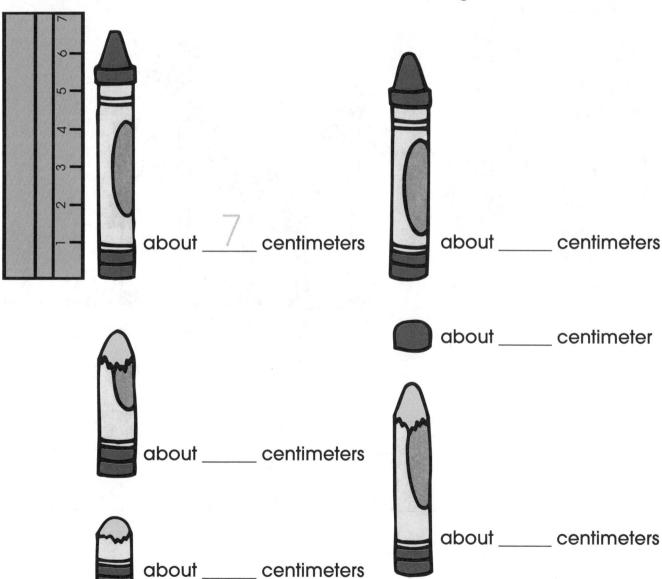

about ___7___ centimeters

about _____ centimeters

about _____ centimeter

about _____ centimeters

about _____ centimeters

about _____ centimeters

Measurement: Centimeters

Directions: The giraffe is about 8 centimeters high. How many centimeters (cm) high are the trees? Write your answers in the blanks.

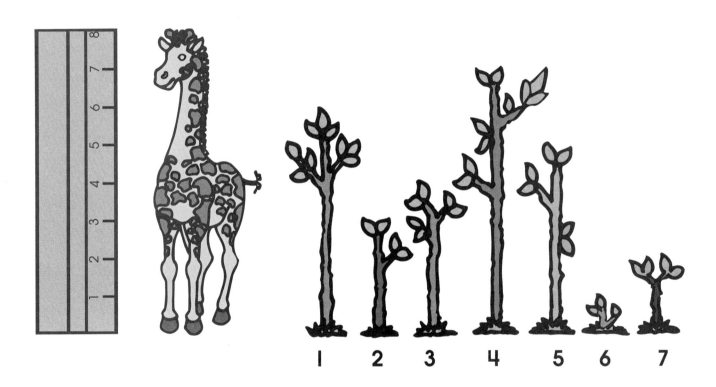

1)_____cm   2)_____cm   3)_____cm

4)_____cm   5)_____cm   6)_____cm   7)_____cm

Buddy the Bee

Directions: Connect the dots from **0** to **60**. Then, color to finish the picture.

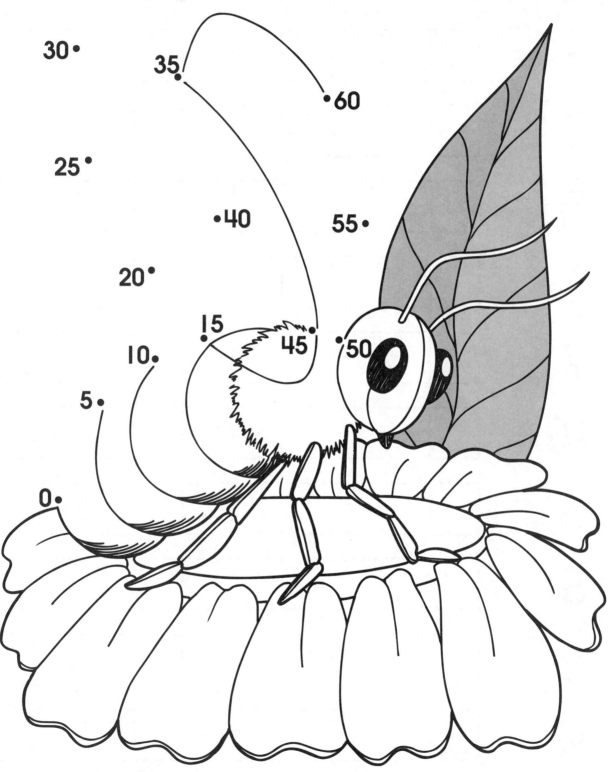

Counting and Color Fun

Directions: Color the correct number of squares.

1

5

9

6

7

10

3

5

2

4

Tending the Garden

Directions: Help the girl water the garden. Color the drops of water in order from **1** to **10**.

Time: Hour, Half-Hour

An hour is sixty minutes. The short hand of a clock tells the hour. It is written **0:00**, such as **5:00**. A half-hour is thirty minutes. When the long hand of the clock is pointing to the six, the time is on the half-hour. It is written **:30**, such as **5:30**.

Directions: Study the examples.
Tell what time it is on each clock.

Examples:

 9:00

The minute hand is on the 12.
The hour hand is on the 9.
It is 9 o'clock.

 4:30

The minute hand is on the 6.
The hour hand is between the 4 and 5.
It is 4:30.

_____   _____   _____   _____   _____

_____   _____   _____   _____   _____

Time: Hour, Half-Hour

Directions: Draw lines between the clocks that show the same time.

Time: Counting by Fives

The minute hand of a clock takes 5 minutes to move from one number to the next. Start at the 12, and count by fives to tell how many minutes it is past the hour.

Directions: Study the examples. Tell what time is on each clock.

Examples:

 ___9:10___  ___8:25___

_____ _____ _____

_____ _____ _____

_____ _____ _____

Time: Quarter Hours

Time can also be shown as fractions. 30 minutes = $\frac{1}{2}$ hour

Directions: Shade the fraction of each clock, and tell how many minutes you have shaded.

Examples:

$\frac{1}{2}$ hour

30 minutes

$\frac{1}{4}$ hour

_____ minutes

$\frac{2}{4}$ hour

_____ minutes

$\frac{3}{4}$ hour

_____ minutes

$\frac{1}{2}$ hour

_____ minutes

Water, Water, Water

Directions: Help the crab get to the tidal pool. Color the sea stars in order from **1** to **10**.

A Pile of Puppies

Directions: Find **11** puppies below. Color them. Then, color the rest of the picture.

Name _____

Sara the Swallowtail Butterfly

Directions: Connect the dots from **0** to **85**. Then, color to finish the picture.

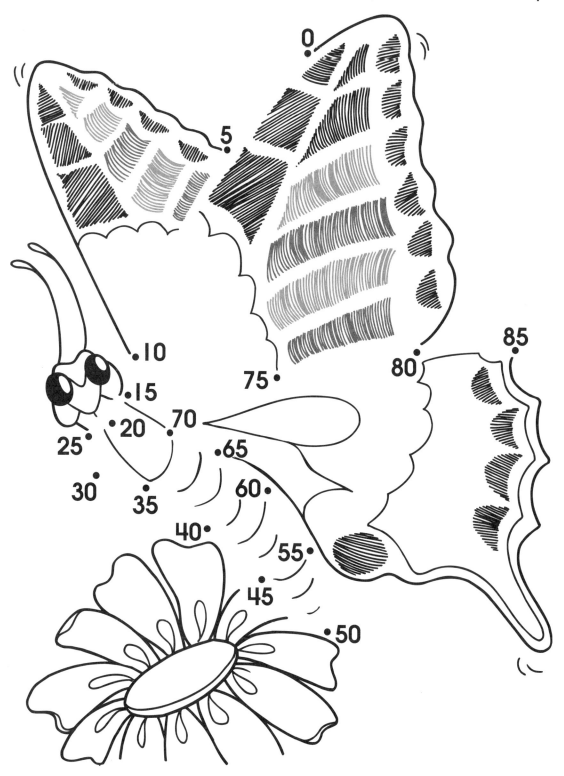

Review

Counting

Directions: Write the number that is:

next.	one less.	one greater.
68, 69, _____	_____, 57	12, _____
786, 787, _____	_____, 650	843, _____

Place Value: Tens and Ones

Directions: Draw a line to the correct number.

4 tens + 7 ones	20
2 tens + 0 ones	51
7 tens + 3 ones	47
5 tens + 1 ones	73

Addition and Subtraction

Directions: Add or subtract.

$$\begin{array}{r} 15 \\ + 5 \\ \hline \end{array} \qquad \begin{array}{r} 14 \\ - 4 \\ \hline \end{array} \qquad \begin{array}{r} 7 \\ + 3 \\ \hline \end{array} \qquad \begin{array}{r} 8 \\ - 6 \\ \hline \end{array} \qquad \begin{array}{r} 10 \\ + 7 \\ \hline \end{array} \qquad \begin{array}{r} 14 \\ - 5 \\ \hline \end{array}$$

Review

2-Digit Addition and Subtraction

Directions: Add or subtract, remembering to regroup, if needed.

66	38	87	52	40
− 37	+ 18	− 69	− 15	+ 17

84	65	99	61	56
+ 17	+ 14	− 48	− 36	+ 46

Place Value: Hundreds and Thousands

Directions: Draw a line to the correct number.

4 hundreds + 3 tens + 2 ones	7,201
6 hundreds + 7 tens + 6 ones	290
5 thousands + 3 hundreds + 7 tens + 2 ones	432
4 hundreds + 3 tens + 2 ones	676
7 thousands + 2 hundreds + 0 tens + 1 ones	5,372

3-Digit Addition and Subtraction

Directions: Add or subtract, remembering to regroup, if needed.

458	793	822	528	697	569
− 248	− 414	− 460	+ 319	+ 108	+ 288

Review

Multiplication

Directions: Solve the problems. Draw groups if necessary.

$$\begin{array}{c} 2 \\ \underline{\times 8} \end{array} \qquad \begin{array}{c} 6 \\ \underline{\times 4} \end{array} \qquad \begin{array}{c} 3 \\ \underline{\times 2} \end{array} \qquad \begin{array}{c} 8 \\ \underline{\times 4} \end{array} \qquad \begin{array}{c} 5 \\ \underline{\times 3} \end{array} \qquad \begin{array}{c} 2 \\ \underline{\times 2} \end{array}$$

Fractions

Directions: Circle the correct fraction of each shape's white part.

$$\frac{1}{2} \quad \frac{1}{3} \quad \frac{1}{4}$$

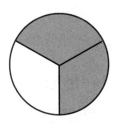

$$\frac{1}{4} \quad \frac{1}{3} \quad \frac{1}{2}$$

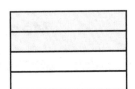

$$\frac{2}{3} \quad \frac{2}{4} \quad \frac{1}{3}$$

$$\frac{1}{4} \quad \frac{1}{2} \quad \frac{3}{4}$$

Graphs

Directions: Count the flowers. Color the pots to make a graph that shows the number of flowers.

1 2 3 4 5 6 7 8

Review

Geometry

Directions: Match the shapes.

rectangle

square

circle

triangle

Measurement

Directions: Look at the ruler. Measure the objects to the nearest inch.

_____ inches

_____ inches

_____ inches

Time

Directions: Tell what time is on each clock.

_____   _____   _____   _____

What a Fall!

Directions: Subtract. Use the differences to answer the riddle.

What falls often but never gets hurt?

____ ____ ____ ____ !
7   8   9   6

G	O
12 – 8 = _____	18 – 9 = _____
P	**L**
14 – 9 = _____	11 – 9 = _____
T	**S**
12 – 9 = _____	15 – 8 = _____
W	**N**
13 – 7 = _____	17 – 9 = _____

An Animal Friend

Directions: This animal purrs when it's happy. Connect the dots from **1** to **20**. Then, color to finish the picture.

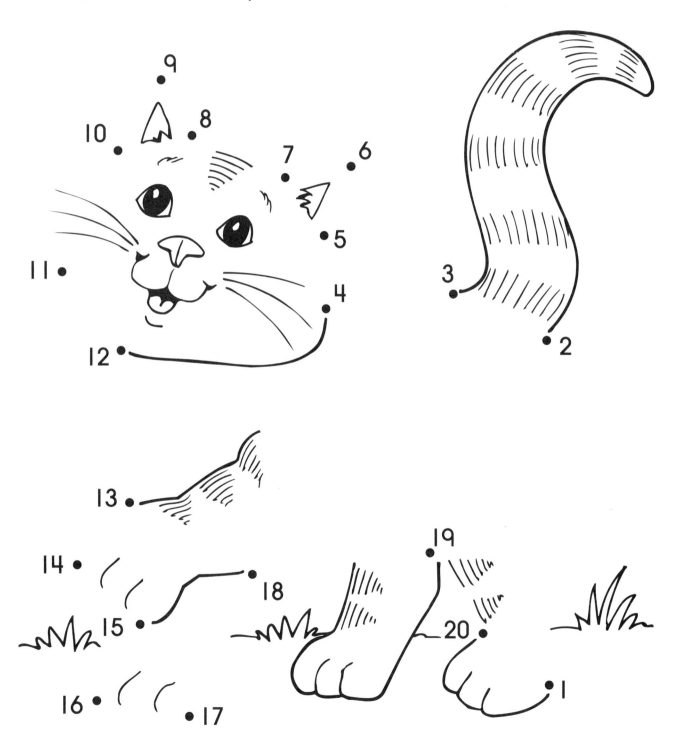

A Starry Night

Directions: Help Kevin find **21** stars ☆. Color them yellow. Then, color the rest of the picture.

The Pied Piper

Directions: Connect the dots from **20** to **85**. Then, color to finish the picture.

Leaves Are Falling

Directions: Find the differences to complete the paths.
Start at the top and go down.

Yoli the Yellow Jacket

Directions: Connect the dots from **15** to **90**. Then, color to finish the picture.

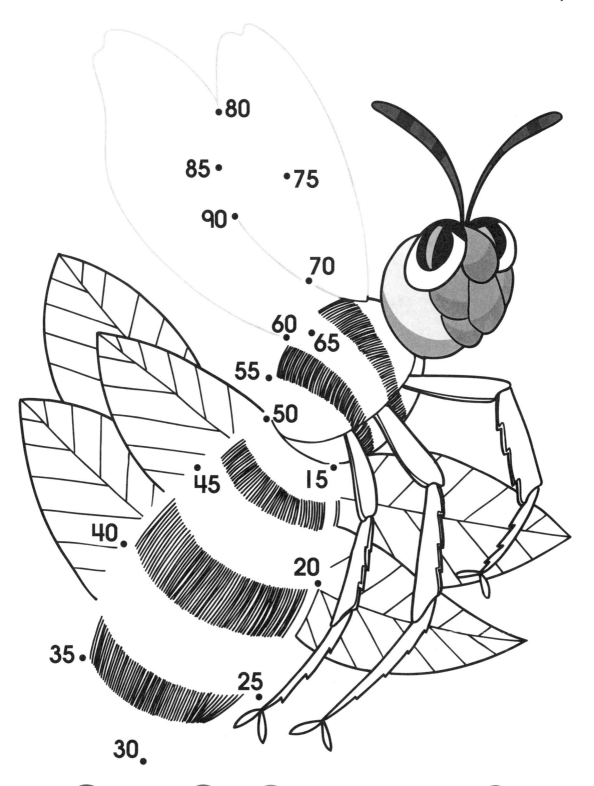

School Spirit

Directions: Count the items. Write the number words in the puzzle. Use the word box to help you.

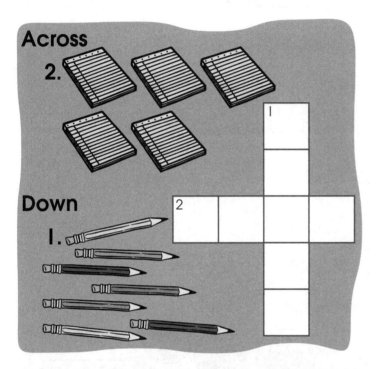

Across

2.

Down

1.

> seven   eight   one
>
> two   four   five

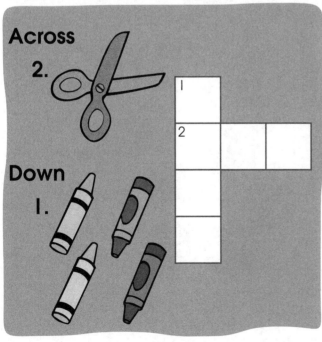

Across

2.

Down

1.

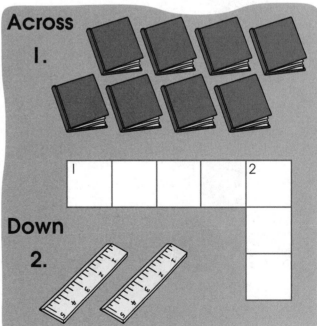

Across

1.

Down

2.

Money: Penny, Nickel

Penny 1¢   Nickel 5¢

Directions: Count the coins and write the amount.

Example:

_____ ¢

5¢   1¢   1¢   1¢

_____ ¢

_____ ¢

_____ ¢

_____ ¢

Money: Penny, Nickel, Dime

Penny 1¢   Nickel 5¢   Dime 10¢

Directions: Count the coins and write the amount.

Example:

 ___16___ ¢

 _____ ¢    _____ ¢

 _____ ¢    _____ ¢

Money: Penny, Nickel, Dime

Directions: Draw a line from the toy to the amount of money it costs.

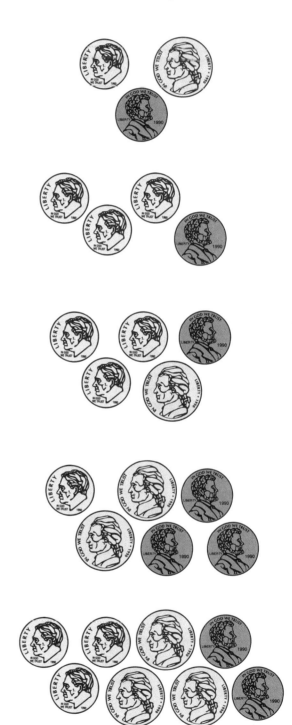

Money: Penny, Nickel, Dime

Directions: Draw a line to match the amounts of money.

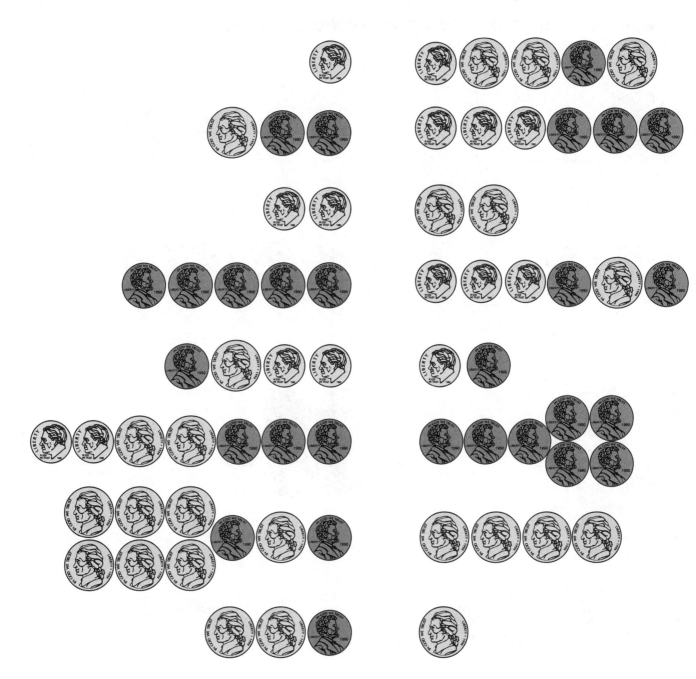

Money: Quarter

A quarter is worth 25¢.

Directions: Count the coins, and write the amounts.

 _____ ¢

 _____ ¢

 _____ ¢

 _____ ¢

 _____ ¢

 _____ ¢

 _____ ¢

 _____ ¢

Money: Decimals

A **decimal** is a number with one or more places to the right of a decimal point, such as 6.5 or 2.25. Money amounts are written with two places to the right of the decimal point.

25¢   10¢   5¢   1¢
$.25 $.10 $.05 $.01

Directions: Count the coins, and circle the amount shown.

Example:

 23¢ $.07

$.50   51¢   61¢

$.28   36¢   42¢

37¢   43¢ $.47

Money: Decimals

Directions: Draw a line from the coins to the correct amount in each column.

3¢ $.55

55¢ $.41

31¢ $.37

37¢ $.31

41¢ $.03

Money: Dollar

One dollar equals 100 cents. It is written $1.00.

Directions: Count the money, and write the amounts.

 $ ____ . ____

 $ ____ . ____

 $ ____ . ____

 $ ____ . ____

  $ ____ . ____

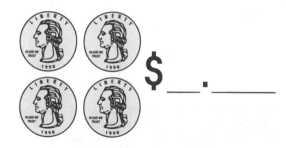 $ ____ . ____

  $ ____ . ____

 $ ____ . ____

Adding Money

Directions: Write the amount of money using decimals. Then, add to find the total amount.

Example:

$$
\begin{array}{r}
\$1.00 \\
.05 \\
+ \ \ .02 \\
\hline
\$1.07
\end{array}
$$

$$
\begin{array}{r}
\$\_\_.\_\_ \\
\$\_\_.\_\_ \\
\$\_\_.\_\_ \\
+\$\_\_.\_\_ \\
\hline
\_\_.\_\_
\end{array}
$$

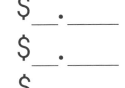

$$
\begin{array}{r}
\$\_\_.\_\_ \\
\$\_\_.\_\_ \\
\$\_\_.\_\_ \\
+\$\_\_.\_\_ \\
\hline
\_\_.\_\_
\end{array}
$$

$$
\begin{array}{r}
\$\_\_.\_\_ \\
\$\_\_.\_\_ \\
+\$\_\_.\_\_ \\
\hline
\_\_.\_\_
\end{array}
$$

$$
\begin{array}{r}
\$\_\_.\_\_ \\
\$\_\_.\_\_ \\
\$\_\_.\_\_ \\
+\$\_\_.\_\_ \\
\hline
\_\_.\_\_
\end{array}
$$

Money

Directions: Add the money, and write the total.

 _____ ¢

 _____ ¢

 $ _____ . _____

 _____ ¢

  $ _____ . _____

What Shark Is This?

Directions: Connect the dots from **24** to **72**. Then, color to finish the picture.

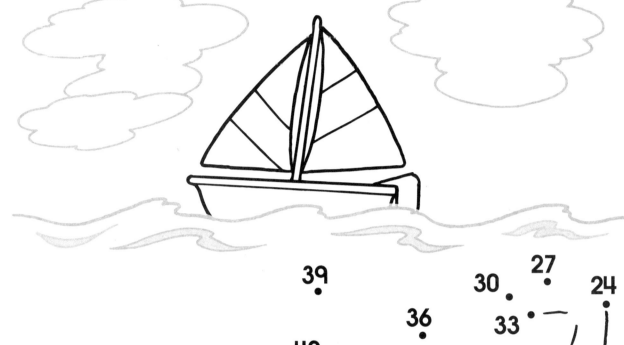

39

27

30   24

36   33

42   72

48   51

45   69

54   63

60

66

57

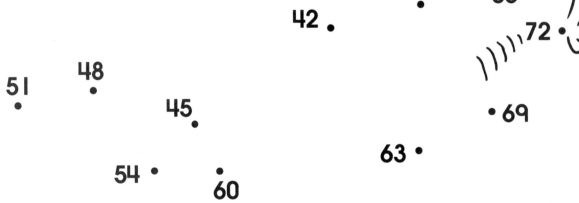

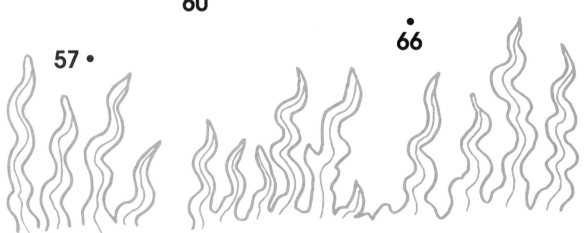

Helen Housefly

Directions: Connect the dots from **0** to **100**. Then, color to finish the picture.

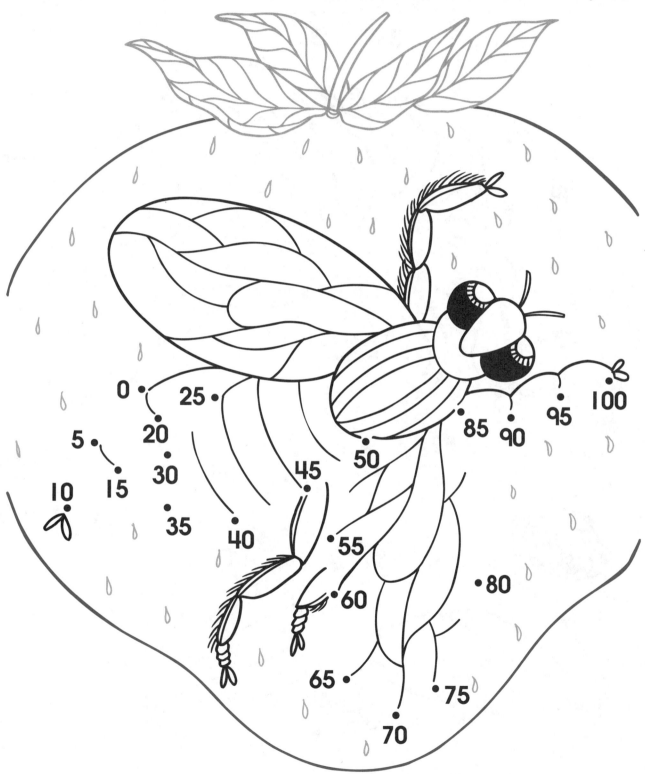

Name _____

A Tiger Shell

Directions: Connect the dots from **26** to **60**. Then, color to finish the picture.

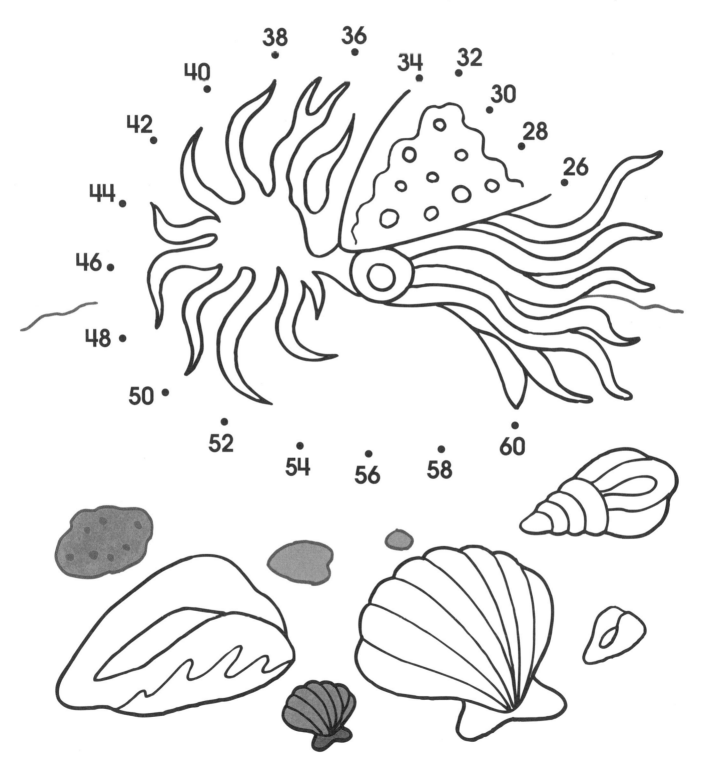

Name _____

Jack and the Beanstalk

Directions: Connect the dots from **5** to **60**. Then, color to finish the picture.

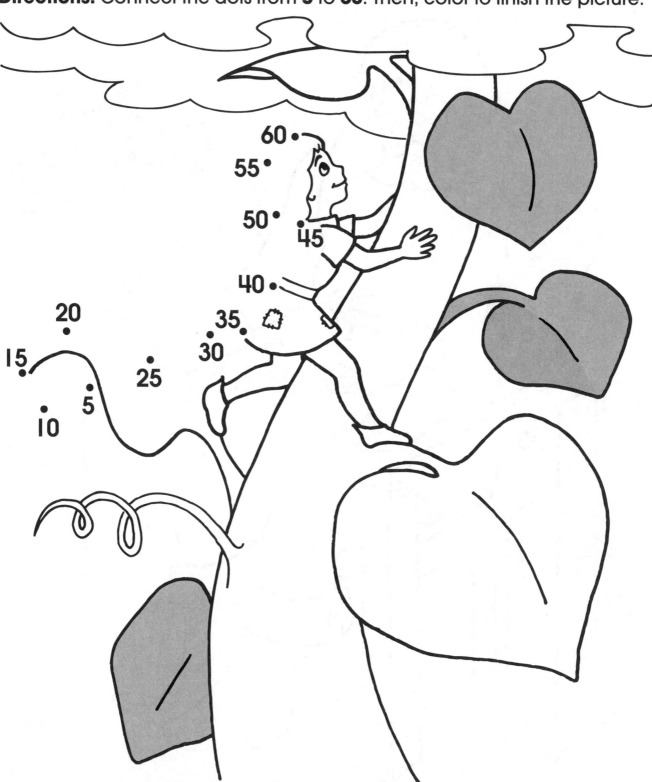

Name _____

The Giant

Directions: Connect the dots from **10** to **65**. Then, color to finish the picture.

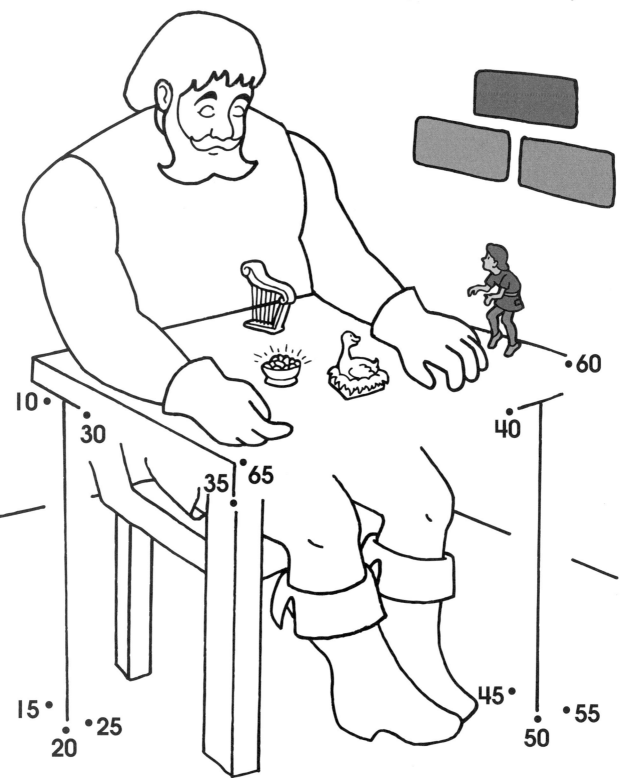

Cloud Watch

Directions: Find the numbers **1** to **10**. Color them. Then, color the rest of the picture.

Rapunzel

Directions: Connect the dots from **5** to **70**. Then, color to finish the picture.

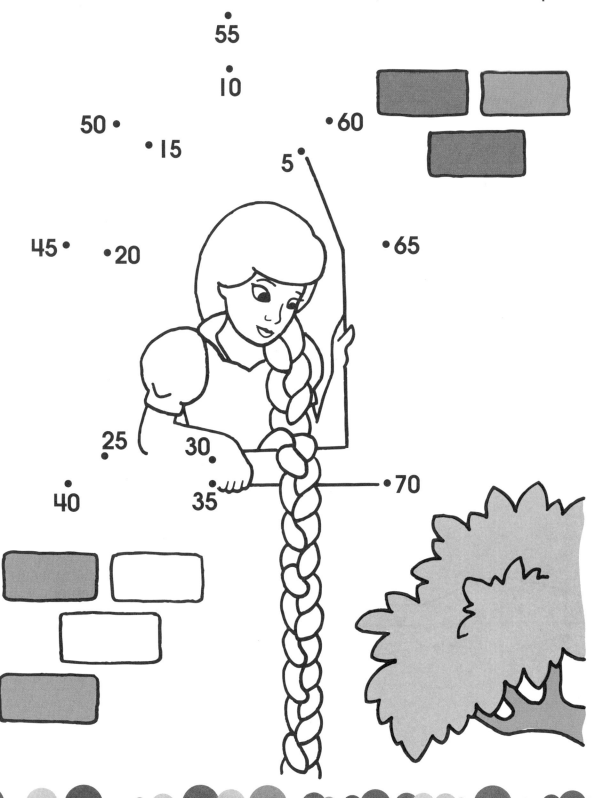

Name _____

Problem Solving

Directions: Tell whether you should add or subtract. **In all** is a clue to add. **Left** is a clue to subtract. Draw pictures to help you.

Example:

Jane's dog has 5 bones. He ate 3 bones. How many bones are left?

subtract

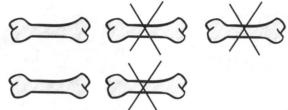

$$\begin{array}{r} 5 \\ \boxed{-}\ 3 \\ \hline 2 \end{array}$$

_____ bones

Lucky the cat had 5 mice. She got 4 more for her birthday. How many mice did she have in all?

_____

☐

_____ mice

Sam bought 6 fish. She gave 2 fish to a friend. How many fish does she have left?

_____

☐

_____ fish

Problem Solving: Addition, Subtraction, Multiplication

Directions: Tell if you add, subtract, or multiply. Then, write the answer

Example:
There were 12 frogs sitting on a log by a pond, but 3 frogs hopped away. How many frogs are left?

___subtract___   __9__ frogs

There are 9 flowers growing by the pond.
Each flower has 2 leaves.
How many leaves are there?

_____ _____ leaves

A tree had 7 squirrels playing in it.
Then, 8 more came along.
How many squirrels are there in all?

_____ _____ squirrels

There were 27 birds living in the trees around the pond, but 9 flew away.
How many birds are left?

_____ _____ birds

Problem Solving: Fractions

A **fraction** is a number that names part of a whole, such as $\frac{1}{2}$ or $\frac{1}{3}$.

Directions: Read each problem. Use the pictures to help you solve the problem. Write the fraction that answers the question.

Simon and Jessie shared a pizza.
Together they ate $\frac{3}{4}$ of the pizza.
How much of the pizza is left? _____

Sylvia baked a cherry pie. She gave $\frac{1}{3}$
to her grandmother and $\frac{1}{3}$ to a friend.
How much of the pie did she keep? _____

Ahmad erased $\frac{1}{2}$ of the blackboard
before the bell rang for recess.
How much of the blackboard does
he have left to erase? _____

Directions: Read the problem. Draw your own picture to help you solve the problem. Write the fraction that answers the question.

Yoko mowed $\frac{1}{4}$ of the yard before lunch.
How much does she have left to mow? _____

Problem Solving: Time

Directions: Solve each problem.

Addy wakes up at 7:00. She has 30 minutes before her bus comes. What time does her bus come?

_____ : _____

Vera walks her dog for 15 minutes after supper. She finishes supper at 6:30. When does she get home from walking her dog?

_____ : _____

Diego practices the piano for 30 minutes when he gets home from school. He gets home at 3:30. When does he stop practicing?

_____ : _____

Tanya starts mowing the grass at 4:30. She finishes at 5:00. For how many minutes does she mow the lawn?

_____ minutes

Aiden does his homework for 45 minutes. He starts his work at 7:15. When does he stop working?

_____ : _____

Problem Solving: Money

Directions: Read each problem. Use the pictures to help you solve the problems.

Ben bought a ball. He had 11¢ left.
How much money did he have at the start?

_____ ¢

Tara has 75¢. She buys a car.
How much money does she have left?

_____ ¢

Leah wants to buy a doll and a ball. She has 80¢.
How much more money does she need?

_____ ¢

Jacob has 95¢. He buys the car and the ball.
How much more money does he need to
buy a doll for his sister?

_____ ¢

Pilar paid three quarters, one dime,
and three pennies for a hat.
How much did it cost?

_____ ¢

Ready to Land

Directions: Count from **1** to **20** to take the plane to the hangar.

4	2	1						
6	3	8	7	8	9	10	7	12
5	4	5	6	3	15	11	8	13
9	2	11	13	14	13	12	1	2
10	14	17	16	15	9	13	4	
3	16	5	17	18	19			
15	11	8	9	13	20			

Violet the Violin Beetle

Directions: Connect the dots from **10** to **75**. Then, color to finish the picture.

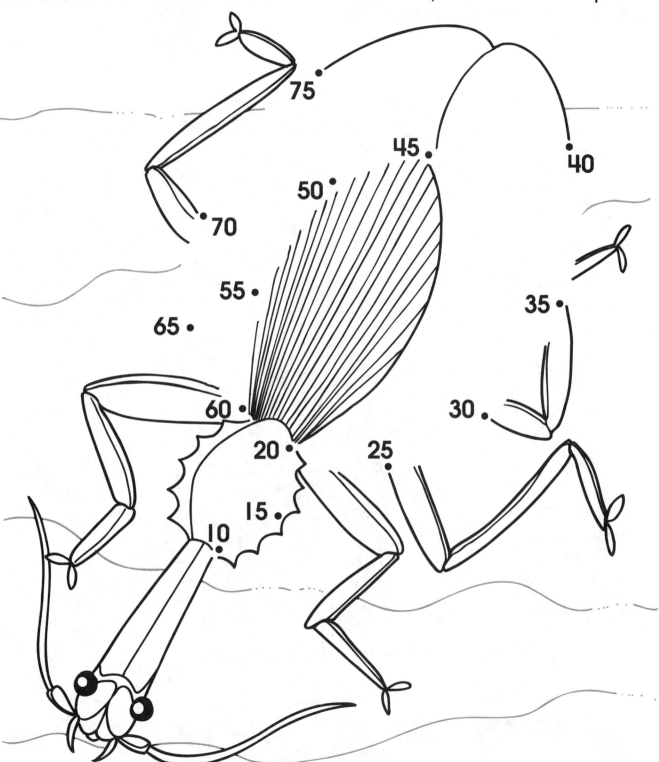

Apples, Apples, Everywhere ...

Directions: Find **16** apples below. Color them **red**. Then, color the rest of the picture.

Time to Paint

Directions: Color the spaces with odd numbers to make a path to the paint.

2	18	6	26	7	3
6	28	9	11	4	2
4	17	4	10	2	16
1	6	4	15	2	12

8	23	5	24	3	14	14	18	16	22
8	6	20	22	17	16	19	20	20	18
24	4	8	12	25	21	12	29	18	16
10	8	6	28	10	20	26	22	7	24
10	14	2	26	8	25	3	14	1	12

15	7	28	17	28	27	18
26	30	24	21	10	5	22

3	11	13

PAINT

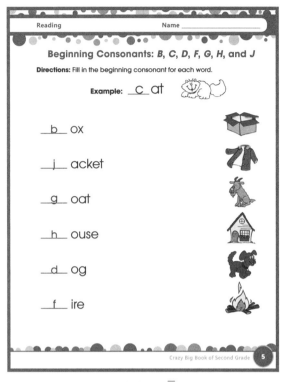

page 5

page 6

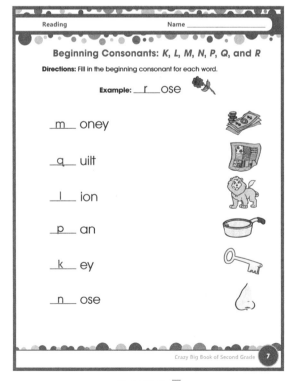

page 7

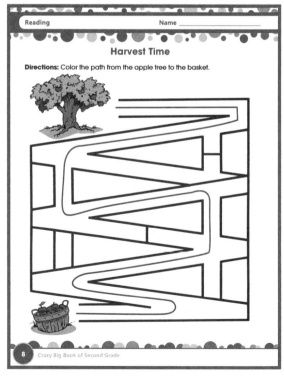

page 8

Answer Key

What Swims Fast?

Directions: Color the spaces with **A** blue. Color the spaces with **a** yellow.

page 9

Beginning Consonants: *S, T, V, W, X, Y,* and *Z*

Directions: Write the letter that makes the beginning sound for each picture.

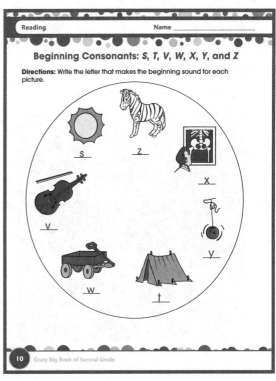

page 10

Beginning Consonants: *S, T, V, W, X, Y,* and *Z*

Directions: Fill in the beginning consonant for each word.

Example: __s__ ock

__z__ ipper

__t__ able

__x__ ray

__v__ ase

__y__ olk

__w__ and

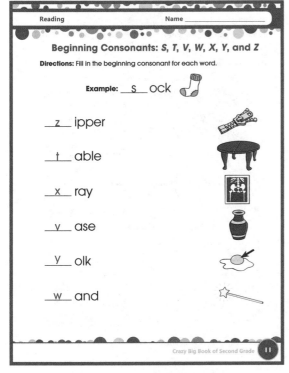

page 11

Winter

Directions: Read the clues and use the words in the word box to complete the puzzle.

Word box:
snowman
skis
ice
sleep
blizzard
indoors
shovel
bare
sled

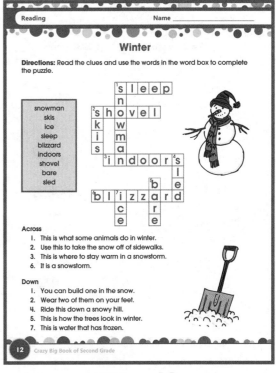

Crossword answers:
- ¹sleep
- ²shovel
- ³indoors
- ⁴sled
- ⁵bare
- ⁶blizzard
- snowman (down)
- skis (down)
- ice (down)

Across
1. This is what some animals do in winter.
2. Use this to take the snow off of sidewalks.
3. This is where to stay warm in a snowstorm.
6. It is a snowstorm.

Down
1. You can build one in the snow.
2. Wear two of them on your feet.
4. Ride this down a snowy hill.
5. This is how the trees look in winter.
7. This is water that has frozen.

page 12

Answer Key

What Waves in the Wind?

Directions: Color to find the hidden picture.

★★★ = purple   ★★
★★ = blue.

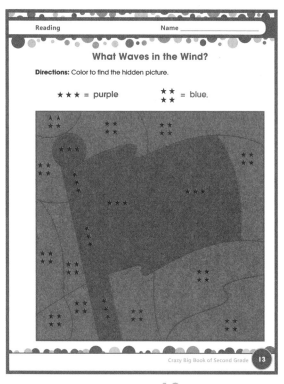

page 13

Ending Consonants: *B*, *D*, *F*, and *G*

Directions: Fill in the ending consonant for each word.

ma __d__

cu __b__

roo __f__

do __g__

be __d__

bi __b__

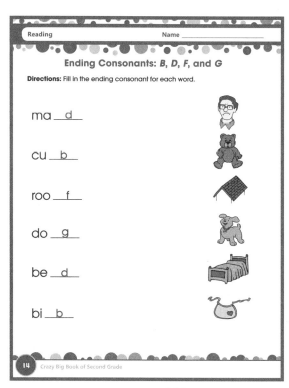

page 14

Ending Consonants: *K*, *L*, *M*, *N*, *P*, and *R*

Directions: Fill in the ending consonant for each word.

nai __l__

ca __n__

gu __m__

ca __r__

truc __k__

ca __p__

pai __l__

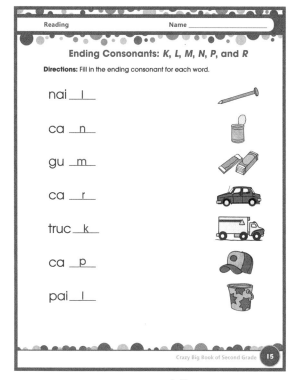

page 15

Home Sweet Home

Directions: Help the bee find its way home.

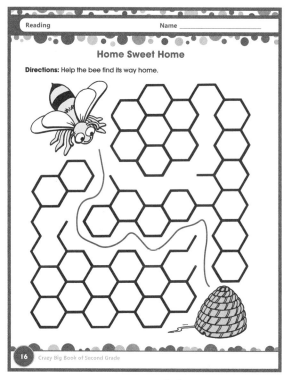

page 16

Answer Key

Reading   Name _____

Plump Pig

Directions: Color each **u** purple. Then, color the rest of the picture.

page 17

Reading   Name _____

Ending Consonants: S, T, and X

Directions: Fill in the ending consonant for each word.

ca __t__

bo __x__

bu __s__

fo __x__

boa __t__

ma __t__

page 18

Reading   Name _____

What Lives in the Forest?

Directions: Color the spaces with **C** green. Color the spaces with **D** yellow.

page 19

Reading   Name _____

Fill Them In

Directions: Write the vowel to complete each word.

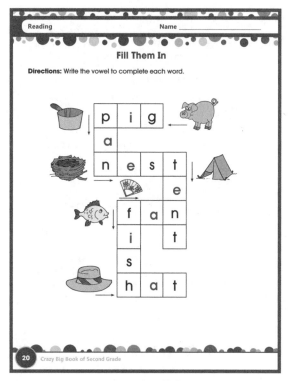

page 20

Answer Key

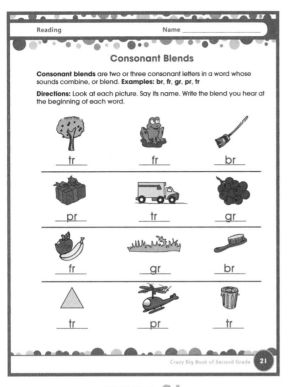

page 21

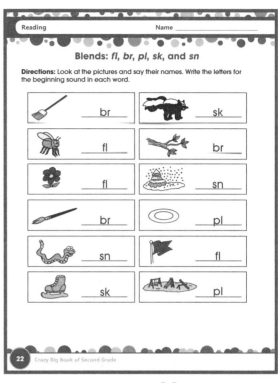

page 22

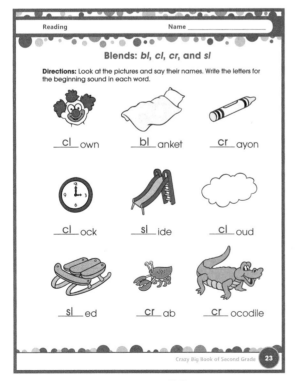

page 23

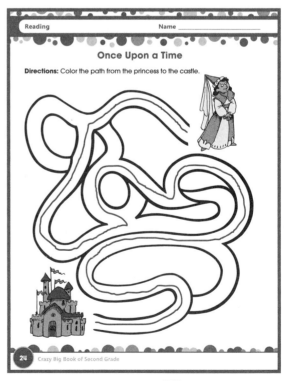

page 24

Answer Key

Up in the Sky

Directions: Write the words in the puzzle.

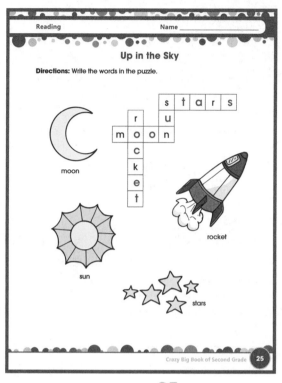

Underline

Directions: Underline all the objects that do not belong in the kitchen.

page 25

page 26

Silent Letters

Some words have letters you can't hear at all, such as the **gh** in **night**, the **w** in **wrong**, the **l** in **walk**, the **k** in **knee**, the **b** in **climb**, and the **t** in **listen**.

Directions: Look at the words in the word box. Write the word under its picture. Underline the silent letters.

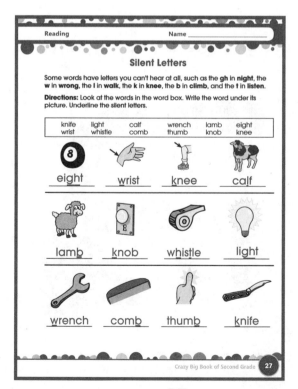

A Sea Giant

Directions: Color the spaces with **M** blue. Color the spaces with **m** black.

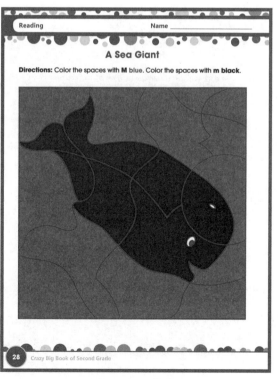

page 27

page 28

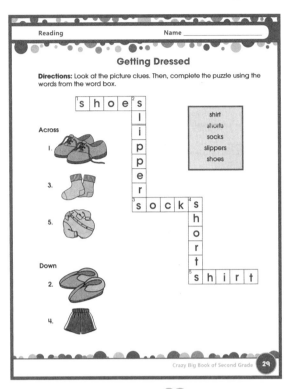

page 29

page 30

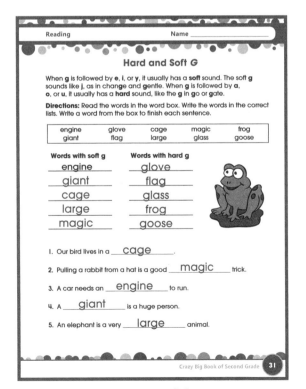

page 31

page 32

Answer Key

page 33

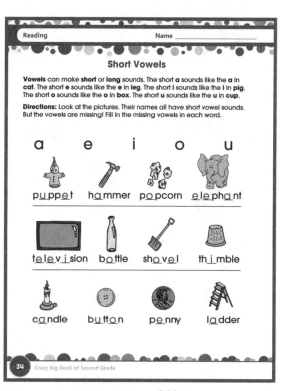

page 34

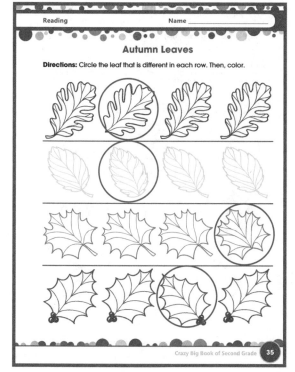

page 35

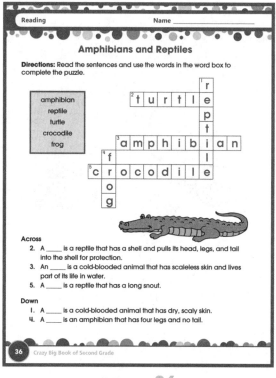

page 36

Answer Key

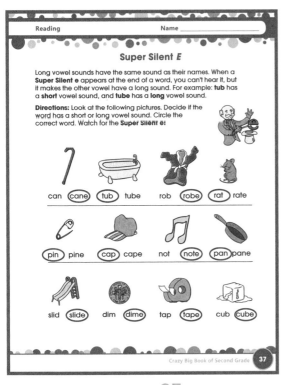

page 37

page 38

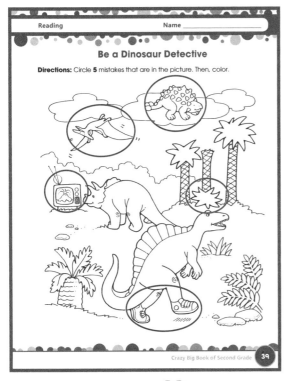

page 39

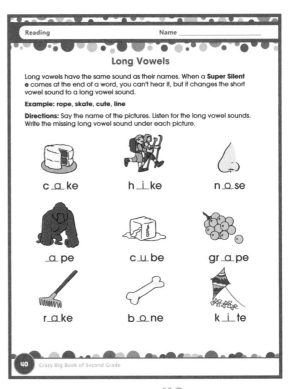

page 40

Answer Key

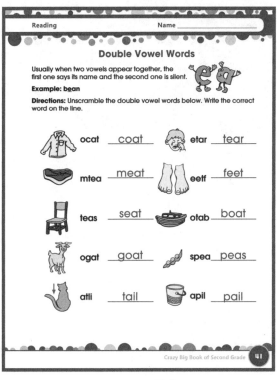

page 41

page 42

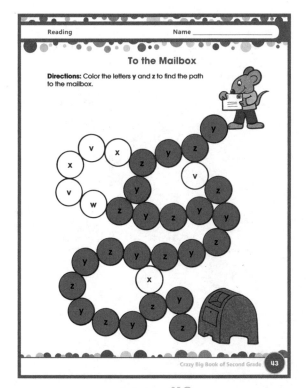

page 43

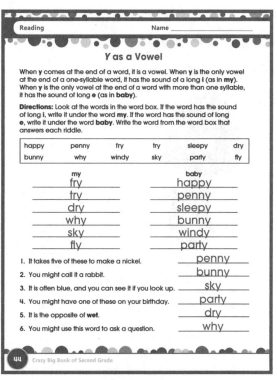

page 44

Answer Key

Y as a Vowel

Directions: Read the rhyming story. Choose words from the box to fill in the blanks.

Larry	Mary
money	funny
honey	bunny

_____Larry_____ and _____Mary_____ are friends.

Larry is selling _____honey_____. Mary needs _____money_____

to buy the honey. "I want to feed it to my _____bunny_____," said

Mary. Larry laughed and said, "That is _____funny_____. Everyone

knows that bunnies do not eat honey."

page 45

Y as a Vowel

Directions: Read the story. Choose words from the box to fill in the blanks.

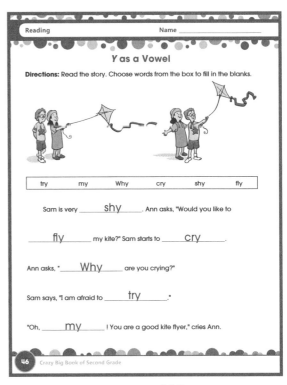

try	my	Why	cry	shy	fly

Sam is very _____shy_____. Ann asks, "Would you like to

_____fly_____ my kite?" Sam starts to _____cry_____.

Ann asks, "_____Why_____ are you crying?"

Sam says, "I am afraid to _____try_____."

"Oh, _____my_____! You are a good kite flyer," cries Ann.

page 46

Living Things

Directions: Read the clues and use the words in the word box to complete the puzzle.

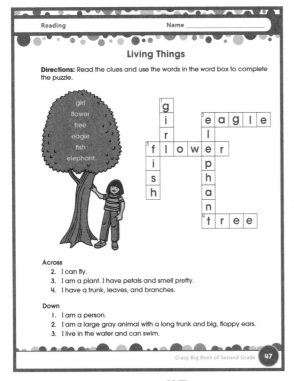

girl
flower
tree
eagle
fish
elephant

Across
2. I can fly.
3. I am a plant. I have petals and smell pretty.
4. I have a trunk, leaves, and branches.

Down
1. I am a person.
2. I am a large gray animal with a long trunk and big, floppy ears.
3. I live in the water and can swim.

page 47

Find the Mystery Picture

Directions: Read each sentence and cross out the picture. What picture is left?

1. It is not a tube.
2. It is not glue.
3. It is not an ice cube.
4. It is not a flute.
5. It is not June.
6. It is not blue.

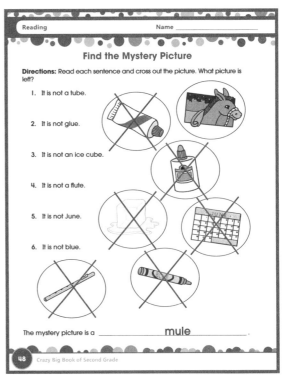

The mystery picture is a _____mule_____

page 48

Answer Key

page 49

Reading   Name _____

School Words

pencil	teacher	crayons
recess	lunchbox	play
fun	math	

Directions: Fill in the blanks with a word from the word box.

1. I need to sharpen my _____ **pencil** _____.
2. I like to _____ **play** _____ at recess.
3. School is _____ **fun** _____ !
4. My _____ **teacher** _____ helps me learn.
5. I need to color the picture with _____ **crayons** _____.
6. I play kickball at _____ **recess** _____.
7. My sandwich is in my _____ **lunchbox** _____.
8. In _____ **math** _____, I can add and subtract.

Crazy Big Book of Second Grade **49**

page 50

Reading   Name _____

A Fast Frog

Directions: Color the circles to help the frog find the fly.

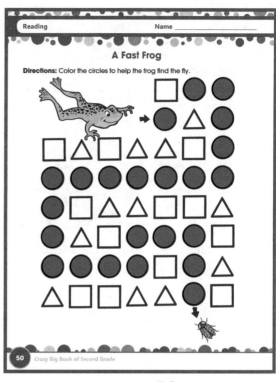

50 *Crazy Big Book of Second Grade*

page 51

Reading   Name _____

Days of the Week

Directions: Write the day of the week that answers each question.

Sunday	Monday	Tuesday
Wednesday	Thursday	Friday
	Saturday	

Days of the week

1. What is the first day of the week?

_____ **Sunday** _____

2. What is the last day of the week?

_____ **Saturday** _____

3. What day comes after Tuesday?

_____ **Wednesday** _____

4. What day comes between Wednesday and Friday?

_____ **Thursday** _____

5. What is the third day of the week?

_____ **Tuesday** _____

6. What day comes before Saturday?

_____ **Friday** _____

7. What day comes after Sunday?

_____ **Monday** _____

Crazy Big Book of Second Grade **51**

page 52

Reading   Name _____

Bugs, Bugs, Bugs

Directions: Read the clues and use the words in the word box to complete the puzzle.

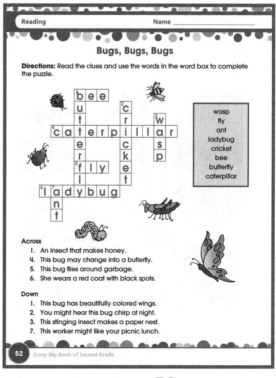

wasp
fly
ant
ladybug
cricket
bee
butterfly
caterpillar

Across
1. An insect that makes honey.
4. This bug may change into a butterfly.
5. This bug flies around garbage.
6. She wears a red coat with black spots.

Down
1. This bug has beautifully colored wings.
2. You might hear this bug chirp at night.
3. This stinging insect makes a paper nest.
7. This worker might like your picnic lunch.

52 *Crazy Big Book of Second Grade*

Answer Key

page 53

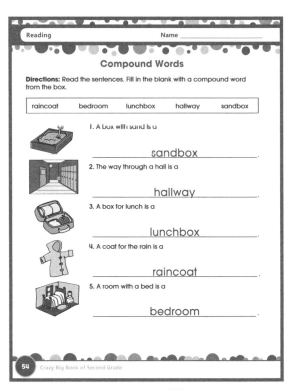

page 54

page 55

page 56

448 Crazy Big Book of Second Grade Activities

Answer Key

Contractions

Contractions are a short way to write two words.

Examples: it is = it's, is not = isn't, I have = I've

Directions: Draw a line from each word pair to its contraction.

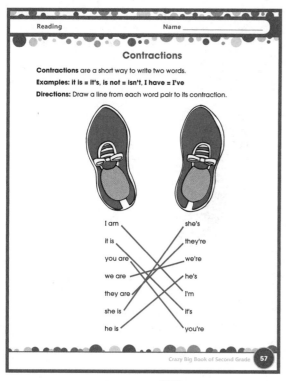

I am	she's
it is	they're
you are	we're
we are	he's
they are	I'm
she is	it's
he is	you're

page 57

Contractions

Directions: Circle the contraction that should replace the underlined words.

Example: were not = weren't

1. The boy was not sad.
   (wasn't)   weren't

2. We were not working.
   wasn't   (weren't)

3. Jen and Caleb have not eaten lunch yet.
   (haven't)   hasn't

4. The mouse has not been here.
   haven't   (hasn't)

page 58

Contractions

Directions: Match the words with their contractions.

would not	I've
was not	he'll
he will	wouldn't
could not	wasn't
I have	couldn't

Directions: Make the words at the end of each line into contractions to complete the sentences.

1. He __didn't__ know the answer.   **did not**
2. __It's__ a long way home.   **It is**
3. __Here's__ my house.   **Here is**
4. __We're__ not going to school today.   **We are**
5. __They'll__ take the bus home tomorrow.   **They will**

page 59

Desert Life

Directions: Read the sentences and use the words in the word box to complete the puzzle.

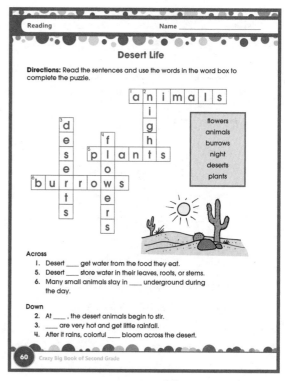

Word box:
flowers
animals
burrows
night
deserts
plants

Across
1. Desert ____ get water from the food they eat.
5. Desert ____ store water in their leaves, roots, or stems.
6. Many small animals stay in ____ underground during the day.

Down
2. At ____ , the desert animals begin to stir.
3. ____ are very hot and get little rainfall.
4. After it rains, colorful ____ bloom across the desert.

page 60

A Big Eater

Directions: Color the spaces with **B** purple. Color the spaces with **b** green.

Crazy Big Book of Second Grade **61**

page 61

Forest Life

Directions: Read the sentences and use the words in the word box to complete the puzzle.

sunlight	forest
insects	trees
squirrels	deer

Across
3. ____ climb trees and eat acorns.
5. Many ____ crawl along the forest floor.
6. Many ____ grow in the forest.

Down
1. A little bit of ____ shines through the trees.
2. It is cool and dark in the ____ .
4. A ____ nibbles on the sweet green plants.

62 Crazy Big Book of Second Grade

page 62

Syllables

Words are made up of parts called **syllables**. Each syllable has a vowel sound. One way to count syllables is to clap as you say the word.

Example: cat   1 clap   1 syllable
table   2 claps   2 syllables
butterfly   3 claps   3 syllables

Directions: "Clap out" the words below. Write how many syllables each word has.

movie __2__   dog __1__

piano __3__   basket __2__

tree __1__   swimmer __2__

bicycle __3__   rainbow __2__

sun __1__   paper __2__

cabinet __3__   picture __2__

football __2__   run __1__

television __4__   enter __2__

Crazy Big Book of Second Grade **63**

page 63

Syllables

Dividing a word into syllables can help you read a new word. You also might use syllables when you are writing if you run out of space on a line. Many words contain two consonants that are next to each other. A word can usually be divided between the consonants.

Directions: Divide each word into two syllables. The first one is done for you.

kitten	kit ten
lumber	lum ber
batter	bat ter
winter	win ter
funny	fun ny
harder	har der
dirty	dir ty
sister	sis ter
little	lit tle
dinner	din ner

64 Crazy Big Book of Second Grade

page 64

Answer Key

Syllables

One way to help you read a word you don't know is to divide it into parts called **syllables**. Every syllable has a vowel sound.

Directions: Say the words. Write the number of syllables. The first one is done for you.

straw • ber • ry

bird	1	rabbit	2
apple	2	elephant	3
balloon	2	family	3
basketball	3	fence	1
breakfast	2	ladder	2
block	1	open	2
candy	2	puddle	2
popcorn	2	Saturday	3
yellow	2	wind	1
understand	3	butterfly	3

page 65

Syllables

When a double consonant is used in the middle of a word, the word can usually be divided between the consonants.

Directions: Look at the words in the word box. Divide each word into two syllables. Leave space between each syllable. One is done for you.

butter	puppy	kitten	yellow
dinner	chatter	ladder	happy
pillow	letter	mitten	summer

but ter   din ner   pil low
pup py   chat ter   let ter
kit ten   lad der   mit ten
yel low   hap py   sum mer

Many words are divided between two consonants that are not alike.

Directions: Look at the words in the word box. Divide each word into two syllables. One is done for you.

window	doctor	number	carpet
mister	winter	pencil	candle
barber	sister	picture	under

win dow   mis ter   bar ber
doc tor   win ter   sis ter
num ber   pen cil   pic ture
car pet   can dle   un der

page 66

Syllables

Directions: Write **1** or **2** on the line to tell how many syllables are in each word. If the word has two syllables, draw a line between the syllables.

Example: sup|per

dog	1	tim|ber	2
bed|room	2	cat	1
slip|per	2	street	1
tree	1	chalk	1
bat|ter	2	blan|ket	2
chair	1	mar|ker	2
fish	1	brush	1
mas|ter	2	rab|bit	2

page 67

Touchdown

Directions: Color the path to the airport.

page 68

Answer Key

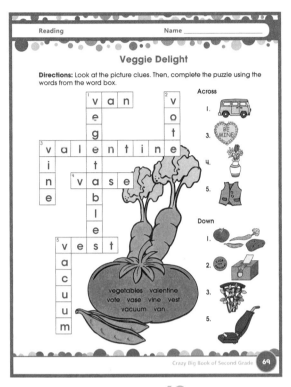

page 69

page 70

page 71

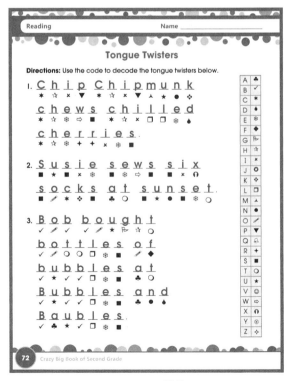

page 72

Answer Key

Haiku

A **haiku** is a form of Japanese poetry. Most haiku are about nature.

first line: 5 syllables
second line: 7 syllables
third line: 5 syllables

Example: The squirrel is brown.
He lives in a great big tree.
He eats nuts all day.

Directions: Write your own haiku. Draw a picture to go with it.

_____ Answers will vary. _____

_____

page 73

Shape Code

Directions: Write the missing letters **m, n, o, p,** or **s** for each word. Use the code to help you.

1. o cto p u s
2. p a p er
3. m o ther
4. m ule
5. p e n cil
6. m o u s e
7. m a p
8. s u n

m	n	o	p	s
□	△	○	▱	⬡

page 74

Suffixes

A **suffix** is a letter or group of letters that is added to the end of a word to change its meaning.

Directions: Add the suffixes to the root words to make new words. Use your new words to complete the sentences.

help + ful =   helpful
care + less =   careless
build + er =   builder
talk + ed =   talked
love + ly =   lovely
loud + er =   louder

1. My mother _talked_ to my teacher about my homework.
2. The radio was _louder_ than the television.
3. Madison is always _helpful_ to her mother.
4. A _builder_ put a new garage on our house.
5. The flowers are _lovely_.
6. It is _careless_ to cross the street without looking both ways.

page 75

Suffixes

An **ing** at the end of an action word shows that the action is happening now. An **ed** at the end shows that the action happened in the past.

Directions: Look at the words in the word box. Underline the root word in each one. Write a word to complete each sentence.

snowing	wished	played	looking	crying
talking	walked	eating	going	doing

1. We like to play. We _played_ yesterday.
2. Is that snow? Yes, it is _snowing_.
3. Do you want to go with me? No, I am _going_ with my friend.
4. The baby will cry if we leave. The baby is _crying_.
5. We will walk home from school. We _walked_ to school this morning.
6. Did you wish for a new bike? Yes, I _wished_ for one.
7. Who is doing the dishes? I am _doing_ them.
8. Did you talk to your friend? Yes, we are _talking_ now.
9. Will you look at my book? I am _looking_ at it now.
10. I like to eat pizza. We are _eating_ it for lunch.

page 76

Answer Key

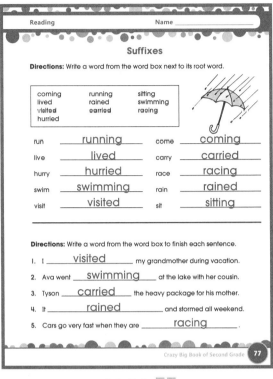

page 77

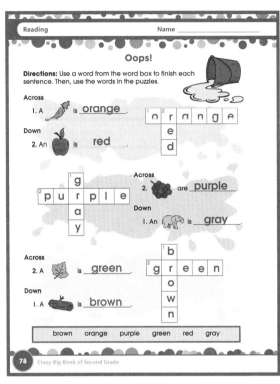

page 78

page 79

page 80

Answer Key

Prefixes: The Three Rs

A **prefix** is a letter or group of letters that is added to the beginning of a word to change its meaning. The prefix **re** means "again."

Directions: Read the story. Then, follow the instructions.

Kim wants to find ways she can help our planet. She studies the "three Rs"—reduce, reuse, and recycle. **Reduce** means "to make less." Both **reuse** and **recycle** mean "to use again."

Add **re** to the beginning of each word below. Use the new words to complete the sentences.

___re___ build   ___re___ fill
___re___ read   ___re___ tell
___re___ write   ___re___ run

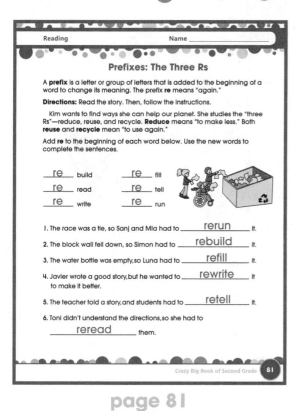

1. The race was a tie, so Sanj and Mia had to _____ **rerun** _____ it.
2. The block wall fell down, so Simon had to _____ **rebuild** _____ it.
3. The water bottle was empty, so Luna had to _____ **refill** _____ it.
4. Javier wrote a good story, but he wanted to _____ **rewrite** _____ it to make it better.
5. The teacher told a story, and students had to _____ **retell** _____ it.
6. Toni didn't understand the directions, so she had to _____ **reread** _____ them.

page 81

Prefixes

Directions: Change the meaning of the sentences by adding the prefixes to the **bold** words.

The boy was **lucky** because he guessed the answer **correctly**.
The boy was (un) ___unlucky___ because he guessed the answer (in) ___incorrectly___ .

When Jada **behaved**, she felt **happy**.
When Jada (mis) _____ **misbehaved** _____ .
she felt (un) _____ **unhappy** _____ .

Mike wore his jacket **buttoned** because the dance was **formal**.
Mike wore his jacket (un) **unbuttoned** because the dance was (in) _____ **informal** _____ .

Cameron **understood** because he was **familiar** with the book.
Cameron (mis) **misunderstood** because he was (un) ___unfamiliar___ with the book.

page 82

Prefixes

Directions: Read the story. Change the story by removing the prefix **re** from the **bold** words. Write the new words in the new story.

Repete is a **rewriter** who has to **redo** every story. He has to **rethink** up the ideas. He has to **rewrite** the sentences. He has to **redraw** the pictures. He even has to **retype** the pages. Who will **repay** **Repete** for all the work he **redoes**?

_____ **Pete** _____ is a _____ **writer** _____ who has to _____ **do** _____ every story. He has to _____ **think** _____ up the ideas. He has to _____ **write** _____ the sentences.
He has to _____ **draw** _____ the pictures.
He even has to _____ **type** _____ the pages.
Who will _____ **pay** _____ **Pete** _____ for all the work he _____ **does** _____ ?

page 83

Dinosaur Crossword

Directions: Look at the picture clues. Then, complete the puzzle using the words from the word box.

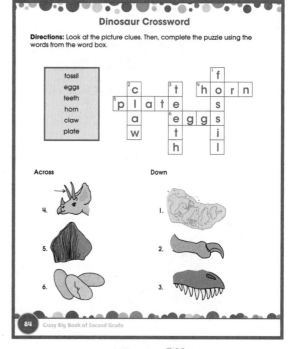

Word box:
fossil, eggs, teeth, horn, claw, plate

Crossword answers:
- horn (4 across)
- plate (5 across)
- eggs (6 across)
- fossil (1 down)
- teeth (2 down)
- claw (3 down)

Across
4.
5.
6.

Down
1.
2.
3.

page 84

Answer Key

Spouting About

Directions: To find the mystery letter, color the spaces with the following letters yellow.

e   m   c   q   y   r   o   j   a

e	b	s	d
q	k	t	f
c	a	m	i
o	g	y	n
r	h	j	p

Circle the mystery letter.   d   (h)   m

Crazy Big Book of Second Grade   85

page 85

Crack the Code

Directions: Write the missing letters for each word. Use the code to help you.

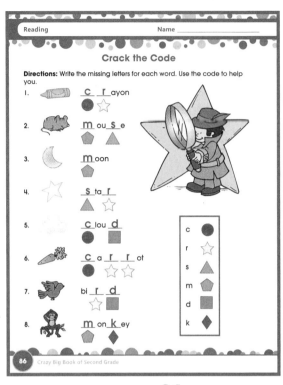

1. c r ayon
2. m ou s e
3. m oon
4. s ta r
5. c lou d
6. c a r r ot
7. bi r d
8. m on k ey

c	●
r	☆
s	△
m	⬠
d	▢
k	◆

86   Crazy Big Book of Second Grade

page 86

Parts of a Book

A book has many parts. The **title** is the name of the book. The **author** is the person who wrote the words. The **illustrator** is the person who drew the pictures. The **table of contents** is located at the beginning to list what is in the book. The **glossary** is a little dictionary in the back to help you with unfamiliar words. Books are often divided into smaller sections of information called **chapters**.

Directions: Look at one of your books. Write the parts you see below.

Answers will vary.

The title of my book is _____

The author is _____

The illustrator is _____

My book has a table of contents.   Yes   No

My book has a glossary.   Yes   No

My book is divided into chapters.   Yes   No

Crazy Big Book of Second Grade   87

page 87

Springtime

Directions: Color the butterfly's path to the flower.

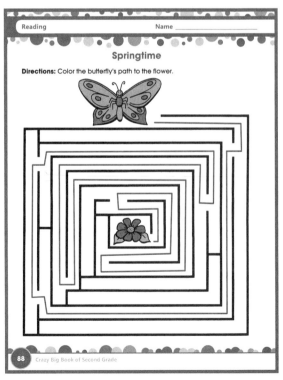

88   Crazy Big Book of Second Grade

page 88

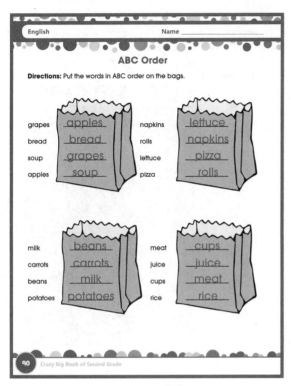

English   Name _____

ABC Order

Directions: Put the words in ABC order on the bags.

grapes — apples
bread — bread
soup — grapes
apples — soup

napkins — lettuce
rolls — napkins
lettuce — pizza
pizza — rolls

milk — beans
carrots — carrots
beans — milk
potatoes — potatoes

meat — cups
juice — juice
cups — meat
rice — rice

90   Crazy Big Book of Second Grade

page 90

English   Name _____

ABC Order

Directions: Write each group of words in alphabetical order. If two words start with the same letter, look at the second letter in each word.

Example: **lamb**   **Lamb** comes first because **a** comes before **i**
        light   in the alphabet.

tree — branch
branch — leaf
leaf — tree

dish — bone
dog — dish
bone — dog

rain — cloud
umbrella — rain
cloud — umbrella

mail — mail
stamp — slot
slot — stamp

Crazy Big Book of Second Grade   91

page 91

English   Name _____

Sequencing: ABC Order

Directions: Write 1, 2, 3, or 4 on the lines in each row to put the words in ABC order.

Example:
1. __1__ bell   __4__ well   __2__ smell   __3__ tell
2. __1__ bite   __2__ kite   __4__ write   __3__ might
3. __4__ tar   __2__ car   __3__ far   __1__ bar
4. __4__ sand   __3__ land   __1__ band   __2__ fanned
5. __3__ sweet   __2__ meat   __1__ eat   __4__ treat
6. __1__ hair   __2__ pear   __3__ tear   __4__ wear
7. __2__ lake   __1__ bake   __3__ rake   __4__ take
8. __3__ round   __4__ sound   __2__ pound   __1__ found

92   Crazy Big Book of Second Grade

page 92

English   Name _____

Megan's Birthday Present

Directions: Write a word from the word box to complete each sentence.

1. Megan got a new **b i k e**.
2. It was a birthday **g i f t**.
3. The color is **g r e e n**.
4. Megan wears a **h e l m e t** when she rides her bike.
5. She wears elbow **p a d s**.
6. She wears **k n e e** pads, too.

| green | bike | pads |
| helmet | knee | gift |

Crazy Big Book of Second Grade   93

page 93

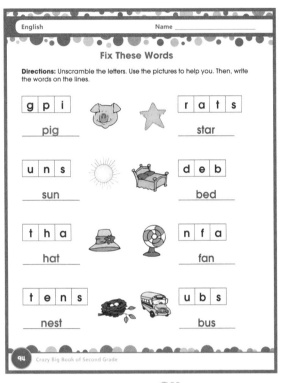

page 94

page 95

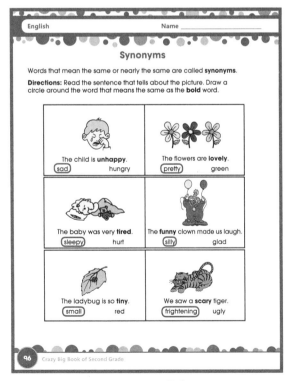

page 96

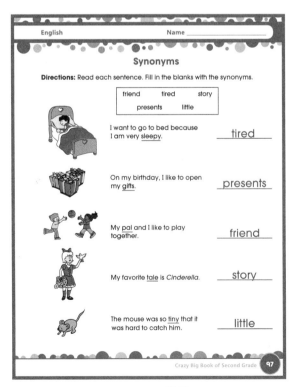

page 97

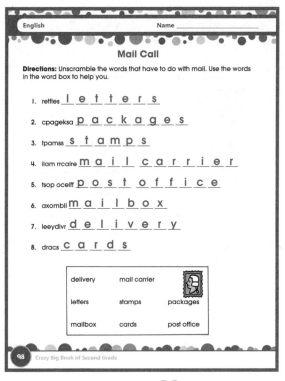

page 98

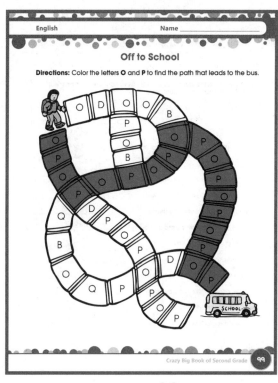

page 99

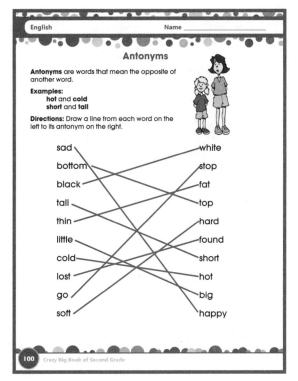

page 100

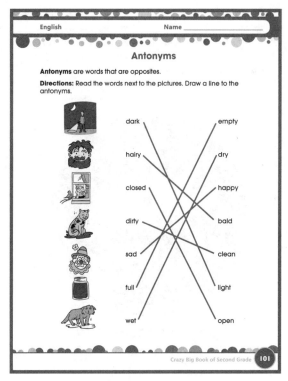

page 101

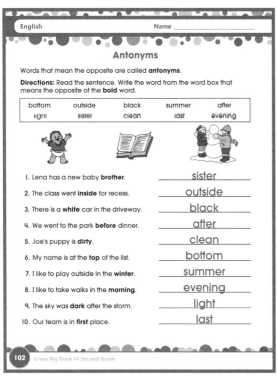

page 102

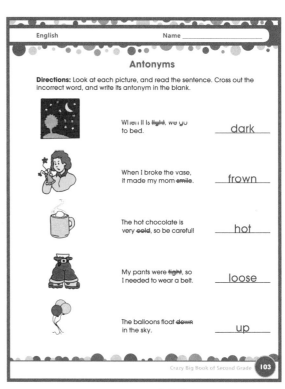

page 103

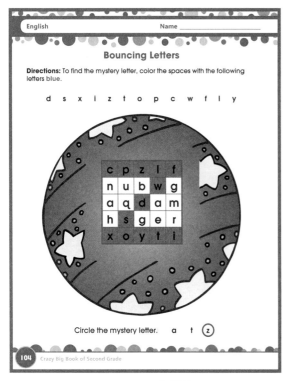

page 104

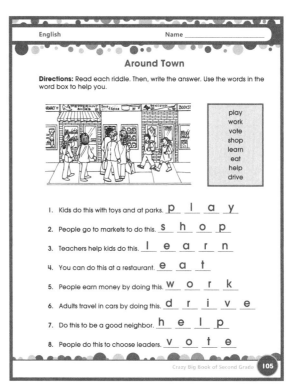

page 105

Answer Key

page 106

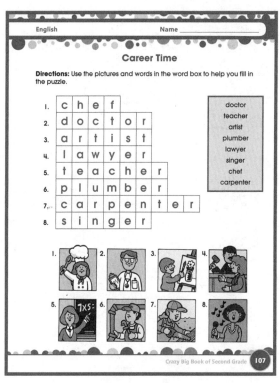

page 107

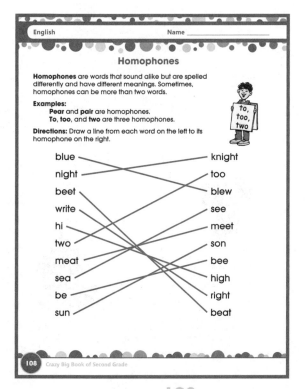

page 108

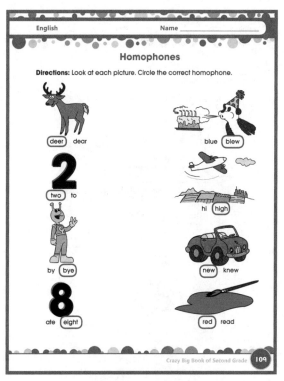

page 109

Answer Key

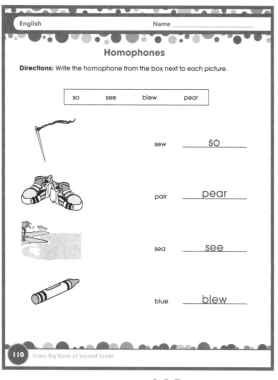

page 110

page 111

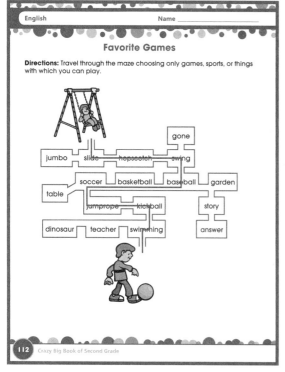

page 112

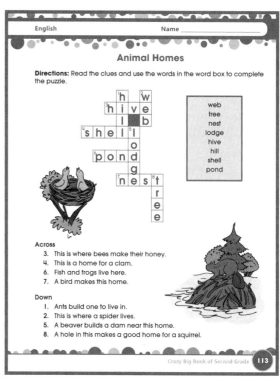

page 113

Answer Key

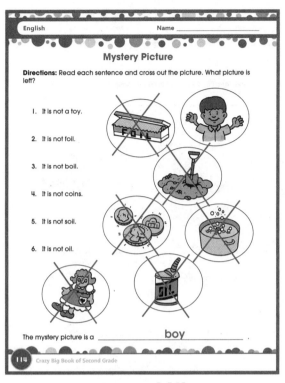

page 114

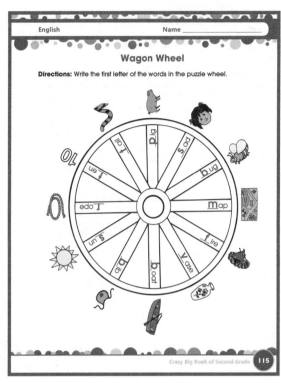

page 115

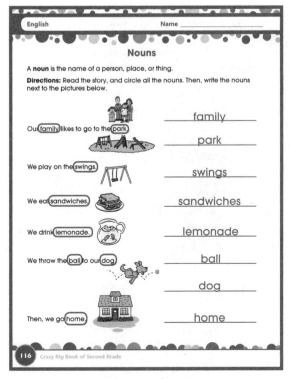

page 116

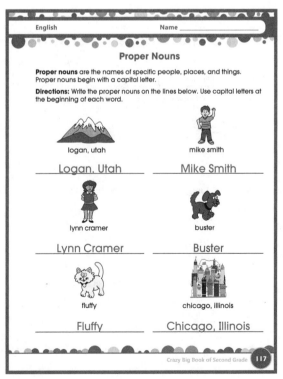

page 117

Answer Key

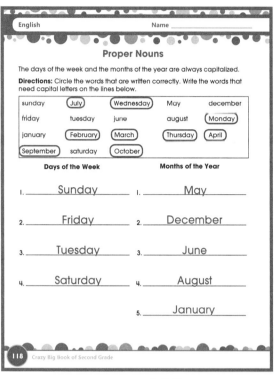

page 118

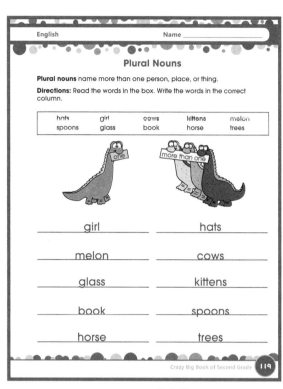

page 119

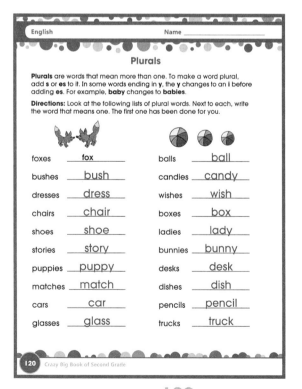

page 120

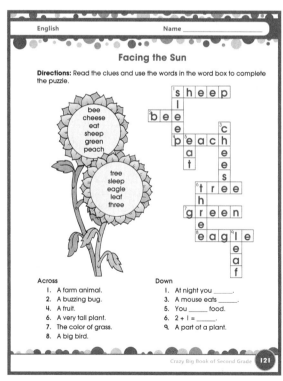

page 121

Answer Key

page 122

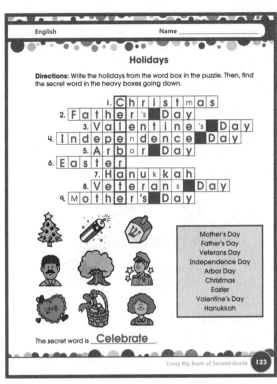

page 123

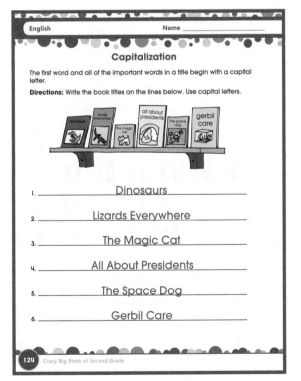

page 124

page 125

Answer Key

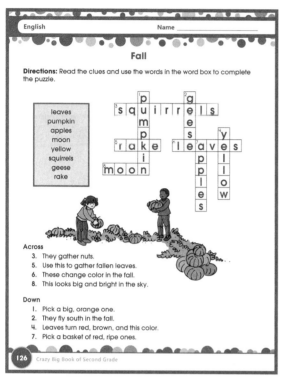

page 126

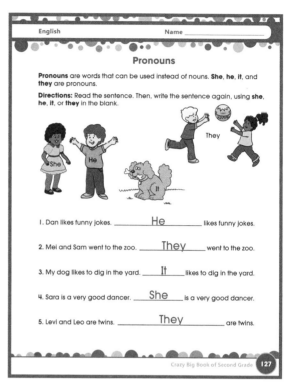

page 127

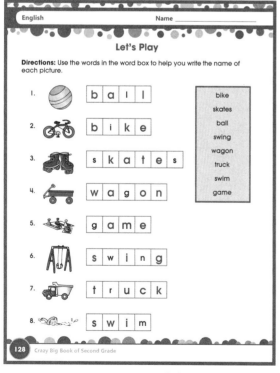

page 128

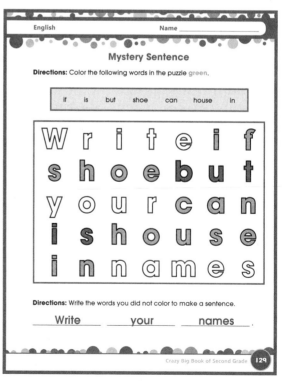

page 129

Answer Key

page 130

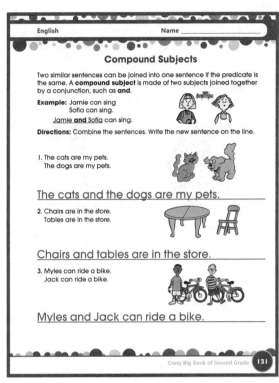

page 131

page 132

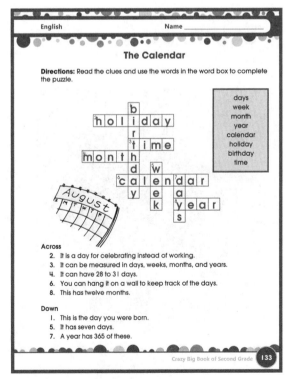

page 133

Answer Key

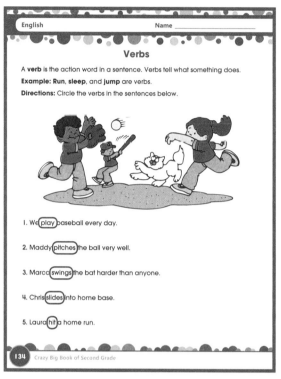

page 134

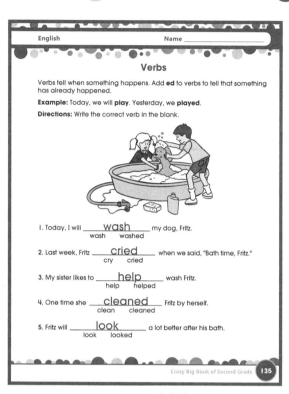

page 135

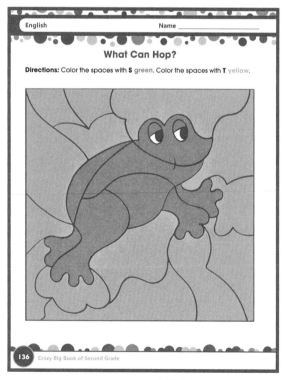

page 136

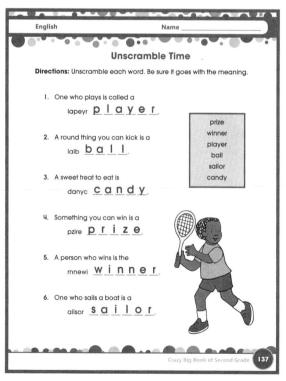

page 137

Answer Key

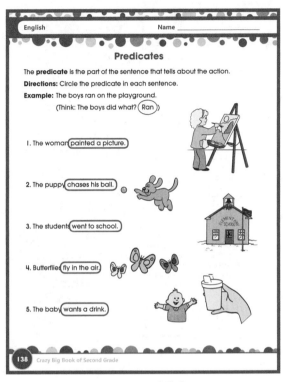

page 138

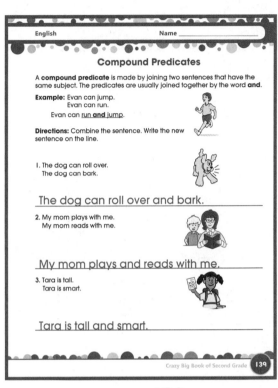

page 139

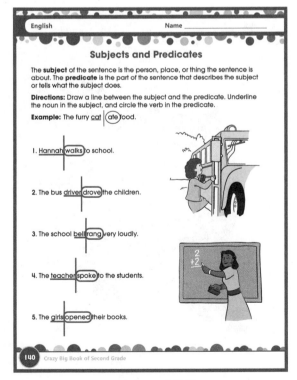

page 140

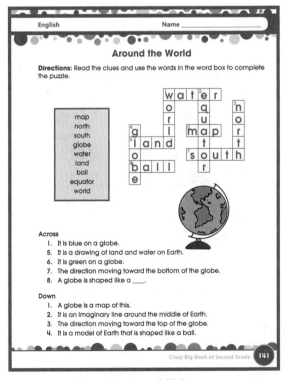

page 141

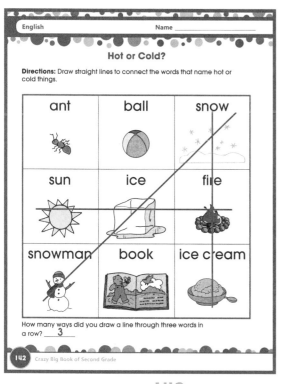

page 142

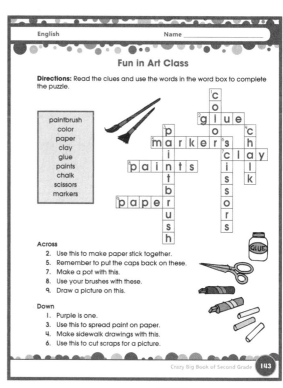

page 143

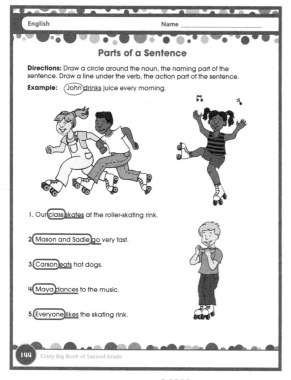

page 144

page 145

Answer Key

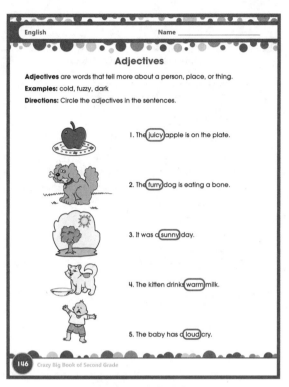

page 146

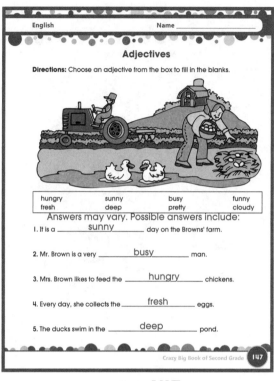

page 147

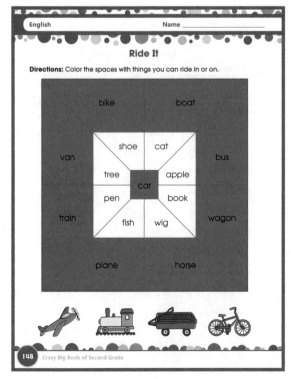

page 148

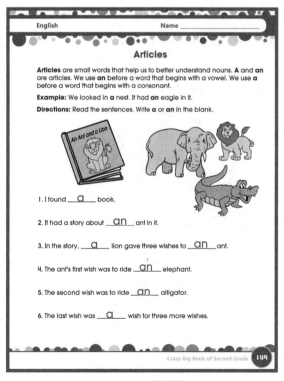

page 149

Answer Key

Mystery Picture

Directions: Read each sentence and cross out the picture. What picture is left?

1. It is not Earth.
2. It is not an astronaut.
3. It is not a shuttle.
4. It is not a helmet.
5. It is not a satellite.
6. It is not a rover.
7. It is not the moon.

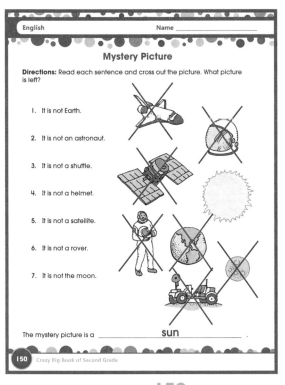

The mystery picture is a _____ sun

page 150

Sentences and Non-Sentences

A **sentence** tells a complete idea. It has a noun and a verb. It begins with a capital letter and has punctuation at the end.

Directions: Circle the group of words if it is a sentence.

1. (Grass is a green plant.)
2. Mowing the lawn.
3. (Grass grows in fields and lawns.)
4. Tickle the feet.
5. (Sheep, cows, and horses eat grass.)
6. We like to play in.
7. (My sister likes to mow the lawn.)
8. A picnic on the grass.
9. (My dog likes to roll in the grass.)
10. Plant flowers around.

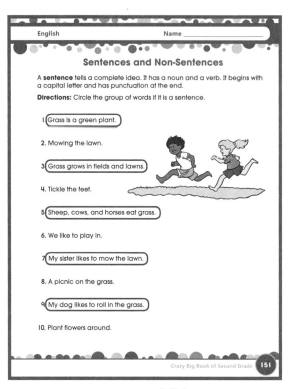

page 151

Statements

Statements are sentences that tell us something. They begin with a capital letter and end with a period.

Directions: Write the sentences on the lines below. Begin each sentence with a capital letter, and end it with a period.

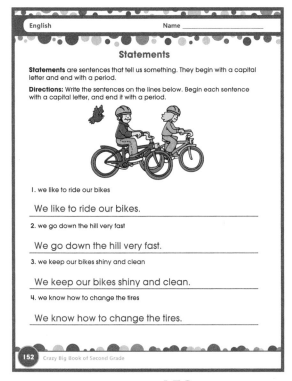

1. we like to ride our bikes

We like to ride our bikes.

2. we go down the hill very fast

We go down the hill very fast.

3. we keep our bikes shiny and clean

We keep our bikes shiny and clean.

4. we know how to change the tires

We know how to change the tires.

page 152

Surprising Sentences

Surprising sentences tell a strong feeling and end with an exclamation point. A surprising sentence may be only one or two words showing fear, surprise, or pain. **Example: Oh, no!**

Directions: Put a period at the end of the sentences that tell something. Put an exclamation point at the end of the sentences that tell a strong feeling. Put a question mark at the end of the sentences that ask a question.

1. The cheetah can run very fast .
2. Wow !
3. Look at that cheetah go !
4. Can you run fast ?
5. Oh, my !
6. You're faster than I am .
7. Let's run together .
8. We can run as fast as a cheetah .
9. What fun !
10. Do you think cheetahs get tired ?

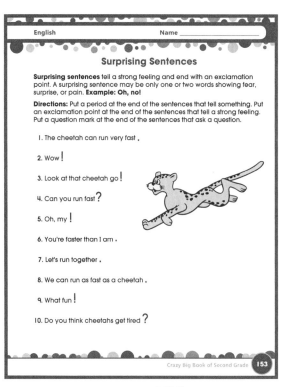

page 153

Answer Key

English   Name _____

Commands

Commands tell someone to do something. **Example: Be careful.**
It can also be written as "Be careful!" if it tells a strong feeling.

Directions: Put a period at the end of the command sentences. Use an exclamation point if the sentence tells a strong feeling. Write your own commands on the lines below.

1. Clean your room .

2. Now!

3. Be careful with your goldfish .

4. Watch out!

5. Be a little more careful!

Answers will vary.

_____

_____

154   Crazy Big Book of Second Grade

page 154

English   Name _____

Questions

Questions are sentences that ask something. They begin with a capital letter and end with a question mark.

Directions: Write the questions on the lines below. Begin each sentence with a capital letter, and end it with a question mark.

1. will you be my friend

Will you be my friend?

2. what is your name

What is your name?

3. are you eight years old

Are you eight years old?

4. do you like rainbows

Do you like rainbows?

Crazy Big Book of Second Grade   155

page 155

English   Name _____

Shining Bright

Directions: To find the mystery letter, color the spaces with the following letters red.

Q F V P G O M N U S

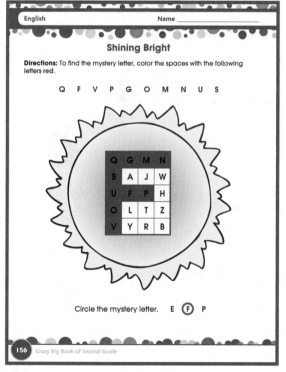

Circle the mystery letter.   E   **(F)**   P

156   Crazy Big Book of Second Grade

page 156

English   Name _____

Making Inferences: Writing Questions

Toban and Sean use many colors when they paint.

Directions: Write two questions for each answer.

Questions will vary.

Answer: It is red.

1. _____ ?

_____ ?

Answer: It is purple.

2. _____ ?

_____ ?

Answer: It is green.

3. _____ ?

_____ ?

Crazy Big Book of Second Grade   157

page 157

English · Name _____

Making Inferences: Point of View

Chelsea likes to pretend she is meeting famous people. She would like to ask them many questions.

Directions: Write a question you think Chelsea would ask if she met these people.

Questions will vary.

1. an actor in a popular new film _____
_____?

2. an Olympic gold medal winner _____
_____?

3. an alien from outer space _____
_____?

Directions: Now, write the answers these people might have given to Chelsea's questions.   **Answers will vary.**

4. an actor in a popular new film _____
_____

5. an Olympic gold medal winner _____
_____

6. an alien from outer space _____
_____

158 Crazy Big Book of Second Grade

page 158

English · Name _____

Making Inferences: Point of View

Ellen likes animals. Someday, she might want to be a veterinarian.

Directions: Write one question you think Ellen would ask each of these animals if she could speak their language.

Questions will vary.

1. a giraffe _____?
2. a mouse _____?
3. a shark _____?
4. a hippopotamus _____?
5. a penguin _____?
6. a gorilla _____?
7. an eagle _____?

Directions: Now, write the answers you think these animals might have given Ellen.   **Answers will vary.**

8. a giraffe _____
9. a mouse _____
10. a shark _____
11. a hippopotamus _____
12. a penguin _____
13. a gorilla _____
14. an eagle _____

Crazy Big Book of Second Grade 159

page 159

English · Name _____

Going Places

Directions: Read the clues and use the words in the word box to complete the puzzle.

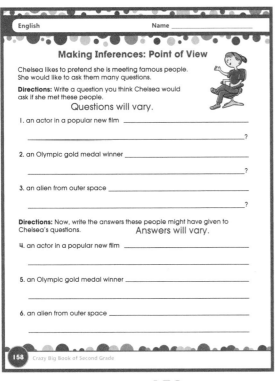

Word box:
airplane
train
bike
bus
car
truck
boat
horse
balloon

Across
1. It is an automobile.
4. Hot air makes it rise into the sky.
7. This can carry heavy loads on the road.
8. It has a saddle.

Down
2. This flies people from city to city.
3. This carries people and big loads on water.
4. It has two wheels and pedals.
5. This takes many people around the city.
6. It runs on tracks.

160 Crazy Big Book of Second Grade

page 160

English · Name _____

Ownership

Add **'s** to nouns (people, places, or things) to tell who or what owns something.

Directions: Read the sentences. Fill in the blanks to show ownership.

Example: The doll belongs to **Sara**.
It is **Sara's** doll.

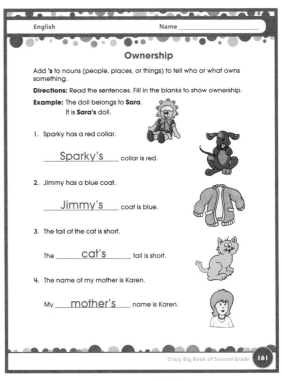

1. Sparky has a red collar.

_____Sparky's_____ collar is red.

2. Jimmy has a blue coat.

_____Jimmy's_____ coat is blue.

3. The tail of the cat is short.

The _____cat's_____ tail is short.

4. The name of my mother is Karen.

My _____mother's_____ name is Karen.

Crazy Big Book of Second Grade 161

page 161

Answer Key

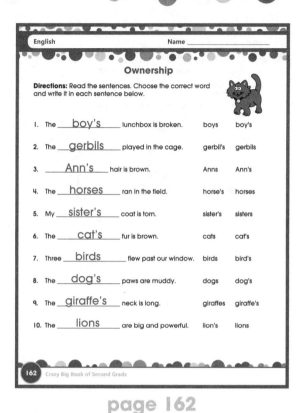

page 162

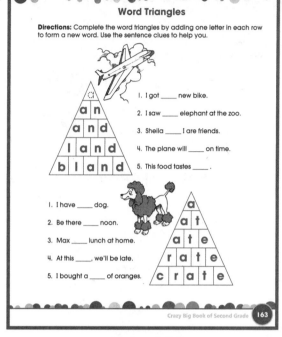

page 163

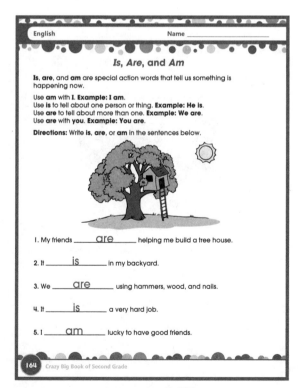

page 164

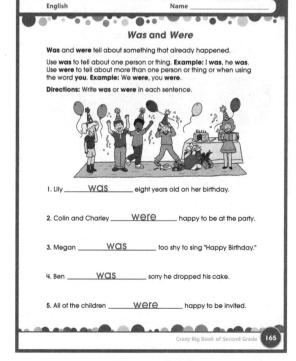

page 165

Answer Key

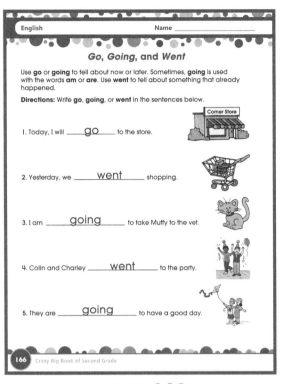

page 166

page 167

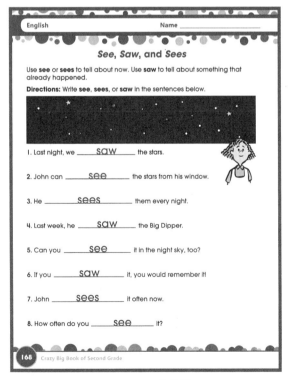

page 168

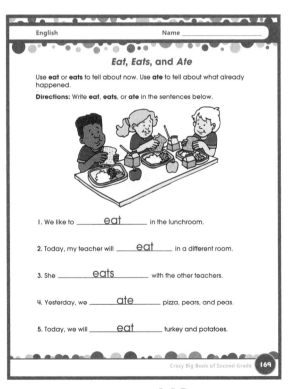

page 169

Answer Key

Leave, Leaves, and Left

Use **leave** and **leaves** to tell about now. Use **left** to tell about what already happened.

Directions: Write **leave**, **leaves**, or **left** in the sentences below.

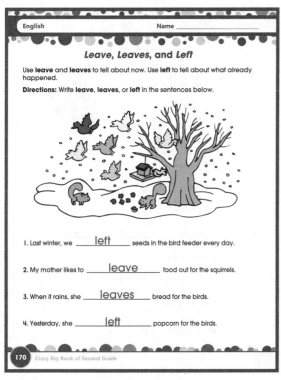

1. Last winter, we ___left___ seeds in the bird feeder every day.

2. My mother likes to ___leave___ food out for the squirrels.

3. When it rains, she ___leaves___ bread for the birds.

4. Yesterday, she ___left___ popcorn for the birds.

170 Crazy Big Book of Second Grade

page 170

Short A Words: Rhyming Words

Short a is the sound you hear in the word **math**.

Directions: Use the **short a** words in the box to write rhyming words.

lamp	fat	bat	van
path	can	cat	man
math	stamp	fan	sat

1. Write four words that rhyme with **mat**.

___fat___   ___cat___

___bat___   ___sat___

2. Write two words that rhyme with **bath**.

___path___   ___math___

3. Write two words that rhyme with **damp**.

___lamp___   ___stamp___

4. Write four words that rhyme with **pan**.

___can___   ___fan___

___van___   ___man___

172 Crazy Big Book of Second Grade

page 172

Short A Words: Sentences

Directions: Use a word from the box to complete each sentence.

fat	path	lamp	can
van	stamp	man	math
sat	cat	fan	bat

Example:

1. The ___lamp___ had a pink shade.

2. The bike ___path___ led us to the park.

3. I like to add in ___math___ class.

4. The cat is very ___fat___.

5. The ___can___ of beans was hard to open.

6. The envelope needed a ___stamp___.

7. He swung the ___bat___ and hit the ball.

8. The ___fan___ blew air around.

9. My mom drives a blue ___van___.

10. I ___sat___ in the backseat.

Crazy Big Book of Second Grade 173

page 173

Long A Words

Long a is a vowel sound that says its own name. **Long a** can be spelled **ai**, as in the word **mail**, **ay**, as in the word **say**, and **a** with a **silent e** at the end of a word, as in the word **same**.

Directions: Say each word, and listen for the **long a** sound. Then, write each word, and underline the letters that make the **long a** vowel sound.

mail	bake	train
game	day	sale
paint	play	name
made	gray	tray

1. ___mail___

2. ___game___

3. ___paint___

4. ___made___

5. ___bake___

6. ___day___

7. ___play___

8. ___gray___

9. ___train___

10. ___sale___

11. ___name___

12. ___tray___

174 Crazy Big Book of Second Grade

page 174

Answer Key

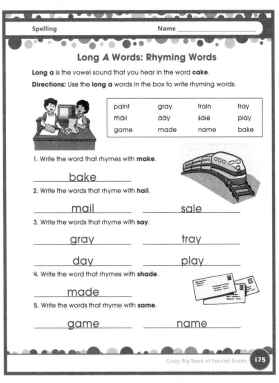

page 175

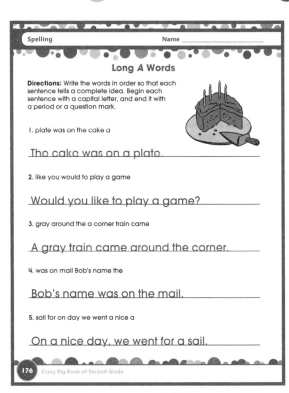

page 176

page 177

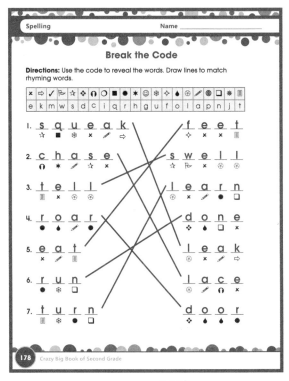

page 178

Answer Key

page 179

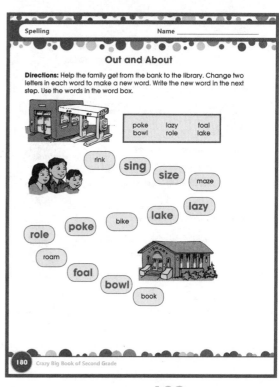

page 180

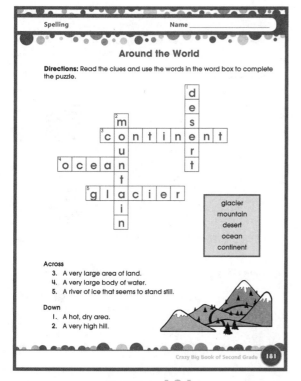

page 181

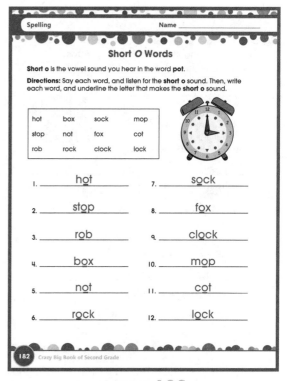

page 182

Answer Key

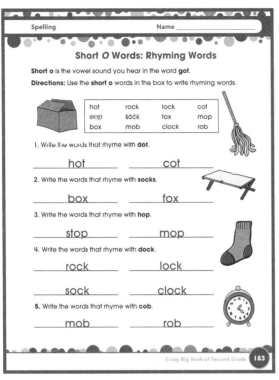

page 183

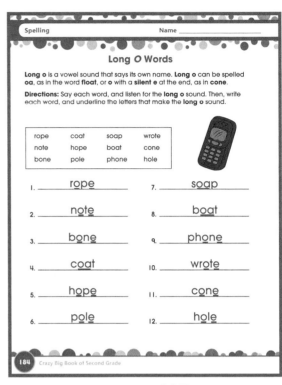

page 184

page 185

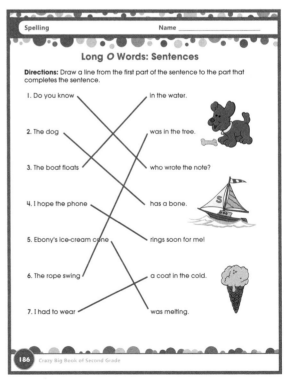

page 186

Answer Key

Giddyup!

Directions: Help the horse find the pasture.

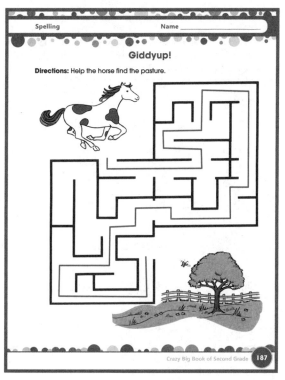

page 187

Weather Watch

Directions: Read the clues and use the words in the word box to complete the puzzle.

word box:
rain
thunder
tornado
wind
sunshine
cloud
storm
lightning
hurricane
fog

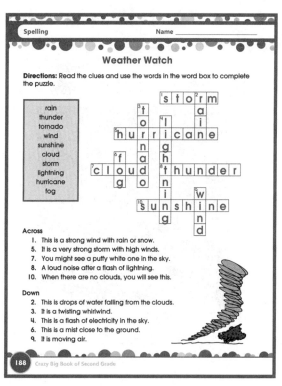

Across
1. This is a strong wind with rain or snow.
5. It is a very strong storm with high winds.
7. You might see a puffy white one in the sky.
8. A loud noise after a flash of lightning.
10. When there are no clouds, you will see this.

Down
2. This is drops of water falling from the clouds.
3. It is a twisting whirlwind.
4. This is a flash of electricity in the sky.
6. This is a mist close to the ground.
9. It is moving air.

page 188

Where's Teddy?

Directions: Help the girl find the teddy bear.

page 189

Fishes

Directions: Read the sentences and use the words in the word box to complete the puzzle.

word box:
colors
ocean
lakes
fins
mouths
gills

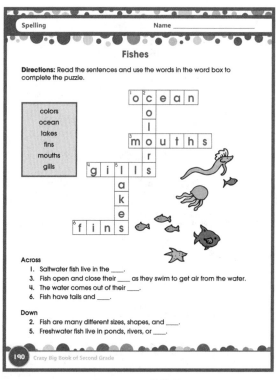

Across
1. Saltwater fish live in the ____.
3. Fish open and close their ____ as they swim to get air from the water.
4. The water comes out of their ____.
6. Fish have tails and ____.

Down
2. Fish are many different sizes, shapes, and ____.
5. Freshwater fish live in ponds, rivers, or ____.

page 190

Answer Key

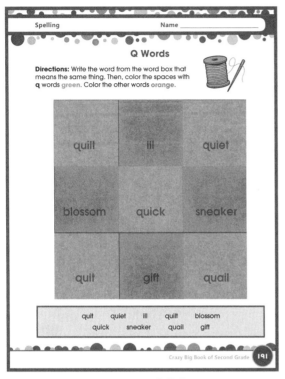

page 191

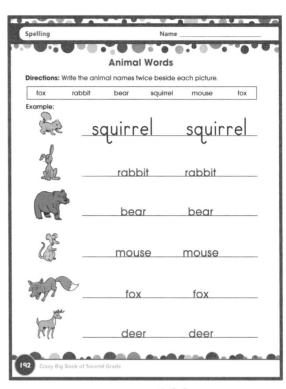

page 192

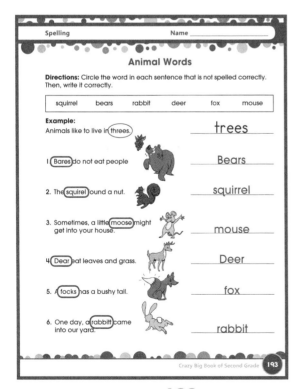

page 193

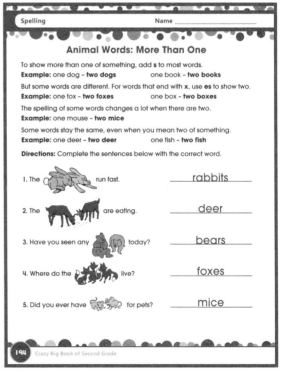

page 194

Answer Key

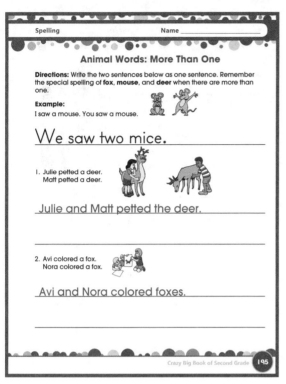

page 195

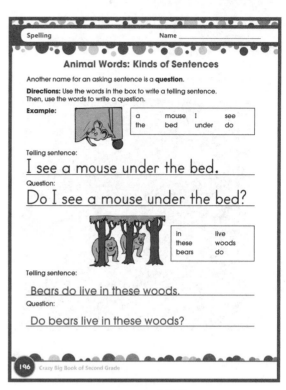

page 196

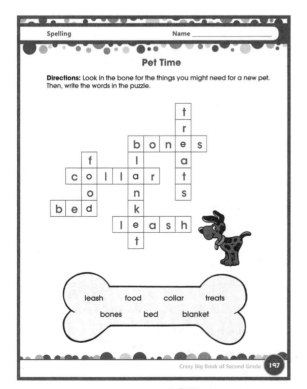

page 197

page 198

Answer Key

page 199

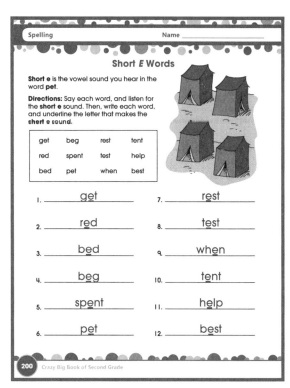

page 200

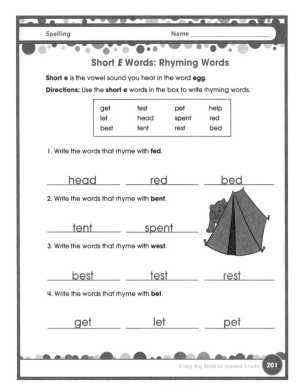

page 201

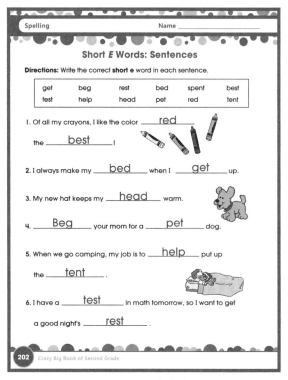

page 202

Answer Key

Long *E* Words

Long e is the vowel sound that says its own name. **Long e** can be spelled **ee**, as in the word **teeth**, **ea**, as in the word **meat**, or **e**, as in the word **me**.

Directions: Say each word, and listen for the **long e** sound. Then, write the words, and underline the letters that make the **long e** sound.

street	neat	treat	feet
sleep	keep	deal	meal
mean	clean	beast	feast

1. str<u>ee</u>t
2. sl<u>ee</u>p
3. m<u>ea</u>n
4. n<u>ea</u>t
5. k<u>ee</u>p
6. cl<u>ea</u>n
7. tr<u>ea</u>t
8. d<u>ea</u>l
9. b<u>ea</u>st
10. f<u>ee</u>t
11. m<u>ea</u>l
12. f<u>ea</u>st

page 203

Long *E* Words: Rhyming Words

Long e is the vowel sound you hear in the word **meet**.

Directions: Use the **long e** words in the box to write rhyming words.

street	feet	neat	treat
keep	deal	sleep	meal
mean	beast	clean	feast

1. Write the words that rhyme with **beat**.

street   neat

feet   treat

2. Write the words that rhyme with **deep**.

keep   sleep

3. Write the words that rhyme with **feel**.

deal   meal

4. Write the words that rhyme with **bean**.

mean   clean

5. Write the words that rhyme with **least**.

beast   feast

page 204

Long *E* Words: Sentences

Directions: Write a word from the box to complete each sentence.

street	feet	neat	treat
keep	deal	sleep	meal
mean	beast	clean	feast

1. I went to ____sleep____ late last night.

2. One of my favorite stories is "Beauty and the ____Beast____."

3. Look both ways when you cross the ____street____.

4. It would be ____mean____ to kick someone.

5. I wear socks and shoes on my ____feet____.

6. The most important ____meal____ of the day is breakfast.

page 205

Morse Code

Directions: Use the code box to decode the messages by substituting the correct letters for the dots and dashes. Then, try to write your own message in Morse code. Ask a friend to solve it.

1. --/---/•/••/•   --•/•--/--••/•   •--/•-/•••

   <u>Morse</u>   <u>code</u>   <u>was</u>

   -••/•/••-/•/•-••/---/•--•/•-•-••   -•••/•--•

   <u>developed</u>   <u>by</u>

   •••/•-/--/••-/•/•-••   --/---/•-•/•••/•

   <u>Samuel</u>   <u>Morse</u>.

2. ••/-   ••/•••   •-   •••/•/•-•/••/•/•••   ---/•-••

   <u>It</u> <u>is</u> <u>a</u> <u>series</u> <u>of</u>

   -••/---/-/•••   •-/-•/-••   -••/•-/•••/••••/•/•••

   <u>dots</u> <u>and</u> <u>dashes</u>

   ••-/•••/•/-••   -/---   •••/•/-•/-••

   <u>used</u> <u>to</u> <u>send</u>

   --/•/•••/•••/•-/--•/•/•••   ---/-•   -/••••/•

   <u>messages</u> <u>on</u> <u>the</u>

   -/•/•-••/•/--•/•-•/•-/•--•/••••

   <u>telegraph</u>

| A •- | B -••• | C -•-• | D -•• | E • | F ••-• | G --• | H •••• | I •• | J •--- | K -•- | L •-•• | M -- | N -• | O --- | P •--• | Q --•- | R •-• | S ••• | T - | U ••- | V •••- | W •-- | X -••- | Y -•-- | Z --•• |

page 206

Answer Key

Spelling   Name _____

Find It

Directions: Look at the two closets. Find and circle **5** objects in the top picture that are not in the bottom picture.

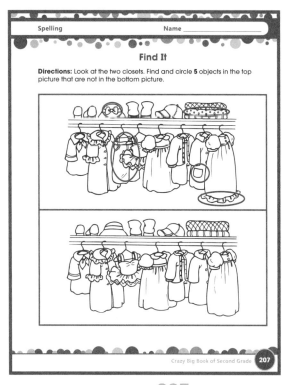

page 207

Spelling   Name _____

Parts of a Book

Directions: Read the clues and use the words in the word box to complete the puzzle.

word box: title, author, illustrator, publisher, date, pages, words, pictures, cover, jacket

Across

5. This is a person who draws the pictures.
7. This is the name of the book.
9. The pieces of paper in a book.
10. The writing in a book.

Down

1. The year the book was made.
2. The drawings or photos in a book.
3. The company that made the book.
4. The outside front and back of the book.
6. The person who wrote the book.
8. A paper cover on the outside of a book.

page 208

Spelling   Name _____

What Might You See?

Directions: When you ride on the highway, what do you see? Draw what you think you might see. Then, color.

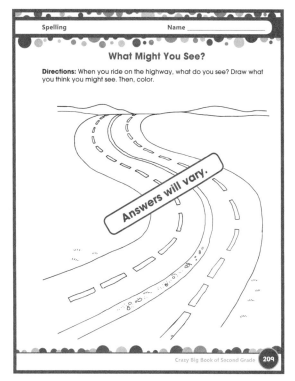

Answers will vary.

page 209

Spelling   Name _____

Camping Out

Directions: Color the letters **R** and **r** to find the path to the tent.

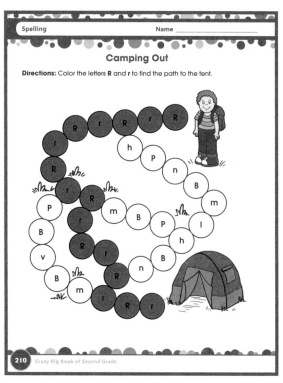

page 210

Answer Key

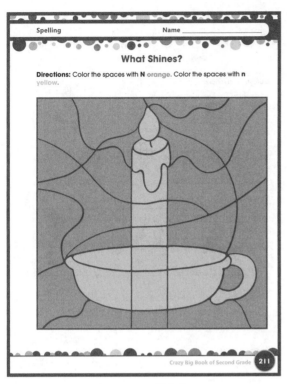

page 211

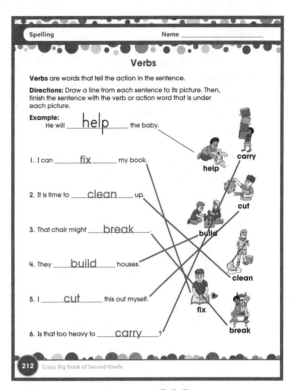

page 212

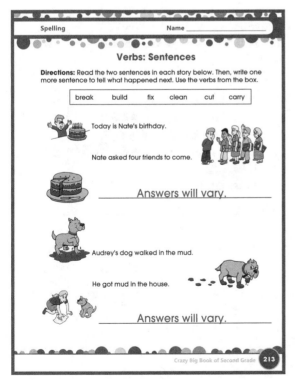

page 213

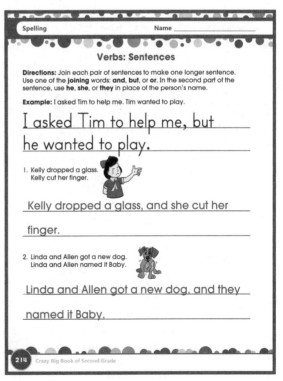

page 214

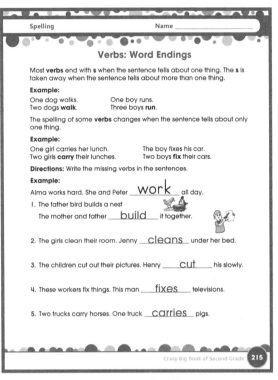

page 215

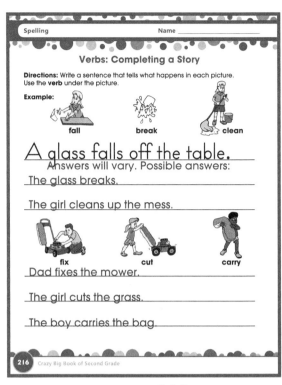

page 216

page 217

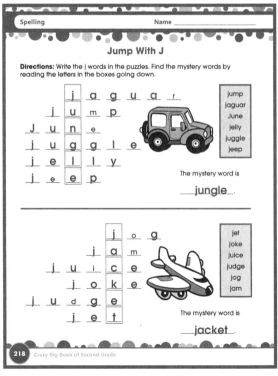

page 218

Answer Key

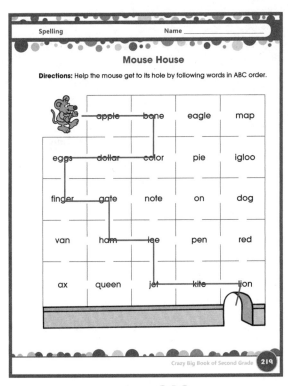

page 219

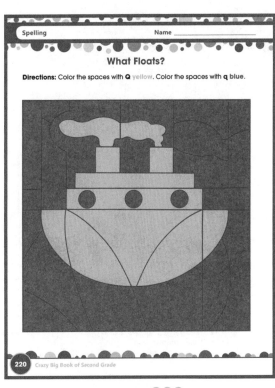

page 220

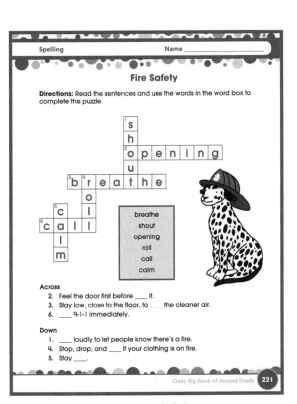

page 221

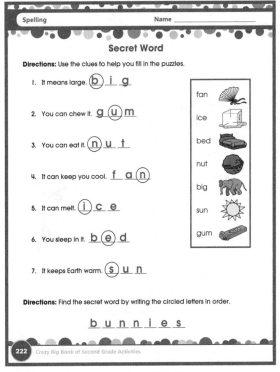

page 222

Answer Key

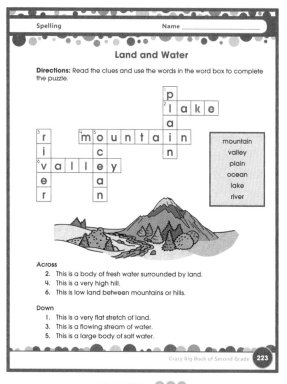

page 223

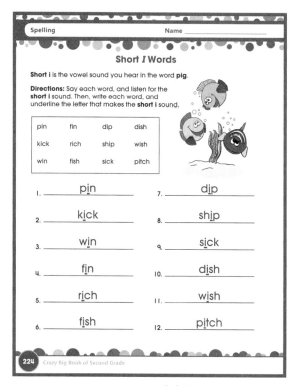

page 224

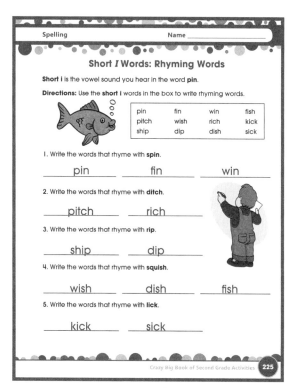

page 225

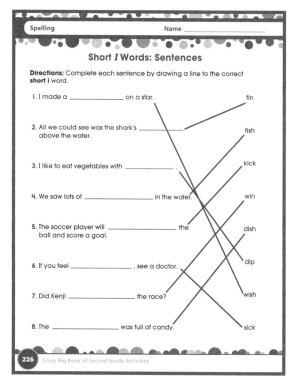

page 226

Answer Key

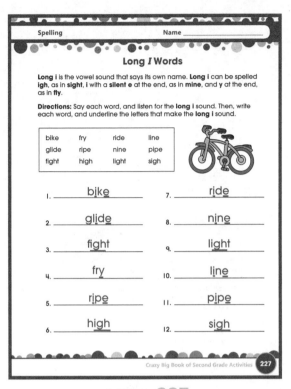

page 227

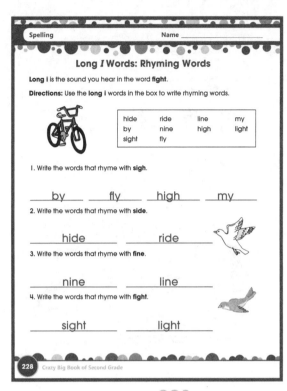

page 228

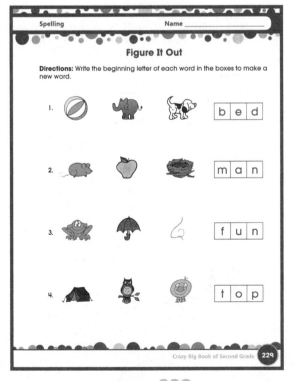

page 229

---

page 230

Answer Key

Picnic

Directions: Find these things that begin with **c**. Color them yellow. Then, color the rest of the picture.

cat   can   cap   cloud   cake

page 231

In Space

Directions: Read the clues and use the words in the word box to complete the puzzle.

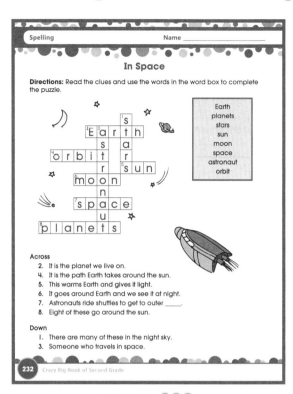

Word box: Earth, planets, stars, sun, moon, space, astronaut, orbit

Across
2. It is the planet we live on.
4. It is the path Earth takes around the sun.
5. This warms Earth and gives it light.
6. It goes around Earth and we see it at night.
7. Astronauts ride shuttles to get to outer _____.
8. Eight of these go around the sun.

Down
1. There are many of these in the night sky.
3. Someone who travels in space.

page 232

Up, Up, and Away

Directions: Color the spaces with things that we eat blue. Color the spaces with things that we wear yellow. Color the spaces with things that we ride in green.

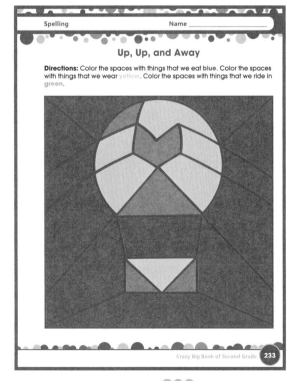

page 233

Location Words

Directions: Use one of the location words from the box to complete each sentence.

between	around	inside	outside	beside	across

Example:
She will hide __under__ the basket.

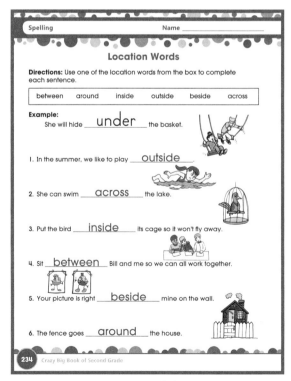

1. In the summer, we like to play __outside__.

2. She can swim __across__ the lake.

3. Put the bird __inside__ its cage so it won't fly away.

4. Sit __between__ Bill and me so we can all work together.

5. Your picture is right __beside__ mine on the wall.

6. The fence goes __around__ the house.

page 234

Answer Key

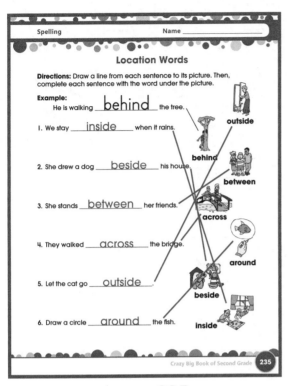

page 235

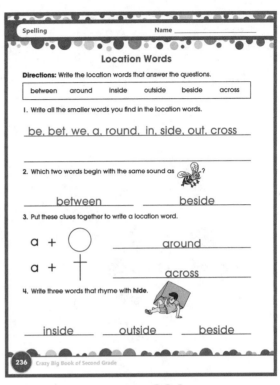

page 236

page 237

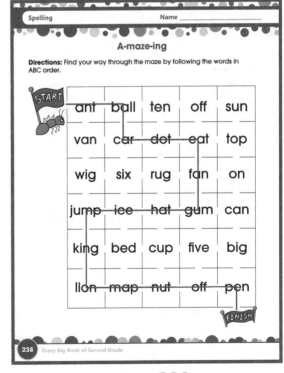

page 238

Answer Key

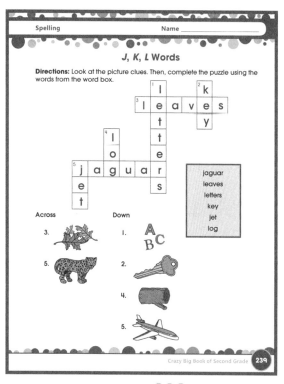

page 239

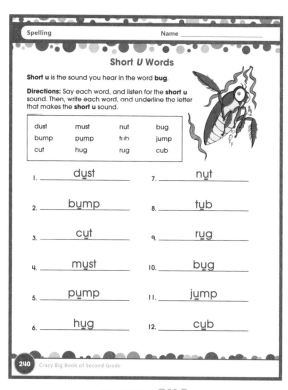

page 240

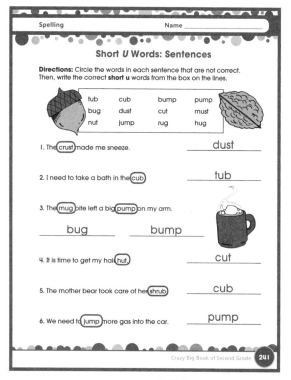

page 241

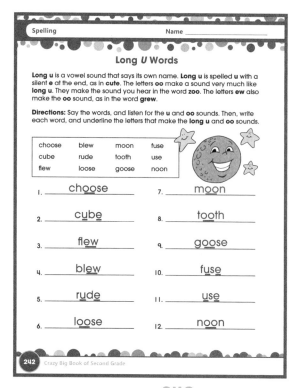

page 242

Answer Key

Long *U* Words: Rhyming Words

Long u is a vowel sound you hear in the word **cube**. Another vowel sound that is very much like the **long u** sound is the **oo** sound you hear in the word **boot**.

Directions: Use the **long u** and **oo** words in the box to write rhyming words

moon	tooth	use	choose
flew	loose	goose	
fuse	noon	blew	

1. Write the words that rhyme with **soon**.

    moon   noon

2. Write the words that rhyme with **lose**.

   fuse   use   choose

3. Write the words that rhyme with **grew**.

   flew   blew

4. Write the words that rhyme with **moose**.

   loose   goose

5. Write the word that rhymes with **booth**.

   tooth

Crazy Big Book of Second Grade **243**

page 243

Long *U* Words: Sentences

Directions: Write the words in the sentences below in the correct order. Begin each sentence with a capital letter, and end it with a period or a question mark.

1. the pulled dentist tooth my loose

   The dentist pulled my loose tooth.

2. ice cubes I choose in my drink to put

   I choose to put ice cubes in my drink.

3. a rude fuse the blew yesterday boy

   The rude boy blew a fuse yesterday.

4. loose the got in garden goose the

   The goose got loose in the garden.

5. flew the goose winter for the south

   The goose flew south for the winter.

6. is full there a moon tonight

   Is there a full moon tonight?

244 *Crazy Big Book of Second Grade*

page 244

Funny Fish

Directions: Can you help Fred Fish find Frieda Fish? Color the pictures that start with **f** to go through the maze.

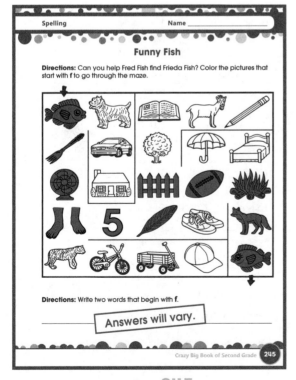

Directions: Write two words that begin with **f**.

_____ | Answers will vary. |

Crazy Big Book of Second Grade **245**

page 245

Safety

Directions: Read the clues and use the words in the word box to complete the puzzle.

| seat belt |
| helmet |
| life jacket |
| stop sign |
| traffic light |

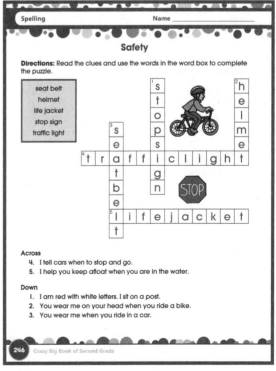

Across
4. I tell cars when to stop and go.
5. I help you keep afloat when you are in the water.

Down
1. I am red with white letters. I sit on a post.
2. You wear me on your head when you ride a bike.
3. You wear me when you ride in a car.

246 *Crazy Big Book of Second Grade*

page 246

Answer Key

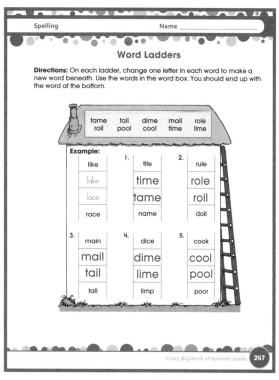

page 247

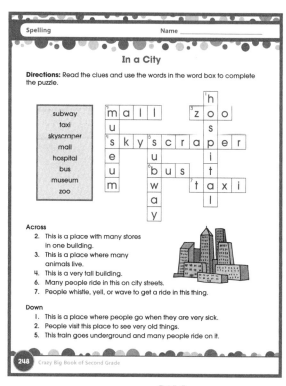

page 248

page 249

Opposite Words

Directions: Opposites are words that are different in every way. Use the opposite words from the box to complete these sentences.

hard	hot	bottom	quickly	happy
sad	slowly	cold	soft	top

Example:
My new coat is blue on ___top___ and red on the ___bottom___.

1. Snow is ___cold___, but fire is ___hot___.

2. A rabbit runs ___quickly___, but a turtle moves ___slowly___.

3. A bed is ___soft___, but a floor is ___hard___.

4. I feel ___happy___ when my friends come and ___sad___ when they leave.

page 250

Answer Key

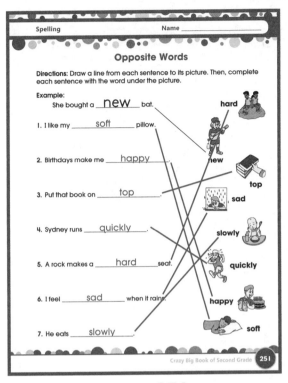

page 251

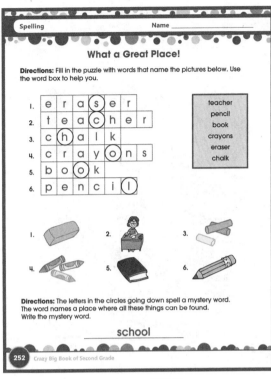

page 252

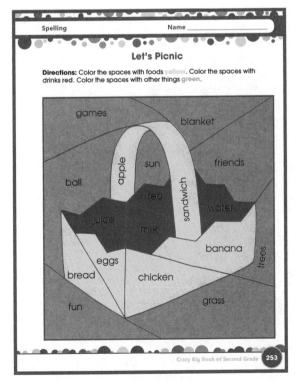

page 253

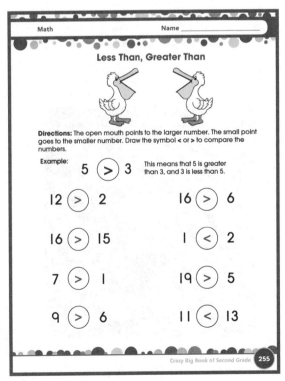

page 255

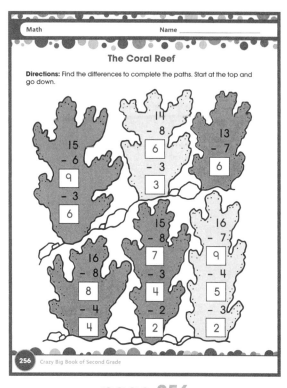

page 256

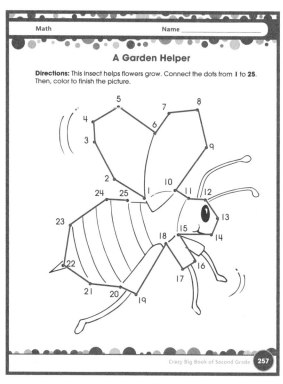

page 257

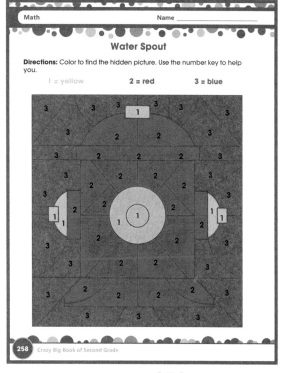

page 258

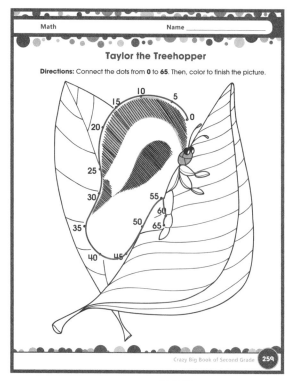

page 259

Answer Key

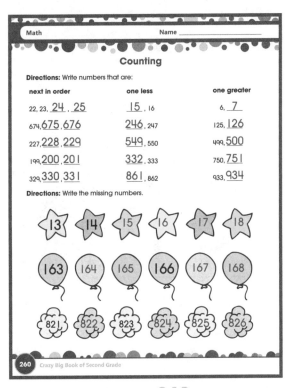

page 260

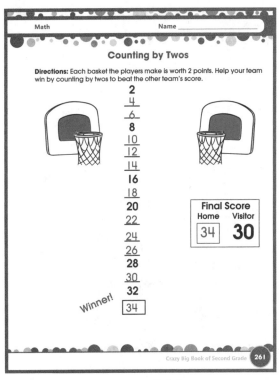

page 261

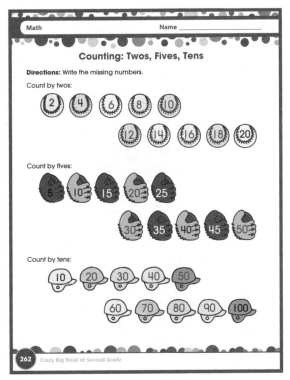

page 262

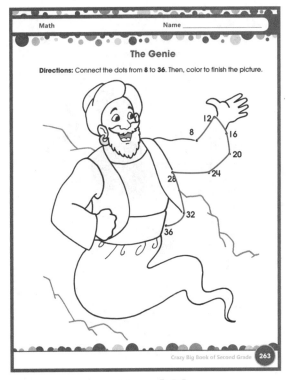

page 263

Answer Key

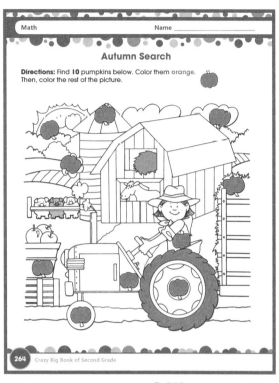

page 264

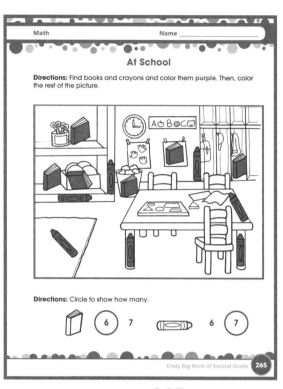

page 265

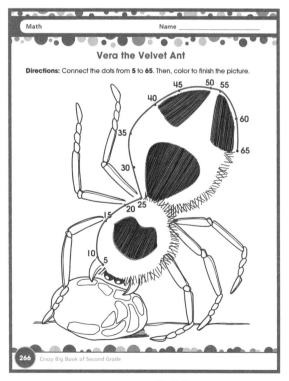

page 266

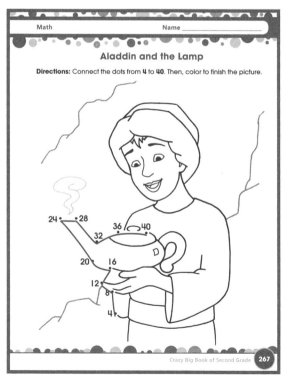

page 267

Answer Key

page 268

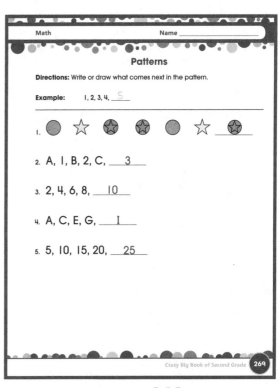

page 269

page 270

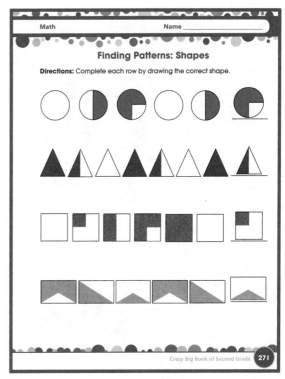

page 271

page 272

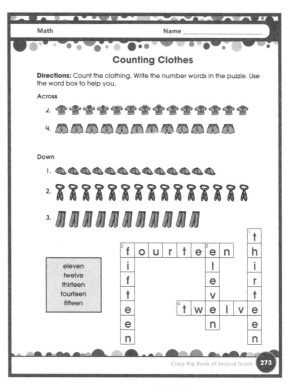

page 273

page 274

page 275

Answer Key

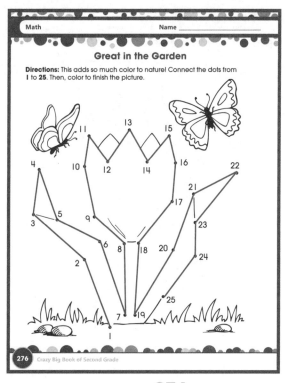

page 276

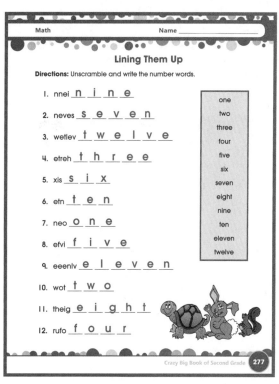

page 277

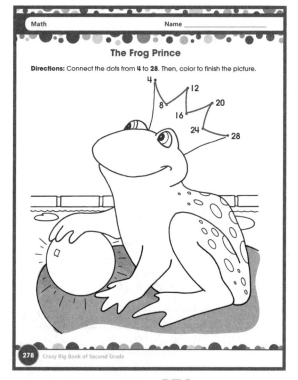

page 278

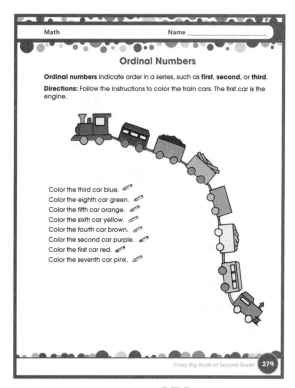

page 279

Answer Key

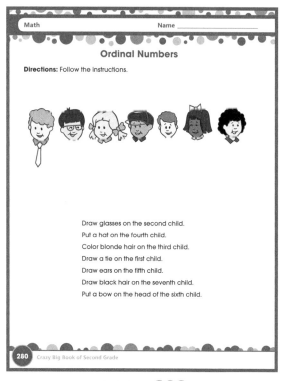

page 280

page 281

page 282

page 283

Answer Key

Hansel and Gretel

Directions: Connect the dots from **4** to **32**. Then, color to finish the picture.

page 284

Addition

Addition is "putting together" or adding two or more numbers to find the sum.

Directions: Add.

Example:

$$\begin{array}{r} 2 \\ +5 \\ \hline 7 \end{array}$$

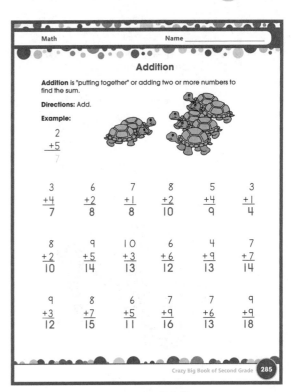

$$\begin{array}{r}3\\+4\\\hline 7\end{array} \quad \begin{array}{r}6\\+2\\\hline 8\end{array} \quad \begin{array}{r}7\\+1\\\hline 8\end{array} \quad \begin{array}{r}8\\+2\\\hline 10\end{array} \quad \begin{array}{r}5\\+4\\\hline 9\end{array} \quad \begin{array}{r}3\\+1\\\hline 4\end{array}$$

$$\begin{array}{r}8\\+2\\\hline 10\end{array} \quad \begin{array}{r}9\\+5\\\hline 14\end{array} \quad \begin{array}{r}10\\+3\\\hline 13\end{array} \quad \begin{array}{r}6\\+6\\\hline 12\end{array} \quad \begin{array}{r}4\\+9\\\hline 13\end{array} \quad \begin{array}{r}7\\+7\\\hline 14\end{array}$$

$$\begin{array}{r}9\\+3\\\hline 12\end{array} \quad \begin{array}{r}8\\+7\\\hline 15\end{array} \quad \begin{array}{r}6\\+5\\\hline 11\end{array} \quad \begin{array}{r}7\\+9\\\hline 16\end{array} \quad \begin{array}{r}7\\+6\\\hline 13\end{array} \quad \begin{array}{r}9\\+9\\\hline 18\end{array}$$

page 285

Addition: Commutative Property

The **commutative property** of addition states that even if the order of the numbers is changed in an addition sentence, the sum will stay the same.

Example: 2 + 3 = 5
           3 + 2 = 5

Directions: Look at the addition sentences below. Complete the addition sentences by writing the missing numerals.

5 + 4 = 9   3 + 1 = 4   2 + 6 = 8
4 + <u>5</u> = 9   1 + <u>3</u> = 4   6 + <u>2</u> = 8

6 + 1 = 7   4 + 3 = 7   1 + 9 = 10
1 + <u>6</u> = 7   3 + <u>4</u> = 7   9 + <u>1</u> = 10

Now, try these:

6 + 3 = 9   10 + 2 = 12   8 + 3 = 11
<u>3</u> + <u>6</u> = 9   <u>2</u> + <u>10</u> = 12   <u>3</u> + <u>8</u> = 11

Answers will vary below. Possible answers:

Look at these sums. Can you think of two number sentences that would show the commutative property of addition?

<u>3</u> + <u>4</u> = 7   <u>5</u> + <u>6</u> = 11   <u>8</u> + <u>1</u> = 9

<u>4</u> + <u>3</u> = 7   <u>6</u> + <u>5</u> = 11   <u>1</u> + <u>8</u> = 9

page 286

Adding 3 or More Numbers

Directions: Add all the numbers to find the sum. Draw pictures or add two numbers together to break up the problem into two smaller problems.

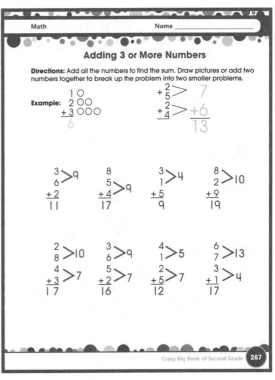

Example:

$$\begin{array}{r}1\\2\\+3\\\hline 6\end{array}$$

$$\begin{array}{r}2\\+5\\\hline\end{array}\!\!\Big\rangle 7 \quad \begin{array}{r}+4\\\hline\end{array}\!\!\Big\rangle \begin{array}{r}+6\\\hline 13\end{array}$$

$$\begin{array}{r}3\\6\\+2\\\hline 11\end{array}\!\Big\rangle 9 \quad \begin{array}{r}8\\5\\+4\\\hline 17\end{array}\!\Big\rangle 9 \quad \begin{array}{r}3\\1\\+5\\\hline 9\end{array}\!\Big\rangle 4 \quad \begin{array}{r}8\\2\\+9\\\hline 19\end{array}\!\Big\rangle 10$$

$$\begin{array}{r}2\\8\\4\\+3\\\hline 17\end{array}\!\Big\rangle 10 \,\Big\rangle 7 \quad \begin{array}{r}3\\6\\5\\+2\\\hline 16\end{array}\!\Big\rangle 9 \,\Big\rangle 7 \quad \begin{array}{r}4\\1\\2\\+5\\\hline 12\end{array}\!\Big\rangle 5 \,\Big\rangle 7 \quad \begin{array}{r}6\\7\\3\\+1\\\hline 17\end{array}\!\Big\rangle 13 \,\Big\rangle 4$$

page 287

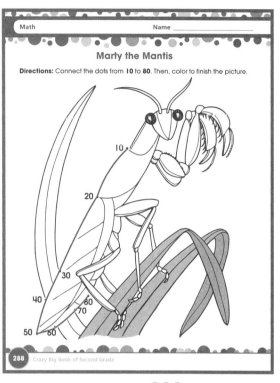

page 288

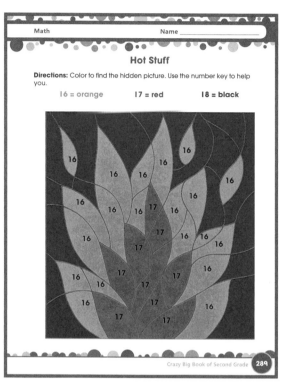

page 289

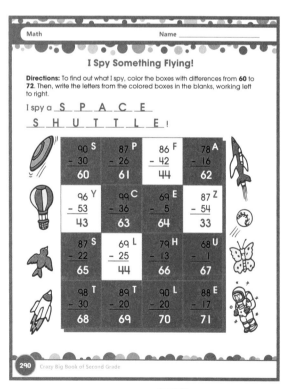

page 290

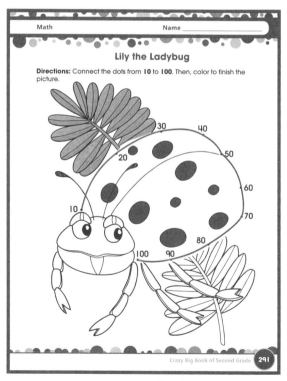

page 291

Answer Key

page 292

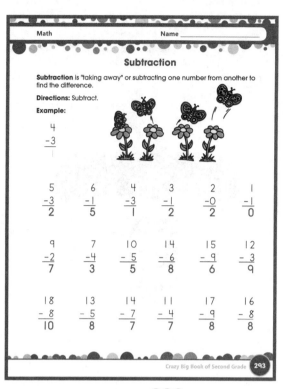

page 293

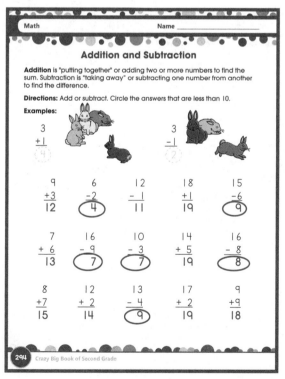

page 294

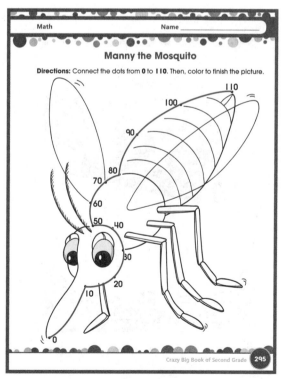

page 295

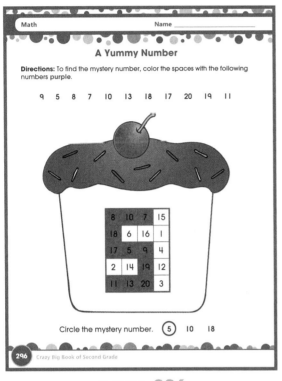

page 296

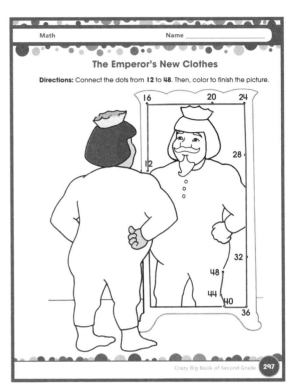

page 297

page 298

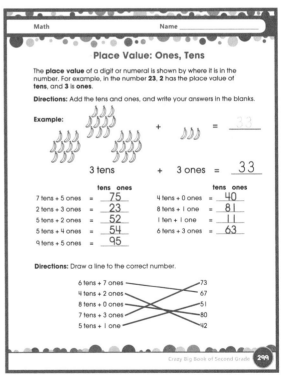

page 299

Answer Key

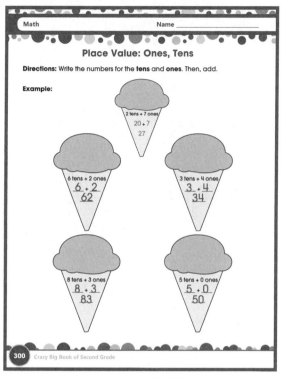

page 300

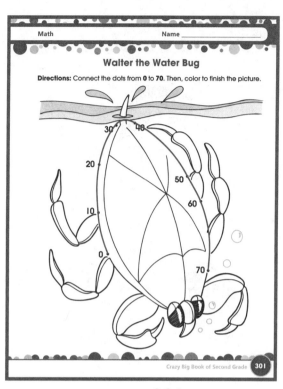

page 301

page 302

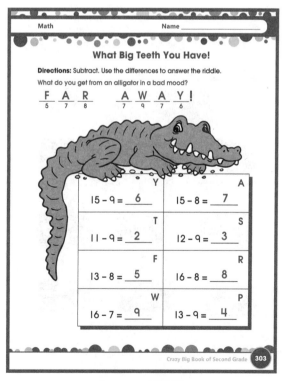

page 303

Answer Key

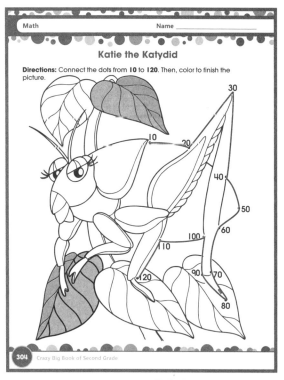

page 304

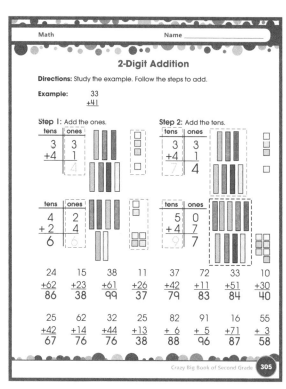

page 305

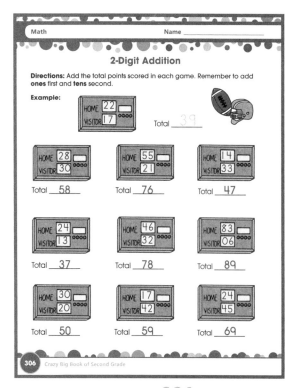

page 306

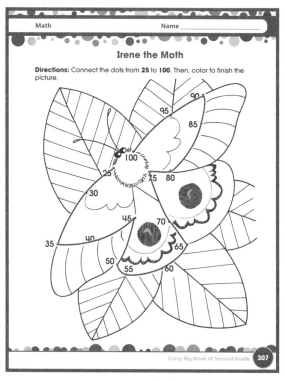

page 307

Answer Key

page 308

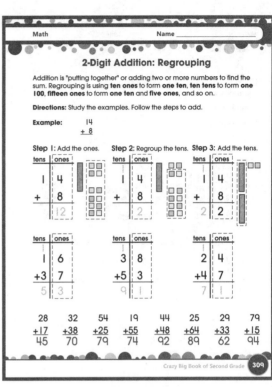

page 309

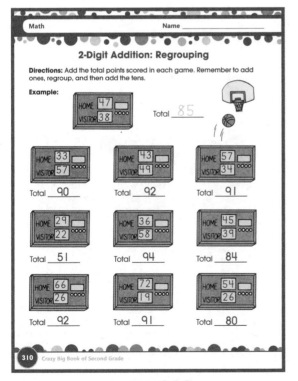

page 310

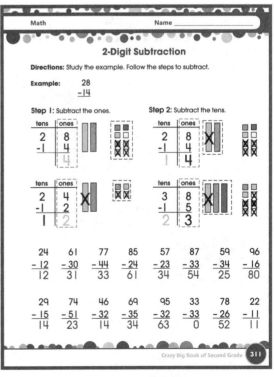

page 311

Answer Key

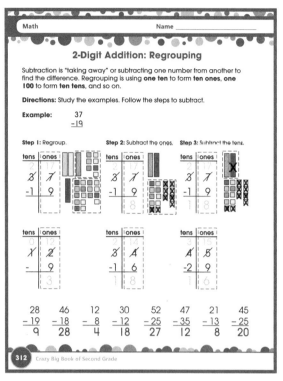

page 312

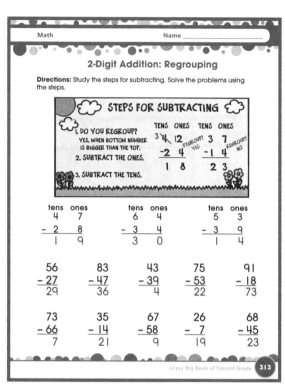

page 313

page 314

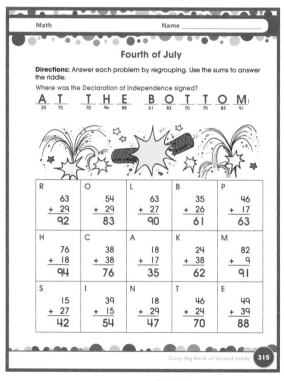

page 315

Answer Key

page 316

page 317

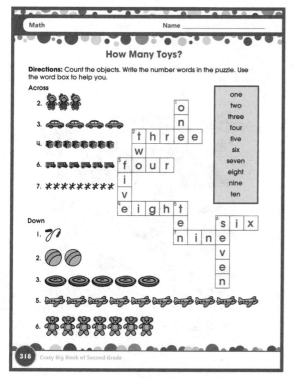

page 318

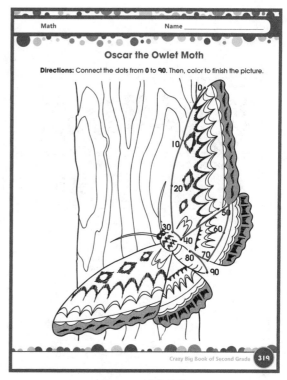

page 319

page 320

Math   Name _____

Bingo!

Directions: Find the differences. Color the answers on the bingo cards. Be careful! Some answers are on both. The first board to be completely covered is the winner!

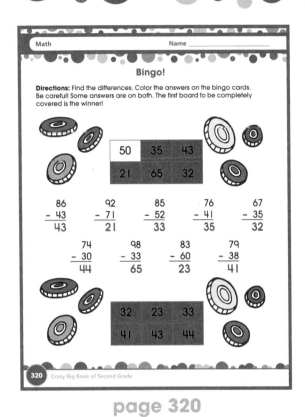

50	35	43
21	65	32

$$\begin{array}{r} 86 \\ -\ 43 \\ \hline 43 \end{array} \quad \begin{array}{r} 92 \\ -\ 71 \\ \hline 21 \end{array} \quad \begin{array}{r} 85 \\ -\ 52 \\ \hline 33 \end{array} \quad \begin{array}{r} 76 \\ -\ 41 \\ \hline 35 \end{array} \quad \begin{array}{r} 67 \\ -\ 35 \\ \hline 32 \end{array}$$

$$\begin{array}{r} 74 \\ -\ 30 \\ \hline 44 \end{array} \quad \begin{array}{r} 98 \\ -\ 33 \\ \hline 65 \end{array} \quad \begin{array}{r} 83 \\ -\ 60 \\ \hline 23 \end{array} \quad \begin{array}{r} 79 \\ -\ 38 \\ \hline 41 \end{array}$$

32	23	33
41	43	44

320 Crazy Big Book of Second Grade

page 321

Math   Name _____

Willy the Walkingstick

Directions: Connect the dots from **0** to **50**. Then, color to finish the picture.

Crazy Big Book of Second Grade 321

page 322

Math   Name _____

The Ball Game

Directions: Which team will win? Find each difference, working from left to right. Shade the answer on a bingo board. The first team to completely cover its card is the winner!

FASTBACKS

46	22	59	71
73	68	35	43

SWANS

21	34	62	32
51	78	23	30

$$\begin{array}{r} 96 \\ -\ 25 \\ \hline 71 \end{array} \quad \begin{array}{r} 43 \\ -\ 20 \\ \hline 23 \end{array} \quad \begin{array}{r} 65 \\ -\ 44 \\ \hline 21 \end{array} \quad \begin{array}{r} 98 \\ -\ 63 \\ \hline 35 \end{array} \quad \begin{array}{r} 74 \\ -\ 52 \\ \hline 22 \end{array}$$

$$\begin{array}{r} 81 \\ -\ 51 \\ \hline 30 \end{array} \quad \begin{array}{r} 57 \\ -\ 23 \\ \hline 34 \end{array} \quad \begin{array}{r} 66 \\ -\ 34 \\ \hline 32 \end{array} \quad \begin{array}{r} 89 \\ -\ 16 \\ \hline 73 \end{array} \quad \begin{array}{r} 68 \\ -\ 25 \\ \hline 43 \end{array}$$

$$\begin{array}{r} 99 \\ -\ 48 \\ \hline 51 \end{array} \quad \begin{array}{r} 98 \\ -\ 36 \\ \hline 62 \end{array} \quad \begin{array}{r} 79 \\ -\ 20 \\ \hline 59 \end{array} \quad \begin{array}{r} 88 \\ -\ 42 \\ \hline 46 \end{array} \quad \begin{array}{r} 99 \\ -\ 31 \\ \hline 68 \end{array}$$

322 Crazy Big Book of Second Grade

page 323

Math   Name _____

Snail Garden

Directions: Color **25** snails brown . Circle to show how many snails are left over.

③   4   5

Crazy Big Book of Second Grade 323

Answer Key

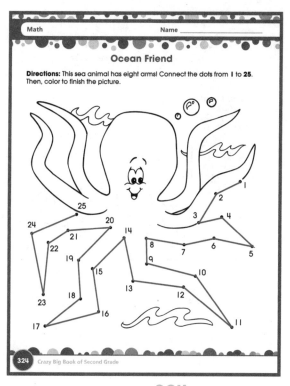

page 324

page 325

page 326

page 327

Answer Key

Tic-Tac-Toe

Directions: Find the differences. Then, mark **X** or **O** over the answers on the tic-tac-toe game to find the winner!

1. 74 − 52 = **22** Mark X.
2. 85 − 53 = **32** Mark O.
3. 98 − 67 = **31** Mark X.
4. 89 − 43 = **46** Mark O.
5. 98 − 43 = **55** Mark X.
6. 75 − 33 = **42** Mark O.
7. 96 − 32 = **64** Mark X.

page 328

The Elves and the Shoemaker

Directions: Connect the dots from **4** to **56**. Then, color to finish the picture.

page 329

So Peaceful

Directions: Grace loves to sit in the shade. Connect the dots from **1** to **25**. Then, color to finish the picture.

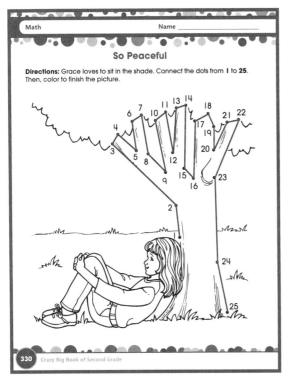

page 330

Add or Subtract

Directions: Add or subtract. Use regrouping when needed. Always do ones first and tens last.

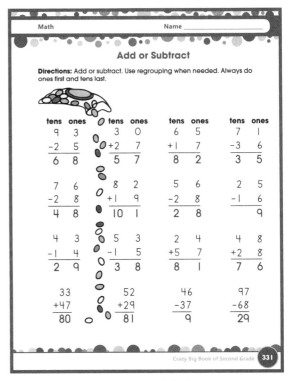

tens ones	tens ones	tens ones	tens ones
9 3	3 0	6 5	7 1
−2 5	+2 7	+1 7	−3 6
6 8	5 7	8 2	3 5
7 6	8 2	5 6	2 5
−2 8	+1 9	−2 8	−1 6
4 8	10 1	2 8	9
4 3	5 3	2 4	4 8
−1 4	−1 5	+5 7	+2 8
2 9	3 8	8 1	7 6
33 +47 = 80	52 +29 = 81	46 −37 = 9	97 −68 = 29

page 331

page 332

page 334

page 333

Math — Name _____

2-Digit Addition and Subtraction

Directions: Add or subtract using regrouping.

23 +48 71	84 −56 28	69 +29 98	41 −17 24
52 −28 24	73 +18 91	84 −27 57	57 −39 18
33 −15 18	64 +17 81	37 +58 95	36 −19 17
65 −28 37	48 −30 18	33 +18 51	25 +35 60

page 333

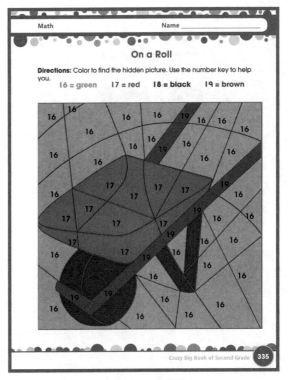

page 335

page 336

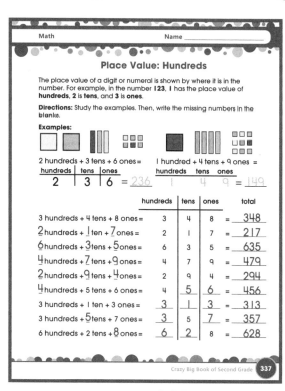

page 337

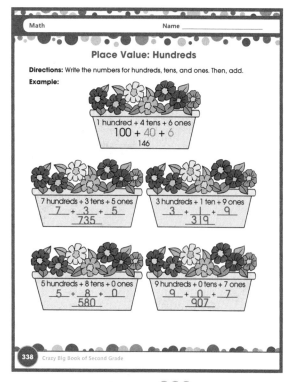

page 338

page 339

Answer Key

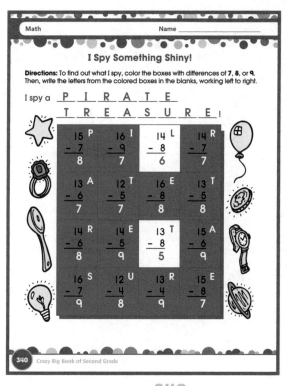

page 340

page 341

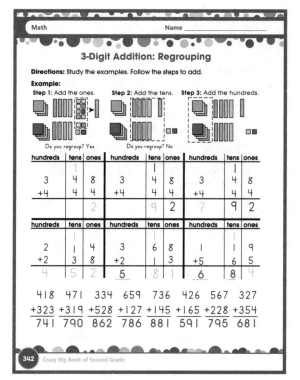

page 342

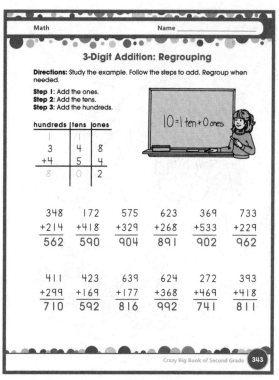

page 343

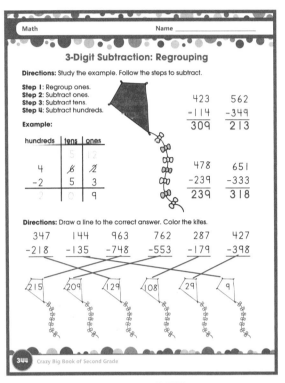

page 344

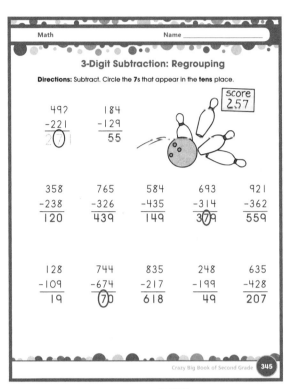

page 345

page 346

page 347

Answer Key

page 348

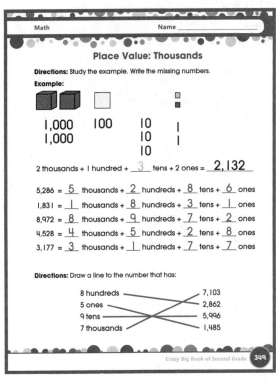

page 349

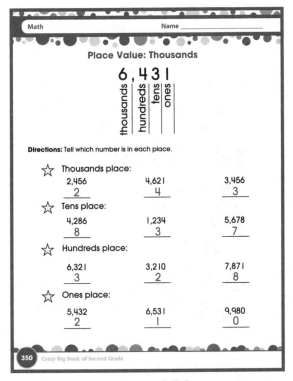

page 350

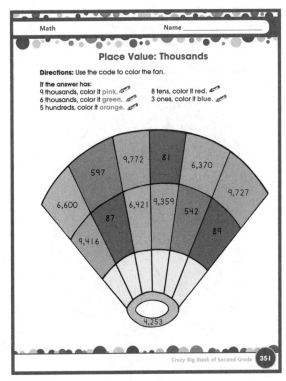

page 351

Answer Key

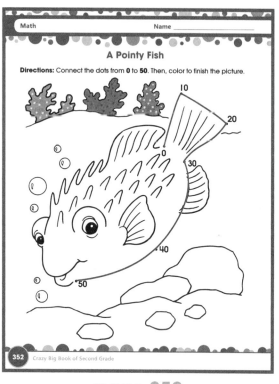

page 352

page 353

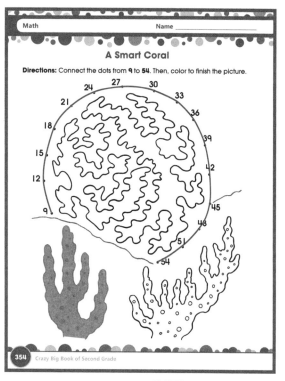

page 354

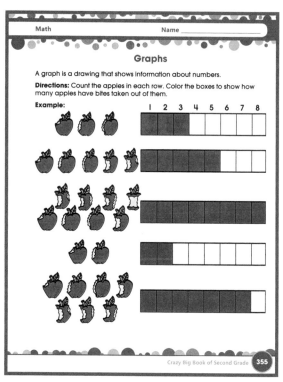

page 355

Answer Key

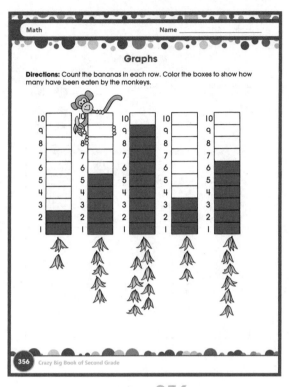

page 356

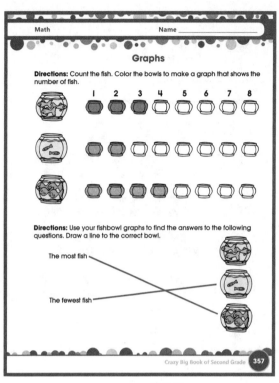

page 357

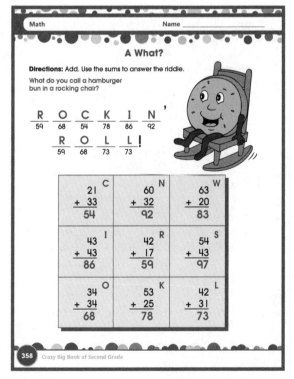

page 358

page 359

Answer Key

Multiplication

Multiplication is a short way to find the sum of adding the same number a certain amount of times. For example, **4 x 7 = 28** instead of **7 + 7 + 7 + 7 = 28.**

Directions: Study the example. Solve the problems.

Example:
$3 + 3 + 3 = 9$
3 threes = 9
$3 \times 3 = 9$

$7 + 7 = 14$
2 sevens = 14
$2 \times 7 = 14$

$4 + 4 + 4 + 4 = 16$
4 fours = 16
$4 \times 4 = 16$

$5 + 5 = 10$
2 fives = 10
$2 \times 5 = 10$

$2 + 2 + 2 + 2 = 8$
4 twos = 8
$4 \times 2 = 8$

$6 + 6 = 12$
2 sixes = 12
$2 \times 6 = 12$

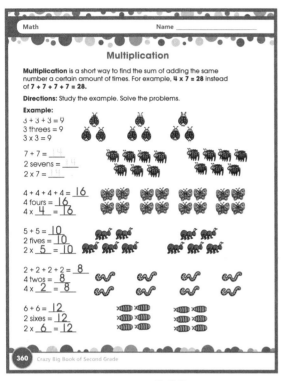

360   Crazy Big Book of Second Grade

page 360

Multiplication

Multiplication is repeated addition.

Directions: Draw a picture for each problem. Then, write the missing numbers.

Example:
Draw 2 groups of 3 apples.

$3 + 3 = 6$
or $2 \times 3 = 6$

Draw 3 groups of 4 hearts.
$4 + 4 + 4 = 12$
or $3 \times 4 = 12$

Draw 2 groups of 5 boxes.
$5 + 5 = 10$
or $2 \times 5 = 10$

Draw 6 groups of 2 circles.
$2 + 2 + 2 + 2 + 2 + 2 = 12$
or $6 \times 2 = 12$

Draw 7 groups of 3 triangles.
$3 + 3 + 3 + 3 + 3 + 3 + 3 = 21$
or $7 \times 3 = 21$

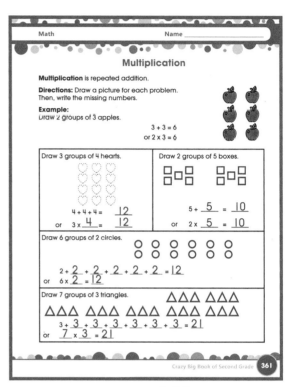

Crazy Big Book of Second Grade   361

page 361

Multiplication

Directions: Study the example. Draw the groups, and write the total.

Example: 3×2
$2 + 2 + 2 = 6$

3×4
$4 + 4 + 4 = 12$

2×5
$5 + 5 = 10$

5×3
$3 + 3 + 3 + 3 + 3 = 15$

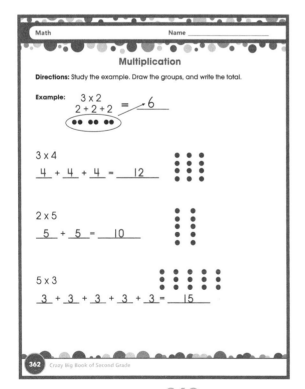

362   Crazy Big Book of Second Grade

page 362

Multiplication

Directions: Solve the problems.

Multiplication saves time. It's faster than addition!

$9 + 9 = 18$
2 nines = 18
$2 \times 9 = 18$

$7 + 7 = 14$
2 sevens = 14
$2 \times 7 = 14$

$4 + 4 + 4 + 4 = 16$
4 fours = 16
$4 \times 4 = 16$

$8 + 8 + 8 + 8 + 8 = 40$
5 eights = 40
$5 \times 8 = 40$

$5 + 5 + 5 = 15$
3 fives = 15
$3 \times 5 = 15$

$9 + 9 = 18$
2 nines = 18
$2 \times 9 = 18$

$6 + 6 + 6 = 18$
3 sixes = 18
$3 \times 6 = 18$

$3 + 3 = 6$
2 threes = 6
$2 \times 3 = 6$

$7 + 7 + 7 + 7 = 28$
4 sevens = 28
$4 \times 7 = 28$

$2 + 2 = 4$
2 twos = 4
$2 \times 2 = 4$

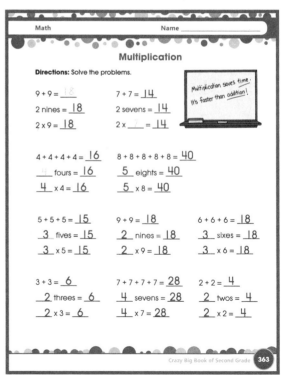

Crazy Big Book of Second Grade   363

page 363

Answer Key

Lynn the Luna Moth

Directions: Connect the dots from **0** to **190**. Then, color to finish the picture.

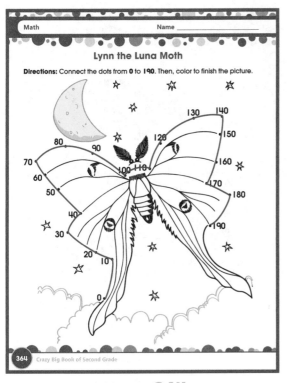

page 364

All Coiled Up

Directions: Color to find the hidden picture. Use the number key to help you.

4 = black   5 = red   6 = yellow

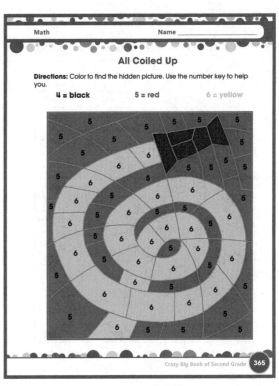

page 365

Out of This World

Directions: Subtract. Use the differences to answer the riddle.

What game do astronauts like to play?

M O O N O P O L Y !
53 36 36 82 36 27 36 41 60

P 38 − 11 = 27	**O** 59 − 23 = 36
R 96 − 71 = 25	**F** 88 − 17 = 71
M 96 − 43 = 53	**N** 93 − 11 = 82
L 77 − 36 = 41	**Y** 99 − 39 = 60

page 366

Carrie the Caterpillar

Directions: Connect the dots from **20** to **190**. Then, color to finish the picture.

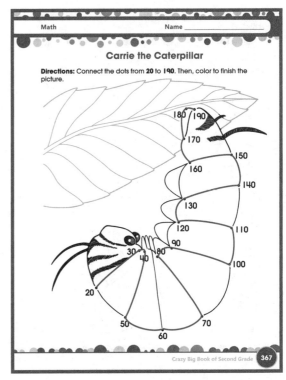

page 367

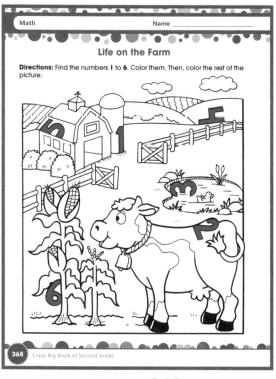

page 368

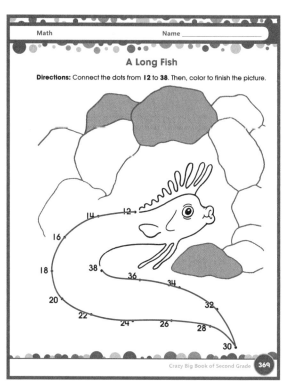

page 369

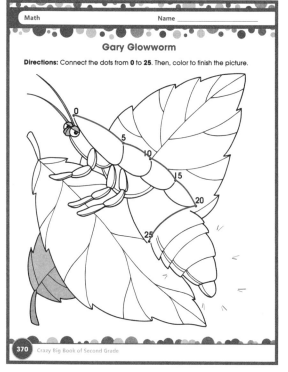

page 370

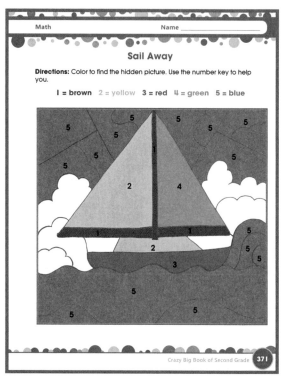

page 371

Answer Key

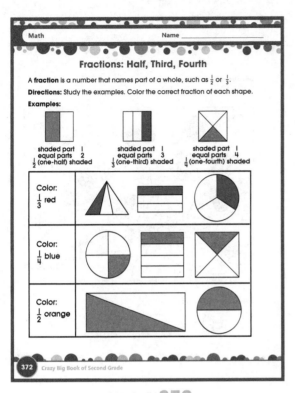

page 372

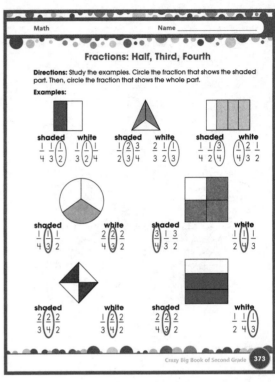

page 373

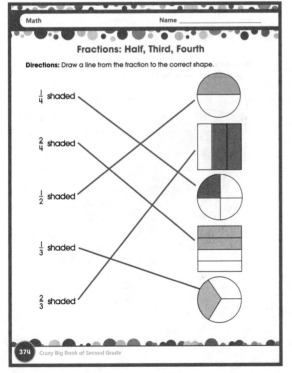

page 374

page 375

Answer Key

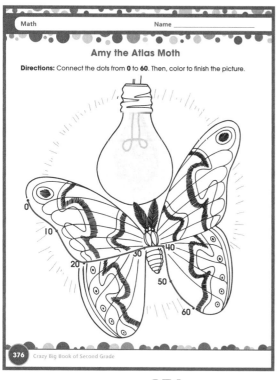

page 376

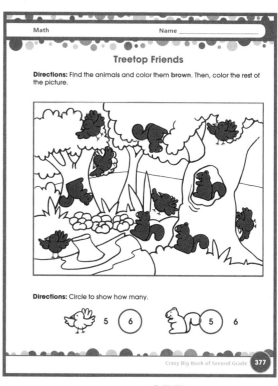

page 377

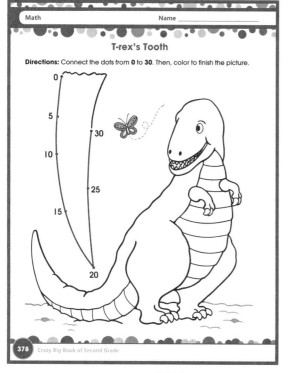

page 378

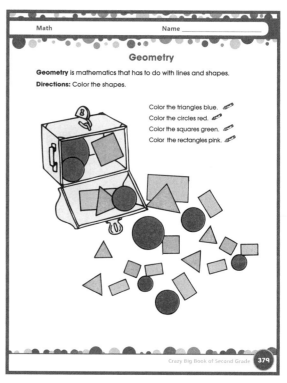

page 379

Answer Key

Geometry

Directions: Draw a line from the word to the shape.

Use a red line for circles.
Use a blue line for squares.
Use a yellow line for rectangles.
Use a green line for triangles.

Circle   **Square**   **Triangle**   **Rectangle**

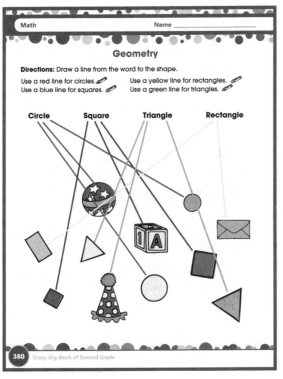

page 380

Numbers 1–10

Directions: Find and circle the words in the puzzle.

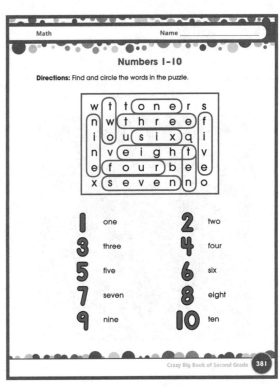

1 one   2 two
3 three   4 four
5 five   6 six
7 seven   8 eight
9 nine   10 ten

page 381

Gardening Counting

Directions: Count the objects. Write the number. Circle the smaller number.

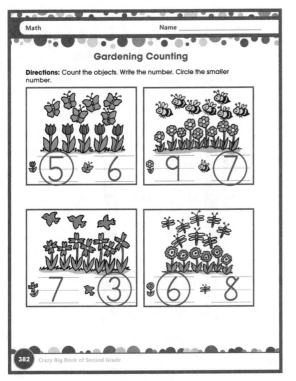

page 382

Swim On!

Directions: Connect the dots from **5** to **30**. Then, color to finish the picture.

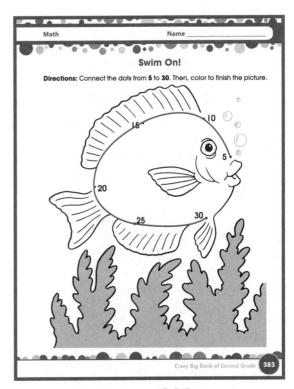

page 383

Answer Key

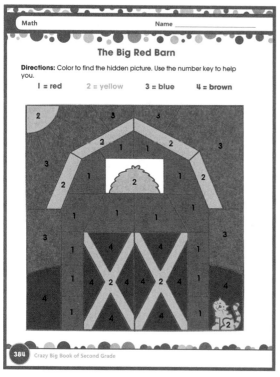

page 384

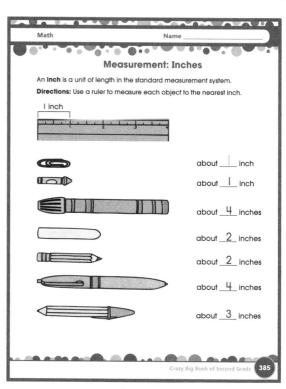

page 385

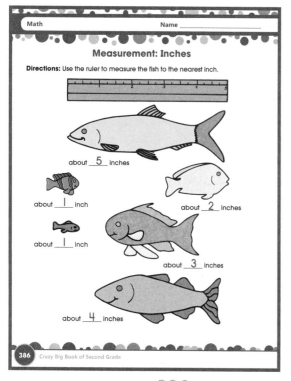

page 386

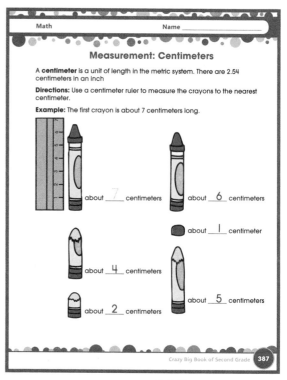

page 387

Answer Key

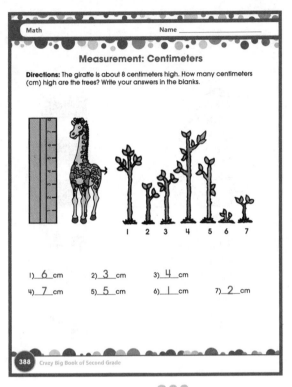

page 388

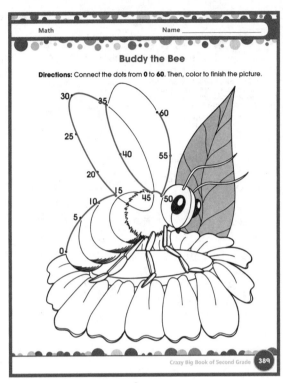

page 389

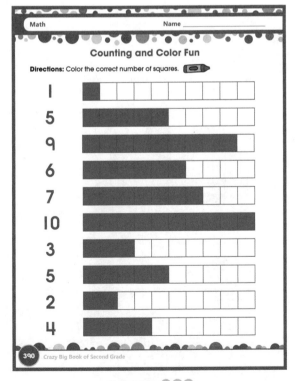

page 390

page 391

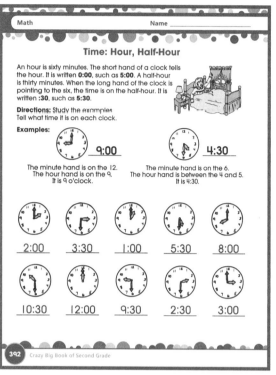

page 392

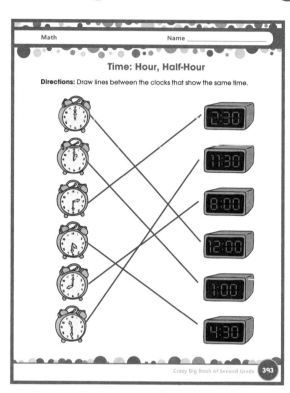

page 393

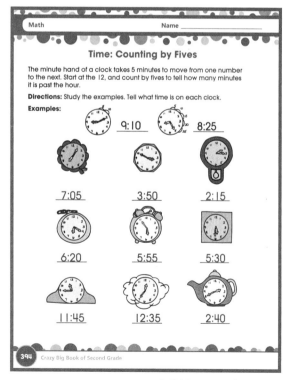

page 394

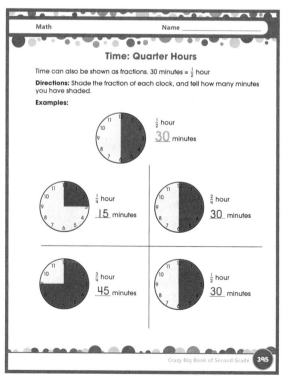

page 395

Answer Key

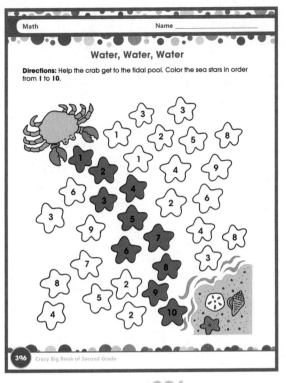

page 396

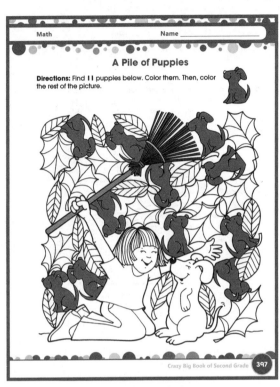

page 397

page 398

Math   Name _____

Review
Counting
Directions: Write the number that is:

next.	one less.	one greater.
68, 69, 70	56, 57	12, 13
786, 787, 788	649, 650	843, 844

Place Value: Tens and Ones
Directions: Draw a line to the correct number.

4 tens + 7 ones — 20
2 tens + 0 ones — 51
7 tens + 3 ones — 47
5 tens + 1 ones — 73

Addition and Subtraction
Directions: Add or subtract.

$\begin{array}{r} 15 \\ +\ 5 \\ \hline 20 \end{array}$ $\begin{array}{r} 14 \\ -\ 4 \\ \hline 10 \end{array}$ $\begin{array}{r} 7 \\ +\ 3 \\ \hline 10 \end{array}$ $\begin{array}{r} 8 \\ -\ 6 \\ \hline 2 \end{array}$ $\begin{array}{r} 10 \\ +\ 7 \\ \hline 17 \end{array}$ $\begin{array}{r} 14 \\ -\ 5 \\ \hline 9 \end{array}$

page 399

Answer Key

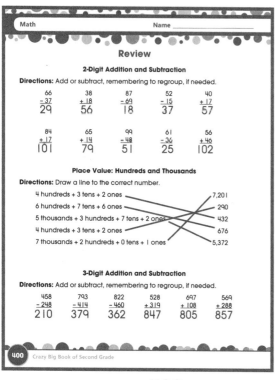

page 400

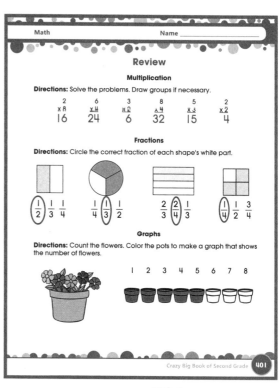

page 401

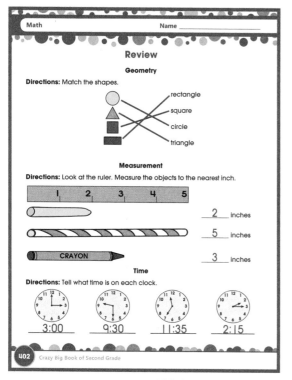

page 402

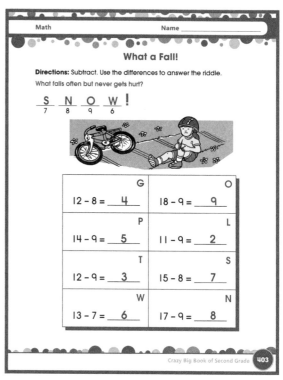

page 403

Answer Key

page 404

page 405

page 406

page 407

Answer Key

Yoli the Yellow Jacket

Directions: Connect the dots from **15** to **90**. Then, color to finish the picture.

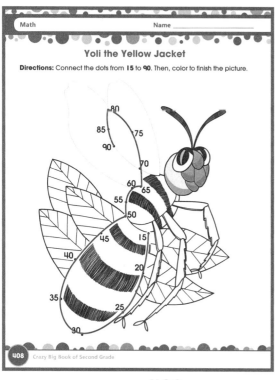

page 408

School Spirit

Directions: Count the items. Write the number words in the puzzle. Use the word box to help you.

page 409

Money: Penny, Nickel

Penny 1¢   Nickel 5¢

Directions: Count the coins and write the amount.

Example:

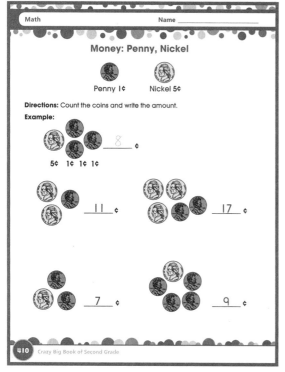

page 410

Money: Penny, Nickel, Dime

Penny 1¢   Nickel 5¢   Dime 10¢

Directions: Count the coins and write the amount.

Example:

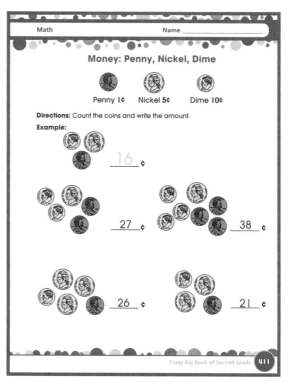

page 411

Answer Key

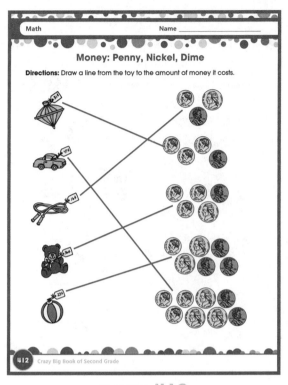

page 412

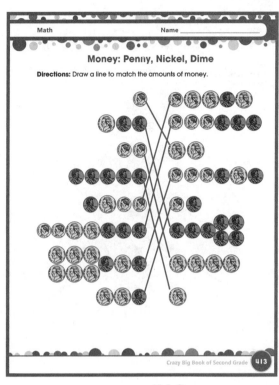

page 413

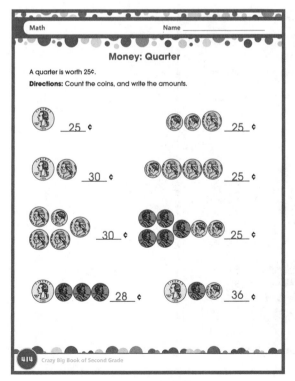

page 414

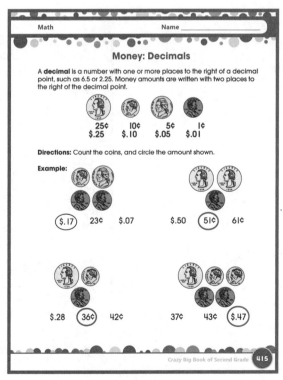

page 415

Answer Key

Money: Decimals

Directions: Draw a line from the coins to the correct amount in each column.

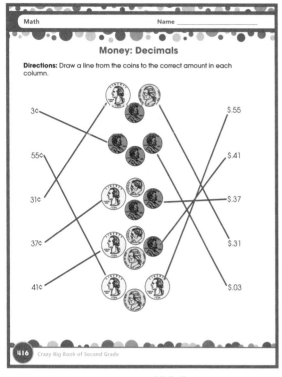

page 416

Money: Dollar

One dollar equals 100 cents. It is written $1.00.

Directions: Count the money, and write the amounts.

$ 1.00 $ .36

$ .71 $ .29

$ 1.25 $ 1.00

$ 1.55 $ 1.21

page 417

Adding Money

Directions: Write the amount of money using decimals. Then, add to find the total amount.

Example:

$$\begin{array}{r} \$1.00 \\ .05 \\ +\ .02 \\ \hline \$1.07 \end{array}$$

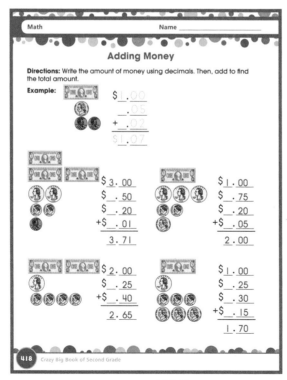

$$\begin{array}{r} \$3.00 \\ \$\ .50 \\ \$\ .20 \\ +\$\ .01 \\ \hline 3.71 \end{array}$$

$$\begin{array}{r} \$1.00 \\ \$\ .75 \\ \$\ .20 \\ +\$\ .05 \\ \hline 2.00 \end{array}$$

$$\begin{array}{r} \$2.00 \\ \$\ .25 \\ +\$\ .40 \\ \hline 2.65 \end{array}$$

$$\begin{array}{r} \$1.00 \\ \$\ .25 \\ \$\ .30 \\ +\$\ .15 \\ \hline 1.70 \end{array}$$

page 418

Answer Key

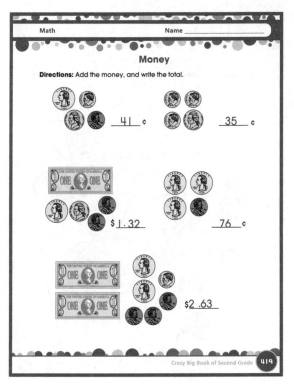

page 419

page 420

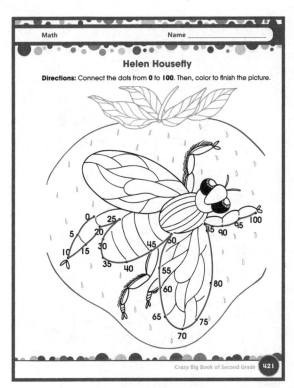

page 421

Answer Key

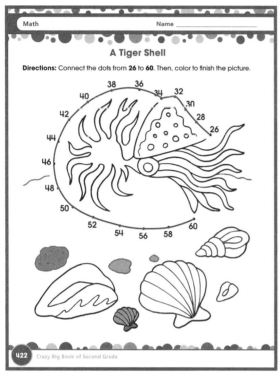

page 422

page 423

page 424

Answer Key

page 425

page 426

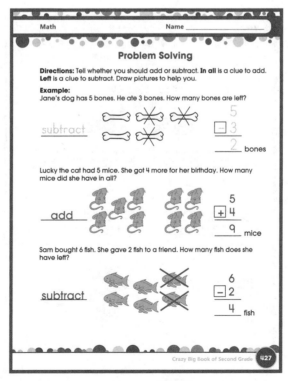

page 427

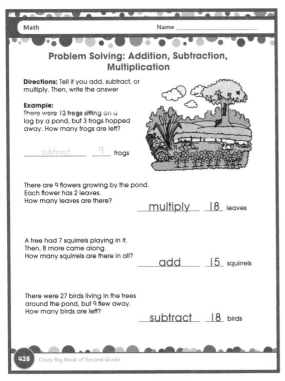

page 428

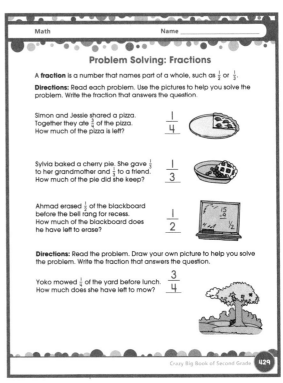

page 429

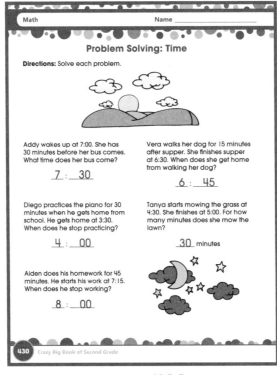

page 430

Answer Key

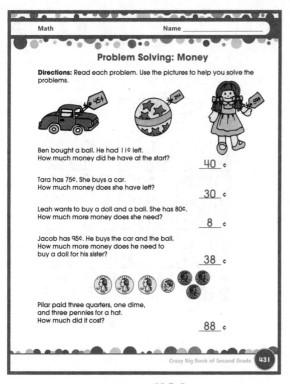

page 431

page 432

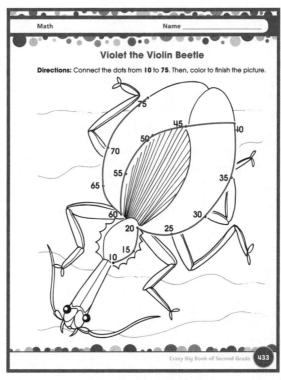

page 433

Answer Key

page 434

page 435